MAY IT PLEASE THE COURT

A Story About One of America's Greatest Trial Lawyers

Charles P. Kocoras

Law Bulletin Publishing Company

For Grace,
For Everything

Law Bulletin Publishing Company
Professional Development
415 North State Street
Chicago, Illinois 60654
312.644.7800
Email: PD@lbpc.con
Visit our website at www.LawBulletin.com

Additional copies can be purchased from our website or by calling us directly. Discounts are available for books ordered in bulk. Inquire by phone or email.

First Edition: February 2015
Includes biographical references and index
ISBN-13: 978-0-910095-01-3
ISBN-10: 0910095019

Printed in the United States of America

Cover, Graphic Design and Layout by Maria Marquez
Edited by Matt Baker, Amy Cook, John Flynn Rooney, Linda Seggelke
Publisher: Peter Mierzwa

TABLE OF CONTENTS

ABOUT THE AUTHOR

Charles P. Kocoras has been a judge in the U.S. District Court for the Northern District of Illinois since his appointment in 1980 by President Jimmy Carter. He served as Chief Judge of the District Court from 2002 to 2006. He also has been an adjunct professor of trial advocacy at The John Marshall Law School since 1975.

Kocoras began his legal career as an associate at Bishop & Crawford. He then served as an Assistant U.S. Attorney in the Northern District of Illinois from 1971 to 1977 where he met Dan Webb. At the U.S. Attorney's office, Kocoras tried 25 cases and conducted grand jury investigations working as a trial attorney, deputy chief of the Criminal and Special Prosecutions divisions, and as First Assistant U.S. Attorney. He also briefly served as the court-appointed U.S. Attorney in 1977. Kocoras was chair of the Illinois Commerce Commission from 1977-79. Immediately prior to becoming a judge, he was a partner at Stone, McGuire, Benjamin & Kocoras.

Kocoras began his professional career at the Internal Revenue Service holding multiple positions from 1962 to 1969. He also served in the Illinois Army National Guard from 1961 to 1967 with active duty in 1961.

He lives in the Chicago area with Grace, his wife of 46 years. They have three sons: Peter, John, and Paul.

ACKNOWLEDGEMENTS

Every book of this kind requires that certain people be particularly acknowledged and rendered special thanks. There are four people to whom I offer this tribute. First is my wife, Grace. More than her constant encouragement, what was deeply appreciated was her hard work in typing the entirety of the draft of the book and its constant revisions. The dedication to her in the front of the book reflects the value of her love and support to me for the many years of our life together. My thanks also go to Chris Heery, the nicest and ablest researcher a lucky author could hope to find. The contributions of those two people made everything else doable.

Peter Mierzwa is the person most responsible for giving life to my dream of writing a book and to, hopefully, give Dan Webb his rightful place as one of the greatest lawyers America has ever produced. Peter not only signed up a novice writer to publish but he also invested himself in the book and oversaw the project from beginning to end. My appreciation for Peter and his involvement is deep and everlasting.

John Flynn Rooney was brought into the project by Peter for his assistance and expertise in the interviewing process. John is a reporter for the Chicago Daily Law Bulletin, a daily Chicago paper about the law, and he agreed to moonlight on the book. While in the midst of his service, John was stricken with a serious illness, ALS (Lou Gehrig's disease). John has publicly acknowledged his battle with ALS, and has displayed a spirit so courageous and indomitable as to inspire the respect and admiration of all who know him.

Both Dan Webb and I met John's father, Ed Rooney, a legendary crime reporter in Chicago, when Dan and I were beginning our careers as Assistant United States Attorneys. The highest tribute I can offer John is to say his own work has added luster to the Rooney name. It is with great appreciation for his contribution to the book and with my deepest wishes for his health and welfare that I offer my thanks.

As was readily apparent to those who read the early drafts of the book, it had more than its share of rough edges. The final version has been touched by the polished hand of the editors at the Law Bulletin Publishing Company. Their ability to improve the manuscript, its readability, and enhance its interest are the source of many pleasures. Thanks to Matt Baker and Amy Cook for their careful and considerate editorial effort and Linda Seggelke for her prowess as proofreader.

There are also acknowledgements of a different sort, the thanks that is due for opportunities far beyond those instrumental to the writing of a book. I had the good fortune to work for four United States Attorneys during my career as an Assistant U.S. Attorney in Chicago, and each contributed to the career in law that has enriched and fulfilled me these last forty plus years.

Judge William J. Bauer started it all with the chance of a lifetime when he hired me. I have been forever grateful, and Bill remains a cherished friend. Governor Jim Thompson is, to me, larger than life in many ways. I have never known a more capable man, nor one so trusting of the abilities of those who worked under him. He gave us small assignments and large ones, and always believed in our abilities to do them all.

Sam Skinner is a lawyer of enormous talent, and there is so much I owe to him. Sam conducted my interview for the AUSA position and recommended my hire. When Sam succeeded Governor Thompson as U.S. Attorney, I became his First Assistant. How can the simple words "thank you" capture the fullness of what he did for me and the depth of my appreciation?

Tom Sullivan succeeded Sam Skinner as the United States Attorney and kept me on as his First Assistant. I have first-hand knowledge of his extraordinary trial skills, having once opposed him in court. When I later served him, I saw the level of decency and the principled way he made all of his prosecutive decisions. Tom recommended me for the judgeship I was later appointed to and blessed with to this very day.

My first year as an AUSA saw me as one of the four members of the Criminal Complaint Unit. Dan Webb, Ty Fahner and Tex Griffin were the other three. The four of us handled the lion's share of new criminal cases that came into the office that year. Each day was a blur of interviews of federal law enforcement agents, preparing affidavits for arrest and search warrants, conducting bond and probable cause hearings, and declining non-meritorious cases. The rewards to us were the trials that ensued from our efforts, often without another AUSA at counsel table.

Tex Griffin was our senior in the unit by a few months. He also had the most worldly experience, having been a highly decorated Vietnam War combatant. No better mentor ever existed. Tex was a special talent and became a special friend. The bonds of friendship were forged in those days among the four of us and have never been broken.

As the months and years unfolded in the office, other strong friendships were formed. Tony Valukas became the de facto leader of an annual week-long trip to Canada for the ostensible purpose of catching some of its fish. We did catch a lot of fish, but it always seemed at weeks-end the empty beer bottles outnumbered the fish. Besides Valukas, the regulars on the trip included Dan Webb, Ty Fahner, Matt Lydon, Jim Montana, and yours truly. Others who ventured north included Howard Hoffmann, Sam Skinner, and Dr. Richard Rovner. Those were special moments with special friends, and it just seems right to acknowledge this group. The passage of time brings those moments into sharper relief than when they occurred. They also warm the memories of the mind.

Another acknowledgement goes to all of the men and women with whom I served in the U.S. Attorney's office from 1971 to 1977. I apologize for not having listed each person who contributed to the success of that office in those years and whose efforts contributed to the collective success which became our legacy. There were many great individual performances then, and it was the beauty of the office that we all shared in it. It mattered less which person was most responsible for which victory—there was plenty of joy to go around to all whenever the occasions arose.

Many of those coworkers were interviewed for this book, and I offer my gratitude to each of them. Of special note were two men who not only possessed great legal skill but also an essential goodness in all that they did. Joel Flaum and Dan Reidy were models for how lawyers should act and how people should live. My last mention of a coworker is Howard Hoffmann. Howard was my trial partner in two major cases. There was no better partner around, and no better friend.

Special thanks also go to Brendan Sullivan. The eloquence of his tribute to Dan Webb in the foreword is matched only by its worthiness to the subject. His assessment is the perfect entrée to Dan's story.

There are four more people I need to specially thank. Three of them are my sons. After reading some early material, my oldest son Peter, a lawyer, offered some observations which were unerringly accurate and instructive. My son John, also a lawyer, devoted considerable time to early editing and constructive criticism. All of it was on the money, and I benefitted greatly. My son Paul, not a lawyer, has for years prodded me to write a book because of my itch to do so. His words of encouragement were finally heeded.

My last acknowledgement is for my judicial secretary from the day of my induction. Even before I became a judge, I made one of the best professional decisions of my life. As a newly appointed Chairman of the Illinois Commerce Commission, I needed to hire a secretary for my Chicago office. The secretary in my Springfield, Illinois office, Ruby Linderman, had served my predecessor. Ruby came with high praise and she stayed on. As for Chicago, I interviewed Jeanette Armstrong. After about a five minute interview, I knew there would be no candidate better than Jeanette. Members of the public, court staff, and other judges are uniform in their praise for her kindness, ability, and pleasant manner. Her characteristics have been my gift for thirty-seven years and a simple "thank you" seems inadequate.

FOREWORD

Dan Webb has a legion of friends and admirers. Any one of them would have been pleased to write the foreword for his biography. As I considered who to ask to do so, a famous Teddy Roosevelt speech came to mind. In "The Man in the Arena," Roosevelt describes the qualities of the man best able to evaluate another.

> It is not the critic who counts; not the man who points out how the strong man stumbles, or where the doer of deeds could have done them better. The credit belongs to the man who is actually in the arena, whose face is marred by dust and sweat and blood; who strives valiantly; who errs, who comes short again and again, because there is no effort without error and shortcoming; but who does actually strive to do the deeds; who knows great enthusiasms, the great devotions; who spends himself in a worthy cause; who at the best knows in the end the triumph of high achievement, and who at the worst, if he fails at least fails while daring greatly, so that his place shall never be with those cold and timid souls who neither know victory nor defeat...The man who does nothing cuts the same sordid figure in the pages of history, whether he be a cynic, or fop, or voluptuary. There is little use for the being whose tepid soul knows nothing of great and generous emotion, of the high pride, the stern belief, the lofty enthusiasm, of the men who quell the storm and ride the thunder.

I thought the person best qualified to write the foreword was not one of his intimates, but someone who was a worthy adversary of Dan's. Someone who knows firsthand what it takes to be a great trial lawyer, and also what it means to be one. One such man is Brendan Sullivan, Jr. His is a household name among the trial lawyers of the country. Sullivan's soul is anything but tepid and he has been known to not only ride the thunder but to create it. Brendan Sullivan, Jr. and Dan Webb have met more than once as adversaries in great battles in the courtroom arenas of the United States, the truest way one man can measure another. This is what he wrote:

> While it has been my unaltered practice NOT to talk about clients or the cases I've been involved in, I am only too happy to talk about Dan Webb. Some random thoughts:
>
> *Brilliance* – Dan can learn and master an extraordinary volume of factual material quickly. Usually presented to him by his team in large binders, he can read the materials as you and I would read the newspaper. Yet once through, the casual read leaves him filled to the brim with salient facts needed to try the case.
>
> *An insatiable appetite for work* – Usually, the brightest among us rely too much on brain power and do little work. Dan is one of the few people who understand that only with hard work can he win the case.
>
> *A visceral feeling against anything unjust* – Dan is repulsed by the injustices which pervade our system. He cannot abide injustice and much of what he does professionally is to prevent it.
>
> *Personable* – Many extremely bright people lack "people skills." Dan is a likeable, masterful advocate. Judges and juries actually like him. He knows how to relate to people. He knows how to make a jury laugh and to cry. Dan would not represent a true rascal (the jury thinks) because Dan is too nice.
>
> *Experience* – When we fly, most prefer the gray-haired pilot who has 27,000 hours in the cockpit. Dan is the most senior "pilot" in America. I doubt one could find another trial lawyer who has spent more hours in a courtroom. He lives there. He tries one case after another. Sometimes, incredibly, he tries two at once.

Instinct – Much of what a trial lawyer does is based on instinct. Dan has the ability to intuit the vulnerability of the witness he cross examines. He knows every legitimate "trick" in the book. No witness is his match, even expert witnesses who usually have more substantive knowledge than a trial lawyer could possibly possess.

Supported by the "A Team" – Dan has picked the best available lawyers to support him in trial. They know what he wants and what he needs to perform his role.

Ego suppressed – If he has one. Most trial lawyers have irrepressible egos which, unbeknownst to them, diminish their effectiveness. Dan is the consummate gentleman. He is professional and polite at all times, with adversaries, judges, co-counsel and his own team. He's entitled to have a big ego, but he doesn't.

Courageous – It takes a certain amount of courage to be a trial lawyer, to go into court and to argue a client's case. No case is certain of outcome. Most have extraordinary challenges and there is always the possibility of an outright loss. Some trial lawyers are terrified of losing and therefore they are not willing to try the hard cases. Dan will try any case when justice and the client require it.

Character and integrity above reproach – I have never heard a bad word or a criticism of Dan. He is the model professional. If he were appointed to the Supreme Court or to the office of the United States Attorney General, there could not be one word of justified criticism from any quarter of the country. There is only one Dan Webb in a generation. We all admire and respect him.

Brendan V. Sullivan, Jr., Williams & Connolly LLP

INTRODUCTION

It may seem odd that a United States District Court Judge would write a book about a practicing lawyer. Part of the reason, as best I can offer it, is that he happens to be a good friend. But truly, any history of the legal times would be incomplete without a recitation of the career of Dan K. Webb.

This book is about the many significant cases that were the canvases upon which Dan displayed his matchless skills in a career still thriving today. For much of his career, I have been a close observer and, in one instance, a co-participant.

My appreciation for Dan began when he and I worked in the same office at similar periods in our careers. We were both hired on the same day as Assistant United States Attorneys (in the U.S. Attorney's office) for the Northern District of Illinois in Chicago. Each of our lives to that point bore little resemblance to the other's but, once hired, those differences never mattered. What brought us together were similar desires and objectives, both personal and professional.

Trying cases, Dan believes, is both science and art. The science involves all of the preparation necessary to perform in the courtroom while the art is the craftsmanship used to present that groundwork and sway judges and juries.

Dan has created a methodology in how to structure and organize the distinct aspects of a trial, including direct examination, cross-examination, opening statement, final argument, and rebuttal argument. Each of these disciplines has its own features and function, and there is no aspect of trial work that Dan does not excel in.

One of the things he acknowledges he has been blessed with is the ability to think on his feet and adapt quickly when things start to go awry. "I have a short distance between my brain and my tongue," he says. No matter how well one has planned for a trial, experience suggests there will be unexpected and unplanned developments that need to be dealt with.

Cross-examining adverse witnesses is, perhaps, the most difficult of all trial functions to perform well. Dan believes it is necessary to develop "lines" of cross-examination, which he says will dictate whether the cross will be effective. This book contains some noteworthy examples of Dan's effectiveness at cross, such as the testimony he was able to extract from Colonel Oliver North during the Iran-Contra trial against Admiral John Poindexter.

Court transcripts are included throughout this book to help provide a full flavor of the cases and exhibit Webb's mastery in the courtroom. The reader should note that many have been edited for brevity and clarity.

During his period as an Assistant U.S. Attorney, Dan Webb first displayed his extraordinary skills in his investigative and pretrial preparation and the brilliance of his courtroom performances. As this book will show, for example, that hard work and readiness was key to securing a bribery conviction for Cook County Clerk Edward Barrett in the 1970s.

The private world of litigation, in most cases, no longer consists of the same intensity of labor or the steady diet of high profile and significant cases. For many, a career of trial successes as a prosecutor is usually enough to bask in for a lifetime. Dan Webb was not one of the many. When the time came to move on, Dan made the transition to a different professional life with ease and, to no one's surprise, his brilliance continued. As a private practitioner, he has represented clients in both private and public disputes of the highest profile and the most serious and far-reaching consequences, from corporate giants Microsoft and GE to former Illinois politicians Dan Rostenkowski and George Ryan.

Such has been his stature that even as his private practice flourished, he has been recalled to public service four times. One of those instances was to oversee the Operation Greylord prosecution which was both unprecedented in scope and came with the risk of disbarment.

I offer anyone the opportunity to appraise the same material addressed in this book in terms of the nature and difficulty of the cases described, their importance in the realm which they occupy, and the final outcomes decreed by respected judges and juries of citizens. The story of great achievement often lacks scientific precision or other objective measure. As such, I recognize that a book like this, written by a friend, may be viewed with suspicion. My hope is that the very friendship which exists will be seen as permitting an insight into events sometimes lacking in other biographical recitations and will serve to add luster to a professional career rather than detract from its uniqueness.

My desire is that the reader will enjoy the same measure of appreciation for Dan's marvelous work as I do. Notwithstanding the untold hours he has spent preparing for and trying cases, he has managed to maintain a balance in his life. Dan and his wife, Laura, have raised five wonderful children together. Dan also has many good friends and rejoices in their companionships and in spending time with them. One of Dan's strongest qualities is his value of loyalty. His good friends will attest to how he regularly practices it.

By any measure, Dan Webb is not only an extraordinary lawyer, he is also an extraordinary person. I have been blessed with his friendship for almost 50 years and realize my good fortune in sharing it. This book is my way of saying thank you. It is also my way of sharing with the world one of the greatest litigators of our time.

Riccardo Muti, the music director of the acclaimed Chicago Symphony Orchestra, was the second recipient of the Birgit Nilsson Prize for classical music. In his acceptance remarks, Muti recalled having risen early one morning to hear Nilsson rehearse a concert performance of Beethoven's opera "Fidelio" with Leonard Bernstein. "Even though, as a Neapolitan, one does not care to rise early, to leave home and travel—we are happy where we are—I had to see this great artist live." In saluting the many great singers from that stage, including Nilsson, Muti said, "We have no singers like this anymore, in part because our world, our careers, our lives move too fast. We need to save our culture, our history, for the future."

It can be no less for the other great artists of our time, including those whose stage is a courtroom. Dan Webb's devotion to the law is complete, inspiring, and is the reason I wrote this book about Dan, the boy from Bushnell.

Dan Webb (left) and Charles P. Kocoras

BUSHNELL
Agriculture
& Industry

CHAPTER 1
THE DEAN'S MISTAKE

Although born in Macomb, Illinois, Dan Webb was raised in the nearby farm town of Bushnell, a rural and isolated community 200 miles southwest of Chicago with little around it. But do not be deceived; there is much to be learned from the town, its people and the land it occupies. When it came time for Webb to leave, he took with him those traits and experiences. In significant respects, they were the essence of his strengths. Webb recognized "my upbringing in a small, rural community and coming from a modest background has grounded me in a way that has aided my success as a trial lawyer."

Webb's father, Keith, worked for a while as a farm-implement dealer, then tried the grocery business, and eventually became a mail carrier. His mother, Phyllis, was both a housewife and dental office secretary. Her principal devotion was to the care of her family. A sister named Diane, three years younger than Webb, rounded out the family.

Diane Hoyle said her brother was competitive at a young age. She described croquet games in which he would launch her ball a couple of backyards away. "He'd get real upset when he didn't [win], but he generally did because he was smart," Hoyle said. "We may have been hayseeds," Webb would say later, "but we understood competition as kids growing up."

Webb got hooked on the fictional lawyer Perry Mason while in high school. It was also during this time when one individual would help set his course in life. During a high school debate class, the school guidance counselor, Josephine Johnson, saw him perform. She told Webb how well he did and presented him with two books

> *The dream of becoming a lawyer had taken deep root at this point, and Webb displayed the first sign of what he would need as a lawyer: persistence.*

about great trial lawyers. One was about the hallowed Chicago attorney, Clarence Darrow. The other was about Earl Rogers, probably the most famous lawyer practicing in California. Webb read those books and, when he was finished, he knew he wanted to become a trial lawyer. This desire was the first demonstration of his single-minded fierceness of purpose and his drive for success.

He decided that a career in the tiny town of Bushnell was not for him and Webb planned his future accordingly. He enrolled at Western Illinois University in nearby Macomb and worked as an assistant manager in a campus residence hall, which covered the cost of room and board. Bushnell also was known as the home of the largest hammer factory in the world, Vaughan & Bushnell, and Webb worked there during the summers to help pay his way through undergraduate school.

At that time, Western Illinois University and the University of Illinois offered a program that permitted a student to matriculate into the law program at the University of Illinois at Urbana-Champaign after only three years of study at Western Illinois. No college degree was required. By the time Webb finished his three years, however, the joint program had been discontinued. The dream of becoming a lawyer had taken deep root at this point, and Webb displayed the first sign of what he would need as a lawyer: persistence.

Rather than accepting his fate and staying at Western Illinois for another year to get a degree, Webb sent applications to a number of Chicago area law schools. All but one of the schools rejected him because he did not have the required college degree. Loyola University was the exception and they offered him an interview. Wasting no time, Webb hopped on a train for his first ever ride to Chicago. He met with the Dean of the Law School, John Hayes, on a rainy Saturday morning. Dean Hayes, apparently looking at Webb's application closely for the first time, discovered the missing fourth year of college and the college degree. Sensing imminent rejection, Webb gave the Dean his first closing argument, emphasizing his high grades and displaying his infectious enthusiasm to become a trial attorney. To his credit and to Loyola University's everlasting benefit, Dean Hayes admitted the school's mistake. Saying he dragged Webb to Chicago because of his own oversight, the Dean told Webb he was going to take a chance on him. Dean Hayes never made a surer bet. Webb was admitted to law school without an undergraduate degree.

In 1967, Webb moved to Chicago and found two other law school students for roommates. Webb must have drawn the short straw because the other two slept in the bedroom while he set up a rollaway bed in a large closet located next to the toilet. With his clothes hanging down on him at night, Webb was usually the first one dressed in the morning. Having a place to sleep, to hang your clothes and to relieve yourself may constitute the comforts of home, but Webb and his mother would have preferred a different configuration. The rural boy from Bushnell tired of the arrangement and because his money was also running out, Webb had to make a change. He switched to night classes and took a day job. The First National Bank of Chicago hired Webb as a paralegal in the trust and probate department and agreed to pay his night-school tuition for the next three years. Webb began to breathe easier in his new apartment, one where the bedroom closet was left to perform its proper function.

Webb's choice of a day job, in addition to easing the living pressures he was dealing with, was also provident for another reason: he realized what he did not want to do when he became a lawyer. He found some of the work he was doing to be boring, and he believed that could never be said of trial work. Webb also felt that he was good on his feet, and the job of working on trust agreements, wills, and the administration of estates left you firmly planted behind a desk. While finishing law school, a brief period of employment at a small probate firm solidified his career choice for trial work that fueled his inner desire sparked by Perry Mason.

After graduating number two in his class in 1970, Webb wanted more than anything to find a job as a trial attorney. While working at the bank, some of the lawyers there told him that he should try to get a job as a federal prosecutor. Webb had never heard of Bill Bauer or Jim Thompson, but he wanted to try cases and was told that the U.S. Attorney's office was where they were doing it.

"I started following federal cases during my last year of law school and decided the best thing to do was to become a federal prosecutor," Webb said. "I went there because I thought I could try cases."

The U.S. Attorney's office was run by two outstanding lawyers who would go on to prominent public careers. William J. Bauer became the United States Attorney for the Northern District of Illinois in 1970, after previously serving as the DuPage County State's Attorney and as a judge on the Circuit Court for the 18th Judicial Circuit. About one year after serving as United States Attorney, Bauer was appointed as a United States District Judge for the Northern District of Illinois. Judge Bauer was later nominated to a seat on the United States Court of Appeals for the Seventh Circuit where he served as Chief Judge from 1986 to 1993, and assumed senior status in 1994.

Judge Bauer was succeeded as U.S. Attorney by James R. Thompson in 1971. Thompson served until 1975 when he resigned to run for governor of Illinois in the 1976 election. He took office in January 1977 for the first of four terms as governor. After leaving public service, Governor Thompson joined Winston & Strawn, a major Chicago-based law firm, where he served as Chairman of the Executive Committee and as Chairman and CEO of the firm.

When Judge Bauer became the United States Attorney, he was authorized to increase the size of the office from 22 lawyers to 32 lawyers. In making that expansion, Judge Bauer and his successor, Thompson, never adopted the practice of favoring politically connected or politically supported candidates for employment. Political favoritism was in vogue in most public offices at the city, county, and state levels in the Chicago area, and was usually the litmus test for employment—something Webb was very much aware of.

That philosophy of political hiring was captured in a memorable expression once directed to Abner J. Mikva. A graduate of the University of Chicago Law School and a former law clerk to a Supreme Court Justice, who later became a Congressman and White House Counsel, Mikva had an interest in politics. While still in law school, Mikva stopped by the headquarters of the Chicago ward in which he lived. Mikva said he walked in, addressed the ward committeeman, and said he wanted to volunteer to work for Adlai Stevenson and Paul Douglas. The ward committeeman took the cigar out of his mouth, glared at Mikva, and said, "Who sent you?" Mikva responded, "Nobody sent me." The ward committeeman put the cigar back in his mouth and said, "We don't want nobody that nobody sent." Neither Judge Bauer nor Thompson smoked cigars and neither was ever heard to utter that phrase. However, Webb did not know that when he interviewed. Thompson said that at the time, Webb was a fresh-faced, wholesome-looking farm boy from western Illinois. "I thought that was a face that would resonate with jurors, particularly mothers," Thompson said.

Webb was interviewed by Deputy Chief of the Criminal Division, Sam Skinner. The interview was going well until Skinner, after carefully examining the resume, asked Webb for his references. This was the question Webb dreaded. He had been told this request was to be code for who his political sponsor was. His resume did not list references of any type. Blurting out that he did not know his ward committeeman or politicians—that he was just a guy from Western Illinois—Skinner burst out laughing and said, "Those days are long gone, I'm asking about law school references that can describe your law school career." With great relief, Webb gave him the name of Dean Hayes and some law professors. He thought to himself, "I have a shot at this job."

Webb had worked hard and had a good academic record, Skinner said. "To do as well as he had in school, I thought he was worth taking a chance on," Skinner said. "The odds were pretty good that he would be successful, but not that successful."

To the district's great benefit and the office's great credit, hiring decisions were based on merit. Although many prosecutors' offices favored applicants with some legal experience, that was not required under Bauer and Thompson. Scholastic achievement, a strong work ethic, and enthusiasm for the mission of the office were sufficient. If a candidate had some legal experience, so much the better, but lack of experience was not a basis for rejection. Webb "impressed the hell out of everybody" when he interviewed to become an Assistant U.S. Attorney, Bauer said.

D. Arthur Connelly was a grizzled veteran in the U.S. Attorney's office. He had gone to law school with Judge Bauer and had made his way to the office long before Thompson and Bauer. Connelly was Chief of the Criminal Division when

Judge Bauer became the U.S. Attorney. He was smart, tough, and no nonsense. Connelly was not given to classroom lectures on how to be a trial lawyer, and he was a little short on offering mock demonstrations or how-to sessions. But he was terrific in skill and experience, and if one watched him perform in the courtroom and listened carefully whenever he spoke, the lessons were invaluable.

One of Connelly's duties was to interview job applicants and offer his judgment on their prospects. "Art had an interesting way of making notations at the bottom of the applications," Bauer recalled. "One of the notations he often used was 'not married, but does not live at home.' Thompson always yelled about that one. He'd say 'What does that mean? I'm not married, but I don't live at home.' And Connelly would always say he never understood why, if somebody wasn't married, he wouldn't stay home and live with his family."

"I thought I knew Art's code pretty well, but when I got Webb's application it said on the bottom 'NBBR.'" Bauer said, "I called him in and said 'NBBR? What the hell does that mean?' Connelly replied, 'Nice boy, but rural.'" Connelly got it right on both prongs. He may have known how those rural qualities of hard work and devotion to the task would be so vital in pretrial investigation and trial preparedness. Webb was hired as an Assistant U.S. Attorney for the Northern District of Illinois in early 1971.

None of our careers started off in any rip-roaring way in the courtroom. There was simply too much to learn, and we all began at the very bottom of the U.S. Attorney's office. In early 1971, Farrel "Tex" Griffin, Dan Webb, Tyrone Fahner, and I started in the Complaint Unit. In terms of the sheer number of cases presented to the U.S. Attorney's office by the federal agencies charged with the investigations of crimes, the four of us were assigned the greatest percentage of cases that came into the office. The agents that referred cases to us were mainly from the Federal Bureau of Investigation, Secret Service, Alcohol Tobacco and Firearms, Drug Enforcement Administration, Postal Inspection Services, and Immigration and Naturalization Service. None of us had any experience in any of the criminal areas represented by the different agencies, each of which had jurisdiction over different types of crimes.

> *We would be getting a million dollars' worth of experience, but it would be shoved down our throats a nickel at a time.*

Many of the presentations involved simple fact situations and only one or two subjects of the investigation. The more complex matters, usually involving more than one suspect, were assigned to other units in the office.

On his first day of work, Webb was reading a manual describing crimes and prosecutions when what would prove to be a typical experience for the unit unfolded. A Secret Service agent entered Webb's office and told him that the case that the agent was presenting had been assigned to him. The first decision that must be made upon an agent's presentation is whether to accept the case or decline to prosecute, in this case a "one check" forgery for a modest amount of money. In assessing the case, Webb was bewildered and appeared so. The agent asked Webb if it was his first day on the job; he confessed that it was. The agent then said that the office always declines to prosecute one-check cases. And so his first prosecutive decision was made—a no go.

In our first year in that unit, the cases came in fast and furious. The hours were long and provided many lessons. Because we had so many cases in court and before so many different judges, we routinely covered for each other. "All of us wanted to be on trial or getting ready for trial," Fahner said. We each tried from 20 to 30 cases during the first year or so, usually before juries, often without another AUSA at the table. It was great experience, but sometimes quite painful. As our supervisor told us, we would be getting a million dollars' worth of experience, but it would be shoved down our throats a nickel at a time.

Webb delivering his closing argument in the Gill/Fahey case as Judge Richard Austin listens.

United States v. Frank J. Gill and James Fahey

CHAPTER 2
THE CHICAGO STRIKE FORCE

Experience leads to confidence, and we all developed some accordingly. Webb was always inexhaustible, and his skill level soon matched his energy. According to Fahner, Webb is happiest when he is getting ready for trial and trying a case in the courtroom. "What makes him tick is his love of the courtroom," Fahner said.

At one point, Webb was prosecuting a man accused of theft from an interstate shipment. He had cut his teeth on those types of cases, and he spent long hours on this one to make sure it was strong. As he stood before the jury to begin his final argument, the defendant stood up and told the judge that he wanted to plead guilty. A prosecutor less certain of the outcome might have stepped aside, allowed the plea of guilty to proceed, and be content with a guaranteed conviction. Not Webb. He had prepared so well for his final argument that he objected to the offer of the guilty plea on the grounds that, "I'm only 10 minutes away from a guilty verdict." The judge looked down with a barely concealed smile masking his look of surprise. In all the years he had presided and even with all the twists and turns that criminal cases often produce, he had never before heard a prosecutor object when a criminal defendant wanted to plead guilty. The judge wisely denied Webb's objection.

During those early years Webb never lost a case that went to trial. As his reputation grew, so did his responsibilities. He was soon entrusted with investigating and prosecuting public officials, including law enforcement officers. Like most citizens, the four of us in the Complaint Unit grew up with the belief that police were honest and deserving of our admiration. Their work was often fraught with peril, and confronting danger as a regular diet of their sworn duties commanded our respect. To question whether police officers were law violators rather than law enforcers did not go down easily, for the oaths we took were similar to the oaths the policemen took: to uphold the law, not to debase it. Nevertheless, the guiding principle of any prosecutor worthy of his or her office was to follow and develop the evidence, wherever it might lead and however distasteful it may personally be.

For probably as long as Chicago has been incorporated as a city and has had a police force, there have been stories about an errant few officers willing to take a bribe and look the other way. Handling small problems on the street for small sums between the private citizen and the beat officer is an efficient, albeit corrupt, way that many such confrontations get resolved. When these infrequent occurrences become more frequent, when the amounts exchanged get larger and larger and the readiness of more and more officers to do business with the citizens they serve increases, the way in which we police and govern ourselves becomes imperiled.

The young Assistant United States Attorneys hired by the Bauer and Thompson administrations were turned loose with all their energies and talents, hell-bent to develop their skills in the courtroom while honoring the commitment to prosecute anybody who violated the law in a serious manner. Leading the charge was Dan Webb.

The United States Department of Justice once had units called Strike Forces in every major city. These units were usually housed in the same offices as the U.S. Attorney's office and while they were both under the direction of the Attorney General, the Strike Force units were much smaller than their counterparts. Originally formed to combat La Cosa Nostra and other types of organized crime, they operated separately from the U.S. Attorney's office and took orders directly from Washington, D.C.

The Chicago Strike Force in the early 1970s was headed by Sheldon Davidson and was composed of a handful of attorneys. The Strike Force developed a case against two police officers, one a lieutenant and one a sergeant. It involved an apparent shakedown of a liquor store owner accused of the sale of liquor to a minor. As presented by Davidson to United States Attorney Jim Thompson, it was not a particularly strong case since it involved the word of the owner of the liquor store and one other person against two ranking officers with little corroboration of the shakedown. Davidson wanted Thompson to loan one of his top lawyers to help try the case. Thompson gave him Webb; it was 1972 and Webb had been at the office less than two years.

"Sure, I gave Webb big cases, but you either had confidence in someone or you didn't," Thompson said. "He was obviously a young kid with ambition. There were no small cases. You had to go with the youngsters you had. And this guy was a very able trial lawyer."

At trial, the government laid out its case. Stojan Kovacevic was the licensee of a combination tavern and liquor store called Chicago-Oak Liquors. Sometime in July 1971, a Chicago police officer named Reddon entered the store and told Kovacevic that he had sold beer to a minor. Kovacevic could not recall the sale so Officer Reddon left the store and returned shortly with the minor to whom the beer had been sold. After a conversation between Kovacevic and Reddon, Reddon left with the minor. A short time later, Lieutenant Frank J. Gill and Sergeant James Fahey entered the store. Gill told Kovacevic that he had sold liquor to a minor.

Kovacevic claimed he could not recall this and suggested that the officers search the minor for an identification card. Gill and Fahey then left and returned shortly and told Kovacevic that they did not find any identification on the minor. Kovacevic insisted that he still did not believe it. Gill then said that he would have to appear before the Liquor Commissioner. Kovacevic asked if something could be done; Gill asked what he meant. Kovacevic then offered Gill $150, but Gill countered with a demand for $500.

A man named Constantine "Dino" Sanichas was in the tavern while Gill and Fahey were there; he was acquainted with Fahey. Approaching Fahey, Sanichas

---

> *"The judge was a grizzled, crew-cut veteran with a reputation for chewing up defense lawyers and mocking young prosecuters."*

asked him what the problem was. Fahey told Sanichas that the owner was caught selling liquor to a minor.

Willing to act as a go-between for Fahey and the owner, Sanichas talked with Boris Kovacevic, the establishment's bartender and Stojan's brother. Returning to Fahey, Sanichas told him that Kovacevic would pay $300 to avoid arrest. Fahey told Sanichas to get the money and meet him on the corner. They met there after Sanichas got the money from Boris Kovacevic, which he then gave to Fahey. Some weeks later, Fahey gave Sanichas $40 for his help.

After joining the prosecution team, Webb assessed the evidence that had been gathered to date. Although the government had two witnesses who could directly testify to the payoff to Gill and Fahey, they were certain to face denials at trial by both of the police officers. In addition to those expected denials of misconduct by Gill and Fahey, the only two government witnesses were in opposition, leaving the government's burden of proving guilt beyond a reasonable doubt to be a difficult if not insurmountable challenge.

It became clear to Webb and Davidson that they would have to make every effort to find the minor who was at the center of the charged extortion. Finding him would be difficult because, not surprisingly, no police report of the incident existed which would have supplied his identification.

Even as the trial began, the FBI agents were searching for the underage customer. The only information they had was his last name and the approximate location of his home. As luck and hard work would have it, he was found as the case was being presented. Webb decided to take a calculated risk and save him for rebuttal evidence in case either or both of the defendants should testify. Not calling the young man as a witness in the government's case in chief meant that he would not have to be listed as a witness in the trial. Witnesses who may or may not testify as government rebuttal witnesses to the defense case do not have to be disclosed.

The defense at trial was as simple as the charged crimes. Gill testified that, indeed, the officers had given the liquor store owner a pass but they did so because the boy was only a few days away from his 21st birthday and by the time the case reached court, the judge would throw it out because the underage customer would

> *It was obvious the judge thought we were just blowing our whole case out of the water. Everybody thought that I was getting killed.*

be of age. Gill testified that no money was taken for the kindness they showed the owner. Both defendants were apparently unaware of the young man's availability as a witness. They were also unaware, or had forgotten, that the young man was only 17 and not days away from being 21.

Judge Richard B. Austin presided over the trial. As described by a 1985 *Chicago Tribune Magazine* article, Judge Austin was "a grizzled, crew-cut veteran with a reputation for chewing up defense lawyers and mocking young prosecutors." Despite his bearish stature, the judge took a liking to Webb and often would spend hours in his chambers giving the nice but rural boy from Bushnell courtroom tips and advice.

During his cross-examination of Gill, Webb's baby face and his obvious youth made it apparent to both the judge and jury that he was not an experienced trial lawyer. Webb turned what might have been a failing to his advantage.

"I played the dumb bumpkin from Southern Illinois," Webb said. "I had Gill repeat his story several times so the jury would know it. Judge Austin just turned around in his chair and turned his back to me and the courtroom. It was obvious he thought we were just blowing our whole case out of the water. Everybody thought that because Gill was so good, I was getting killed. When I was through, Judge Austin turned around and said sarcastically, 'Is there anything else, Mr. Webb?' I said, 'I have one more witness, your honor.'"

A young man who did not even look 17, let alone near 21, entered through the back double doors of the courtroom. The journey by this teenager allowed him to walk slowly and deliberately past the defendants and only a few feet away from the entire jury box. The jurors saw the boy close up while he walked and each juror fixed on his appearance.

By the time the young man reached the witness stand there was little doubt left. His testimony as to his age at the time of the incident was rendered superfluous by his obvious youth. Even before he uttered one word, the jurors knew that the young witness was years shy of 21, not days.

Gill testified—repeatedly, thanks to Webb's constant questioning—that the youth was almost 21. "He looked even younger than he was," Webb said. "It was obvious that Gill's story was false." The jury also knew right then that the defense claims in the case held no water. Both defendants were convicted and sentenced to jail. Gill received a four-year sentence while Fahey received three years.

This thoroughness of preparation and trial strategy would characterize every case Webb ever tried. "[Webb] goes at a pace that would leave others looking for bed rest," Thompson said. "I think it comes from his desire to succeed. He's a very disciplined guy."

The Gill/Fahey trial also highlights another of Webb's strengths. Just as he won with a surprise, 17-year-old witness walking slowly past the jury box, Webb would prove in the years to come to be a master of connecting with juries.

Webb delivering his closing argument in the Barrett case.

United States v. Edward J. Barrett

CHAPTER 3
THE TRUE COST OF FREE ELECTIONS

Edward J. Barrett began his political career as a precinct captain on Chicago's south side. Even with an outgoing personality and a good war record (having enlisted for World War I at the age of 17), Barrett surprised most people when, in 1930, he was elected as the youngest Illinois Treasurer in history. He went on to serve as State Auditor two years later. Barrett reenlisted during World War II and while serving as a Marine Sergeant in Hawaii and the Great Lakes Naval Training Station, he was elected Illinois Secretary of State—without making a single speech.

When Barrett's good friend, Richard J. Daley, was elected mayor of Chicago in 1955, Daley engineered Barrett's appointment to succeed him as Cook County Clerk, a position he held until 1973. The genial Barrett had 44 years of public service, having lost only one election. Although he served into his early 70s, his political popularity had never waned. Yet suspicions of political corruption triggered a federal investigation.

Fresh off its success in the Gill/Fahey case, the Justice Department Strike Force again came calling on U.S. Attorney Thompson. This time, Davidson specifically requested Dan Webb to work on the Barrett investigation and Thompson agreed. The Strike Force had been checking allegations that kickbacks may have been paid for the purchase of voting machines. The investigation had started in Philadelphia and was centered on the Shoup Voting Machine Corporation. Irving H. Meyers, while president of Shoup, had been charged with a mail fraud scheme involving the purchase of used voting machines in Tampa, Florida and their resale at new-machine prices in Houston, Texas.

> *If Barrett chose to testify and denied Meyers' assertions, a likable and popular elderly man with a cherubic face would be pitted against a self-admitted crook engaged in wide-ranging acts of criminality.*

During that time, County Clerk Barrett was a ranking member of the Democratic Party in Chicago and until then, he had never been tainted by scandal during his long public career. With evidence from the Strike Force, Barrett was indicted by a federal grand jury in 1972. There were 16 counts in the indictment with the principal charges accusing Barrett of receiving $180,000 in cash in return for the purchase of 900 Shoup voting machines (bribery) and failing to pay taxes on the bribery money (income tax fraud). Barrett was also alleged to have received kickbacks when buying insurance for the voting machines (mail fraud).

The alleged mail fraud scheme was premised on the notion that a government official has a fiduciary obligation to the office and the citizens he or she serves. Often referred to as a duty of "honest services," this obligation requires complete fidelity to the office. The use of the office to personally enrich him or herself without public disclosure of payments received by virtue of the office is a breach of the loyalty and honest services owed to the office and its citizens.

The indictment of the popular Barrett was one of the first brought by the Thompson administration involving major political corruption. As such, it received considerable press and public interest.

Barrett's attorney was Thomas Foran, who had served as the United States Attorney immediately preceding Judge Bauer during the turbulent 1960s. Foran had been chief trial counsel in the four-month trial known as the Conspiracy Seven case that involved the prosecution of seven men accused of conspiring to incite violence during the 1968 Democratic National Convention in Chicago. As the United States attorney from 1968 to 1970, Foran established a remarkable conviction record in the fight against organized crime. His skill and experience in the courtroom were well established.

The Barrett case was one of the highest profile cases to date during the Bauer and Thompson years. Although Strike Force lead Attorney Sheldon Davidson would be on the trial team, Dan Webb was entrusted with the role of first chair for the government at trial despite having less than two years in the office. In a twist of fate, the Barrett case was randomly assigned to the Honorable Richard B. Austin, the same judge who presided over the Gill/Fahey case.

Webb was assigned the responsibility for Irving Meyers, the government's main witness. In his pretrial preparation, Webb spent hours with Meyers conducting extensive interviews, preparing for the specifics of direct examination, and conducting mock cross-examinations to prepare him for what to expect at trial.

Webb learned that Meyers' corruption began almost immediately after he became president of Shoup in 1965. He would issue checks payable to different professionals as fees for services that they never rendered. The recipients would cash the checks and then return to Meyers 40 or 50 percent, while retaining the balance. Meyers would send each of these recipients a federal tax form 1099 at year-end to insure that the recipients paid tax on their purported earnings. Meyers' illegal currency manipulations enabled him to generate a fund of $700,000. This fund was the source of his bribe payments to Barrett and many others.

When the federal government caught up with Meyers, he did the only thing he could do to help himself, he offered to name all those he had bribed or worked with in his various acts of corruption and testify for the government. He and his counsel engaged in plea bargain discussions with the federal prosecutors in Pennsylvania. At the end of those negotiations, Meyers wound up with an agreement that, fairly analyzed, was as sweet as any deal this side of the purchase of Alaska by the United States of America from Russia. Neither Webb nor Davidson had any involvement in Meyers' plea deal.

Meyers' part of the deal was to plead guilty in Pennsylvania to several counts of conspiracy and mail fraud and to two counts of filing false income tax returns that did not report as income portions of the $700,000 fund. Meyers also agreed to testify in other proceedings about what happened to the $700,000. In return, the government recommended a sentence on all counts of one year and a day, to be imposed under a statute making Meyers immediately eligible for parole, and to be served at the detention facility at Eglin Air Force Base in Florida. The government also granted Meyers transactional immunity to preclude state prosecutions for his many state crimes.

The final concession made by the Pennsylvania prosecutors recommended that the IRS exempt Meyers from civil tax liability on any part of the $700,000 that he would testify under oath he had paid as bribes or political contributions to public officials. Barrett's counsel claimed this last provision requiring testimony against public officials was a violation of Barrett's constitutional due process right to a fair trial. Barrett's counsel moved to bar Meyers from testifying against his client at trial.

The theory of the motion was that the government, in effect, had paid Meyers upwards of $1 million to testify against Barrett and others. Each time he testified, Meyers was relieved of the obligation to pay income tax and fraud penalties on whatever amount of the cash he testified he gave to the official. Barrett's counsel described such testimony as "purchased" by the government and argued it should not be allowed. The trial court denied the motion, but allowed defense counsel to argue to the jury that the civil tax immunity agreement gave Meyers a motive to lie about giving $180,000 to Barrett.

In preparing for trial, it was all too clear to Webb and Davidson that their one witness on whom the trial outcome would depend had the most serious credibility issues that could be imagined. The nature and length of Meyers' own criminality hung like a millstone around his neck. And for every dime he claimed he put in Barrett's pocket, he relieved himself of paying the tax and a 50% penalty on those amounts.

As Meyers explained to Webb in pretrial briefings, only he could describe the manner, amount, and purpose of the payments to Barrett. No other witness or other piece of evidence could buttress the fact, manner, or reasons for the payments to Barrett. If Barrett chose to testify and denied Meyers' assertions, a likable and popular elderly man with a cherubic face would be pitted against a self-admitted crook engaged in wide-ranging acts of criminality with the promise of a direct financial benefit to himself in return for his testimony. It was a daunting prospect for Webb and Davidson.

Because of Meyers' importance as a witness and his credibility issues, Webb needed to corroborate every possible detail of his testimony with any records or documents available. The law enforcement agents assigned to the case were dispatched to gather every piece of available evidence.

Pretrial preparation included the anticipated testimony of Barrett. Just as questions for all government witnesses had to be drafted and structured, the same procedure applied to cross-examination of all conceivable defense witnesses and, especially, for Barrett. This process would not only address his expected denials of receipt of the bribe payments, but would cover all of the records reflecting contacts and meetings between Barrett and Meyers. If the jury didn't believe Meyers, there was little doubt that Barrett would be acquitted. As one of the first major political corruption cases to be brought by the U.S. Attorney's office in many years, its outcome was portentous.

The trial began in February of 1973 and Webb conducted the direct examination of Irving Meyers. Meyers testified that on September 13, 1965, in accordance with Barrett's "request for bids," Meyers proposed on behalf of Shoup to sell 250 voting machines to Cook County at $1,791 each. Having received no response, Meyers came to Chicago in December 1965 and met with Barrett in his office. Barrett told Meyers that the county did not have the funds to purchase the machines at that time but might have the money in the forthcoming budget.

Meyers' trial testimony established the key facts. Meyers told Barrett that any future dealings between Shoup and Cook County would be between Meyers and Barrett. Meyers said he was committed to pay Barrett five percent cash on all voting machine sales to Cook County; Barrett responded that he had already been receiving more than five percent. Meyers said that this was a new ball game, and that is all he could commit to pay. After Barrett then demanded $200 per machine, Meyers told Barrett that the only way he could get $200 per machine would be to raise the price of the voting machine by $100 to the county; Barrett assured him that he could take care of the $100 increase in price because Cook County had obsolete voting machines that needed to be replaced.

When Barrett asked about getting the money, Meyers responded that it would be after Shoup was paid for the machines. Barrett said there would be times when he would need money up front, so Meyers agreed to give Barrett half of the money when Shoup received a solid contract or purchase order from Cook County, and the other half of the money when Shoup received payment. Meyers told

Barrett at the conclusion of the meeting that any dealings would be between the two of them alone, and that Meyers never wanted to be in a position where there was a third party present. This was for his protection and for Barrett's protection.

Barrett ran for re-election in November 1966. Meyers made a personal $1,000 campaign contribution, which Barrett acknowledged in two letters, one prior and one subsequent to the election. After the election, Meyers called Barrett to congratulate him. At that time, Barrett gave Meyers his unlisted home telephone number, which Meyers placed in his personal address book.

Webb meticulously presented the evidence against Barrett before the jury. The essential facts of Barrett's receipt of about $6,000 in insurance commissions for the coverage on the county's voting machines were not seriously in dispute. As for the allegations of his income tax violations, Barrett's defense was inextricably connected to the alleged bribery payments by Meyers. Webb and the government claimed the bribery money had been omitted from Barrett's tax returns. If Barrett was acquitted on the bribery payments, the tax counts would disappear as well. In a real sense, the fate of Barrett at trial depended on whether the jury believed Meyers and it would be up to Webb to establish his credibility.

In preparing Meyers, Webb also spent significant time readying him for the opposition's counter-attack. "Cross-examination is a culture shock," according to Webb. "There is nothing else in the world that simulates the cold, sterile experience of cross-examination. Witnesses, unless they are experts, have never been is this type of situation. They will get defensive. They will feel antagonized. They will show anger. I can tell within two minutes whether a witness has been pre-cross-examined by a skilled lawyer to prepare for my cross. I can see immedi-

---

> *We're trying to build a house with the witness's testimony. If lawyers fail to thoroughly prepare the witness for cross, the house they just built can be destroyed in minutes.*

ately that they are not comfortable with this culture; they don't understand why I am coming at them so strong. They haven't thought through all these issues and been taught to avoid irritation and anger."

Cross-examiners invariably ask "yes" or "no" type questions in order to limit the witness from giving some background or context to the yes or no answer. A witness may tell the cross-examiner that they cannot answer yes or no, and good pretrial preparation should arm them with that response.

Another approach is for the witness to commence their answer to yes or no questions by initially offering the context which makes the answer less harmful to the witness and gives it a greater breadth of comprehension. This approach also permits the lawyer who directly examined the witness to ask on redirect examination what it was that the witness wanted to say earlier when they were cut-off by the cross examiner.

Webb follows a three-step process in preparing his key witnesses for cross-examination. He begins by identifying each major point that will be raised on cross and addresses them with the witness as discrete, three-step modules. Webb calls the first step in the module the "talk through." While sitting at a table with the witness, Webb will discuss the point and how the other side might use it. "We talk through so we understand the point that they are going to make," Webb explains. "Then I suggest to the witness potential ways to respond to those questions to get their view across and we identify 'safe harbors' or talking points that they can use when responding to the cross questions."

Webb's second step is called the "Beat Up." This is an essential step that many lawyers leave out. In this step, Webb would role play with the witness, taking on the role of the cross-examining lawyer. Webb would cross-examine the witness on that point in an aggressive, skilled way. "I will spend hours putting together a binder on the way I think the cross-examination questions will unfold, how they would use the deposition and other evidence, and I perform the cross-examination. And I do so in a harsher way than I think the other lawyer will do it."

The third step is a reverse walk through. After the witness has been through the cross, Webb reviews with the witness what they did right; what they did wrong. If he feels the witness did not survive the cross, he'll do it all again. "What a lot of lawyers don't really understand is that we've worked hours, days, sometimes months with witnesses to get them ready for direct. And that is our job. We're trying to build a house with the witness's testimony. If lawyers fail to thoroughly prepare the witness for cross, the house they just built can be destroyed in 10 minutes."

According to Webb, "the reason I break down cross-examination into these modules is that I want the witness to get focused on each point individually, not the sum total impact. If each point is handled appropriately, individually, the sum total impact will be as minimal as we can make it."

For the Barrett trial, Webb also prepared and delivered a one-hour final argument, in which he highlighted for the jury the effect of corrupt public officials. "Corrupt government, expensive government. If a public official is going to accept bribes, it is going to cost someone eventually, but the saddest thing about this case is that the true victims of this case were the taxpayers of Cook County. Mr. Barrett wasn't satisfied with the normal bribe; he wanted more, and because of that the people of Cook County were defrauded of that money. It is as simple as that. He was too greedy."

Then, Webb focused on establishing Meyers' credibility by carefully demonstrating to the jury how his entire testimony was corroborated by the evidence. Webb began by establishing a concrete timeline of the November 1967 bribe payment. Using detailed charts that referenced key evidence, Webb was able to provide the jury with a clear picture to support Meyers' bribe paid to Barrett. Webb effectively used Meyers' testimony to show step by step that what Meyers had said was true. According to testimony, Meyers called Barrett in the first part of November. "Barrett said, 'Tomorrow the contract is going to be approved.'" Webb would go on to demonstrate that this phone call must have been on November 6th. Meyers continued, "I called him a couple of days later. Barrett said, 'The contract has been approved.'" Webb continued to walk through Meyers' testimony all the while reinforcing his credibility and the truth of his statements by showing the jury corroborating evidence.

Meyers testified, "I thereafter made the reservations and the day before I flew to Chicago, I sent Murray Hirshorn down to one of those safety deposit boxes where we kept the slush fund money and he brought me back $30,000. I made a phone call to Barrett and said I am coming out tomorrow."

"I flew out there the next day and there was Barrett at O'Hare Airport," Meyers said. "We had lunch. I didn't stay very long. I didn't have much time between

> *Corrupt government, expensive government. If a public official is going to accept bribes, it is going to cost someone eventually.*

flights. I was just going there and coming right back to Philadelphia. I met with him. I gave him the $30,000 and then I came back to Philadelphia.'"

Webb directed the jury's attention to his charts to build credibility. As he pointed to each part of the timeline, Webb said, "[Meyers] said he called [Barrett] the day before the contract was approved, and right here is a phone call, 321-5656. This is 11-6 of 1967. This is the 1967 phone bill. If you will look over there you can see that that phone number is the County Clerk's number."

Webb pointed to exhibits that echoed Meyers' testimony and showed that the contract was approved by the Board of Commissioners on November 7th. Webb continued by showing the booking memo for Meyers' travel. "If you will look at this exhibit, you will see that Meyers did exactly what he said he did, he made a reservation and he didn't give himself too much time," Webb said. "He arrives here in Chicago at 12:47 Chicago time. He is departing at 2:10."

Then Webb appealed to the jury's common sense. "Now, if the man were coming to Chicago to conduct any type of legitimate business like going down to the Loop or going anywhere at all, he would have to give himself more time than that. You couldn't catch a cab and leave the airport, go through traffic, get downtown or anywhere else, have any type of a business meeting and get back to the airport in time to catch that plane. It just would not have happened. That is because Meyers did exactly what he said he did, he only met with Barrett at the airport, got off the plane, had lunch, gave him the $30,000 in a blue zipper valise, got back on the plane."

Though Meyers' testimony had been corroborated, Webb saw an opportunity to use Foran's cross-examination and opening statement to further establish Meyers' credibility.

> *I also want to discuss with you a few other factors which prove to you that Irving Meyers did nothing but tell the truth when he*

was on the witness stand. First of all, Irving Meyers was subjected to cross-examination by Tom Foran, a very fine, fine attorney, for two days, a severe cross-examination.

And you saw him testify, you listened to him, you saw his demeanor, and there can be no doubt in your mind that after being cross-examined by Mr. Foran, that he was telling nothing but the truth. Foran threw everything at him but the kitchen sink, and he responded to all the questions in only one way, to tell the truth, because that's all he had to do. He wasn't going to get up there and lie. He went up there and told the truth.

Next, Webb reminded the jury of how Foran had promised in his opening statement that he would prove that Meyers' had squandered his "slush fund" money on gambling and that Barrett had not received any of that money as a bribe. Webb continued,

Then on cross-examination—in some of his questions on cross-examination he tried to imply, through his questions, that certain facts or evidence existed which would prove this to you.

But, ladies and gentlemen, you haven't seen one speck of proof of that. And do you want to know why? Because it doesn't exist. Irving Meyers didn't spend that money on himself. He was bribing public officials all across the country, because that's the way he had to do business in the voting machine industry. It's not very pleasant, and he went to jail over it. But he came in here and he testified about it, and he told you that's what he had to do, and that's where he spent his money.

Now, Foran failed to prove what he said he was going to prove. When he started to cross-examine Irving Meyers, he started asking questions, and when he asked questions, he's not under oath. You can imply anything you want to in a question, but the proof is in the pudding. He has got to put up at some point and show you what the evidence is. He asked the questions, implied certain facts existed, and then didn't prove them to you.

Rather than resting on that statement, Webb reviewed each of Foran's cross-examination suppositions to show how there was no evidence to support what he was suggesting with his questions. "Foran said, 'Didn't you go down to the safety deposit box and steal that slush fund money and put it into your checking account?' Meyers said, 'No, sir, I did not do that.' Foran just left it hanging there. He wanted you people to [infer] that that's what he did." Webb then reminded the jury of the government's redirect examination, during which they provided documentation to back up Meyers' testimony—testimony that Foran was trying to call into question.

Webb told the jury, "But if we hadn't come back and cleared that up for you, based on Mr. Foran's questions you would have thought that—or maybe you would have drawn the inference—that maybe Meyers did do that. But he didn't, and we proved to you that he didn't."

Foran had attempted to show that Meyers was a gambler and had spent the slush fund money on gambling in Las Vegas rather than paying a bribe to Barrett. Webb skillfully deflected these claims by showing that Meyers paid his gambling debts out of his bank account, not his slush fund. Foran also told the jury of some checks that were supposedly paid to Las Vegas payees, but Webb reminded the jury that Foran never produced those checks.

Webb said, "Mr. Foran didn't show him those checks, because those checks don't exist. Mr. Foran was sitting there asking a question, hoping you would draw an inference, an inference that didn't even exist. If Mr. Foran had had more checks payable to Las Vegas payees, he would have shown them to you. He didn't show them, because they didn't exist."

Webb also knew he had to address the plea agreement Meyers had received. Webb characterized Foran's discussion of the plea agreement as another "smoke screen" to show that Meyers lied to receive his plea agreement.

Webb explained to the jury that there was nothing to hide about the plea. The government didn't offer to let him go if he testified.

Irving Meyers took his medicine. Irving Meyers had to plead guilty to four indictments. He's a four-time convicted felon, for bribing public officials and filing false income tax returns, and he went to jail because of it.

You want the government to put him on the stand and let him tell the story, and you make the decision. You are the people that in part elected that man to office, and you can pass judgment on him, and you have a right to hear about corrupt politics, and you heard about it. There's absolutely nothing wrong about the deal entered into between the government and Irving Meyers.

Webb told the jury that something else corroborated Meyers' testimony about the slush fund: the financial records of the "conduits," those who were providing the kickbacks that funded Meyers' bribes to politicians like Barrett.

We read off the testimony in stipulation, which means that everyone agrees that these people existed, they were professional people across the country, they were receiving large sums of money and kicking back money to Irving Meyers so that he could pay off public officials. They paid all the income tax on it, the conduits. The federal government didn't lose anything. The conduits took the money and reported all the income tax on it, and then kicked back money to Irving Meyers. Irving Meyers then paid off the public officials.

Now, if Irving Meyers had taken the witness stand and said, "I paid large sums of money to public officials," you would be asking yourself, "Well, where did you get the money Mr. Meyers?" Well, he told you, "I got the money from a slush fund."

You might say, "Well, what proof of that is there? We just have your word." Well, you don't have his word in this case, you have far beyond that. You have the conduit testimony itself in the form of a stipulation. There is no doubt in your mind that Meyers did accumulate what has been called a slush fund, and did put it in a safety deposit box in Philadelphia. That's not even an issue in this case.

The only issue in this case now is that Mr. Foran told you in his opening statement that he was going to prove that that $800,000 was spent by Mr. Meyers, and he didn't prove one, not one speck of evidence on that. Not one. And there's nothing that you can find that Meyers spent the money himself, because Meyers passed it on to public officials.

Webb also summarized the bribe charges. "We brought in every piece of evidence there was, the documents, the testimony. There can be no doubt in your mind that as to those first 10 counts in the indictment that Edward Barrett is guilty as charged beyond a reasonable doubt."

Webb had prepared Meyers during pretrial briefings to fully supply all relevant information in his dealings with Barrett and to truthfully acknowledge his multiple acts of criminality without attempt at minimization. Meyers was not surprised by any question put to him on cross-examination and his manner of testifying convinced the jury of his truthfulness. The other items of evidence that Webb presented corroborated what Meyers told the jury; they were the background brushstrokes in Webb's clear and convincing picture of the mosaic of bribes.

After the government's case was completed, consisting principally of Meyers' testimony, the defense presented four brief witnesses and rested. Judge Austin said, "The defense rests?" in obvious surprise when Foran and his co-counsel, James J. Casey, made the announcement. While it is every defendant's constitutional right to remain silent and decline to testify, the absence of a direct denial by a prominent public official can be a telling void. When a self-admitted crook says he bribed a public official by giving him $180,000 in cash over time, a reasonable person may expect a strong denial and genuine outrage as the innocent response. When none is forthcoming, the silence is ominous.

The jury convicted Barrett of all 16 counts of the indictment. As the Court of Appeals stated in affirming the conviction, "The only important witness against the defendant on the bribery charges was Irving H. Meyers." Some of the public comments of four of the jurors who chose to speak after the verdict included the following sentiment, "We felt compassion for the 72-year-old county clerk, but the evidence was so strong we had to find him guilty."

Barrett's age and physical condition were obvious to the jury and to the officials in the U.S. Attorney's office. Nevertheless, he was sentenced to three years incarceration and a fine of $15,000. He was suffering from a variety of ailments and the U.S. Bureau of Prisons designated Barrett's home as his place of confinement. Then U.S. Attorney Sam Skinner interceded with the U.S. Parole Board and two days after the Bureau of Prisons' decision, the Parole Board voted to parole the ailing Barrett.

The successful outcome in the Barrett case would launch efforts at uncovering additional evidence of governmental and political corruption. As the Barrett case demonstrated, well developed and well prepared cases could overcome the popularity of high-ranking government officeholders when the evidence is warranted.

Casey, one of the lawyers who defended Barrett, recognized Webb's excellent work in the case, especially his ability to connect with jurors. "His ability makes him a very good trial lawyer," Casey said. "But he's also a regular guy. He's not out to get anybody and I think that makes an impact on juries."

Jim Thompson's early prophecy that Dan Webb had a "face that would resonate with jurors" was prescient, even as it did not go far enough. His face may have been the starting point for the jury's assessment, but the display of his civility, knowledge of the facts, the ease of his courtroom manner and the professionalism of his presentation all made it easy to trust what he said was true. The Barrett jury was just one of many that would validate Webb's trial artistry.

Webb delivering his closing argument in the Braasch case.
United States v. Clarence E. Braasch, et al.

CHAPTER 4
TAKING DOWN THE BIG CLUB

In 1972, around the time of the Gill/Fahey prosecution, whispers of widespread police illegality became louder and louder. The Chicago Strike Force had been investigating rumors of a "club" operated by some Chicago police officers. The investigation focused on the 18th Police District, which operates in an area that includes Chicago's famous Rush Street night life area. These businesses are particularly vulnerable to enforcement because liquor licenses can be revoked for a variety of reasons. Whether over-serving patrons, selling to minors, or failing to prevent fights, nightclub owners can be at the mercy of the police.

Everyone was aware of random incidents of police demanding payments to forego enforcement, but word had filtered to the Strike Force about an organized structure of shakedowns. While the Chicago Police Department has as its motto, "We Serve and Protect," the motto for the 18th Police District vice squad came to be known as "We serve ourselves and protect those who pay us." The investigation revealed that bar owners made monthly payments to the police, who then divided the proceeds among members of the vice squad.

Sheldon Davidson had his plan for the Strike Force and he made his now-familiar trek to U.S. Attorney Thompson's office with a specific request this time: he wanted Webb to be turned loose on the 18th District with a squad of FBI agents and Strike Force personnel under his direction. While some attorneys with fewer than two years in the U.S. Attorney's office were still getting their feet wet, Webb's trial performances already established his capacity to handle whatever assignment he was entrusted with. The investigation he was charged to lead this time would ultimately uncover official corruption of such

> *A team of FBI agents and the strike force went out into the field. We started shaking the trees and the apples fell.*

a widespread nature that Tom Clark, an Associate Justice of the U.S. Supreme Court, called it "a betrayal of public trust of the most alarming type to a free society."

Webb embarked on his mission along with Herb Biegel, an experienced Strike Force attorney then handling the investigation. The prosecutors would be aided considerably by recently enacted legislation known as the Organized Crime Control Act, one provision of which allowed the government to bestow "use immunity" to witnesses who refused to testify based on their constitutional right not to incriminate themselves. Use immunity precluded the government's ability to use a person's statements or testimony against them, which therefore eliminated the witness's ability to rely on the right to refuse to testify. In short, a witness given use immunity was forced to testify, with refusal to do so resulting in their being held in contempt of court and jailed until they testified truthfully.

The bar owners had recognized that failure to pay the police would result in frequent visits to their establishments by the officers looking for real or imagined violations, among other instances of harassment. The owners suspected of making payments to the officers were subpoenaed to testify before the investigating grand jury. While Webb viewed the bar owners as "victims" of the police extortion scheme, under the letter of the law, they were guilty of bribery. It therefore came as no surprise that they uniformly refused to testify under the Fifth Amendment. The prosecution team realized they needed to grant them immunity to secure their cooperation and testimony—nabbing the police officers was the priority.

Webb directed the efforts of scores of FBI agents and prosecutors in their work interviewing dozens of bar owners about illegal payments to the police. "A team of FBI agents and the strike force went out into the field," Webb said. "We started shaking the trees and the apples fell." The dimensions of the crime were quickly established. The bar owners named three officers, John "Skippy" Cello, Sal Mascolino, and Eddie Rifkin as the "collectors." At this point, the prosecutors needed to decide whether to indict the collectors on the substantial evidence provided by the bar owners and take them to trial, or to grant them use immunity to go after a larger group of corrupt officers.

Immunizing the collectors would mean that they would escape punishment for their considerable roles in widespread police corruption. However, as Webb suggested, having the collectors testify after immunity would afford prosecutors the ability to charge the largest number of defendants in a single indictment. Webb believed a single conspiracy, appearing before one judge and having only one trial for a group of defendants rather than many different judges was, by far, the superior way to proceed. The U.S. Attorney agreed.

Not surprisingly, the three immunized collectors refused to testify. Cello and Mascolino were promptly sent off to jail with Rifkin following sometime later. The three officers were surrounded by thousands of other inmates—many of whom were incarcerated because of Chicago police officers. They did not have many friends in the crowd.

Sympathetic to the plight of Cello and Mascolino and appreciative of the fact that their silence directly benefited them, other members of the 18th vice squad held a fundraiser to assist the Cello and Mascolino families. When Rifkin joined the two in prison, he told them about the fundraiser, and also that some of the money raised was ripped off and never reached the families. Cello and Mascolino's anger put an end to their silence, and Rifkin followed suit; they began to cooperate with Webb, which was a turning point in the investigation.

Webb was in charge of working with the three main police officers, developing their testimony, and later putting them on the stand at trial. In researching for their testimony, Webb discovered that the organized club he believed existed among the vice squad members was not the only such one in the 18th District, and, surprisingly, not the biggest. The prosecutors were told of a "big club," where everything was collected by one man, Lt. Robert Fischer, and distributed to officers higher up than the vice squad.

The prosecutors summoned Fischer to their offices to confront him and to learn how much further the corruption spread. They bluntly told him what they knew of both the little club and the big club, and that he would be considered for an immunity grant depending on the information he had to offer. Fischer had plenty, and he offered it all.

As he would later testify at trial, Fischer described 10 mob bars in the 18th District that regularly made payments to him through a mob-connected bagman named Bill Gold. The businesses being protected by police included discos, strip joints, and gambling parlors. He detailed how warnings were given to the syndicate bars about vice raids by the police in return for the payments. Fischer explained how the money he collected was distributed to higher-ranking officers, and that is when he surprised Webb and the prosecutors. He identified District Commander Clarence Braasch as one of the primary beneficiaries of the big club corruption payments.

Even as Fischer was telling his story to the prosecutors, Webb was already considering how he would present this testimony to a jury. Fischer was able to describe how payments were made and who was involved, but Webb knew that jurors would assume police officers were law abiding. As shocking and high reaching as the corruption appeared to be from Fischer's story, Webb asked him how a jury could be expected to believe him. Fischer responded with another surprise. He presented Webb with a small, black book. As Webb turned page after page, he realized Fischer had meticulously recorded details of monthly payments made by the establishments. Webb would later call Fischer the best witness he ever put on the stand as a prosecutor.

Webb and the other prosecutors knew they needed to keep the indictment simple and streamlined, or else the trial jury would have difficulty keeping straight a multitude of transactions involving a multitude of defendants. Complexity and confusion can sometimes be the enemy of the prosecution, whose burden is to prove each defendant guilty beyond a reasonable doubt. Consequently, the strategy was to have a main charge that was a single comprehensive conspiracy in which all the defendants were to be named.

In the summer of 1972, the prosecutors began presenting the evidence to the grand jury, and in December of that year, they returned a 16-count indictment against 24 Chicago police officers. The 24 defendants represented the largest number of people ever criminally charged in the Northern District of Illinois in a single indictment.

Webb would serve as lead trial counsel, joined by AUSAs Farrel "Tex" Griffin and James Holderman. Webb and Griffin had little experience in the office and

> *After stating his name he slumped down in the chair, his head sagged, and his hands disappeared. His face was masked with fear, and Webb knew he had to find a way to calm his star witness.*

Holderman had even less. They would be opposed by a veritable who's who of the Chicago criminal defense bar, all of whom had considerable experience and prior successes. They included George Cotsirilos, Patrick Tuite, Harry Busch, Jo Anne Wolfson, David Schippers, R. Eugene Pincham, and Martin Gerber. Every one of these prominent Chicago defense lawyers would become personal friends with Webb. He felt strongly that, "lawyers on the other side of a case are my opponents, not my enemies."

Although Webb was excited by the challenge that the defense counsel would pose, he knew it would be a tough competition. As he later noted, "I was only a year and a half out of law school and I was in awe of those lawyers."

Witnesses from the 53 establishments subject to the vice unit shakedowns were presented after immunized witness Cello described the workings of the criminal conspiracy. All of the immunized witnesses testified in addition to Cello, Mascolino, and Rifkin with Fischer providing almost all of the evidence against Braasch. Although there is no guarantee a defendant will testify, Webb felt certain when the case was indicted that Braasch would testify on his own behalf; thus, Fischer's importance could not be overstated.

When Fischer first sat in the witness chair, things did not go as planned. Fischer looked like anything but a polished police lieutenant and a man of credibility. After stating his name he slumped down in the chair, his head sagged, and his hands disappeared. His face was masked with fear, and Webb knew he had to find a way to calm his star witness. Webb had to change tactics to recover his witness and convince the jury to believe his testimony.

Temporarily abandoning his intended line of relevant questioning, Webb asked Fischer a lengthy series of questions about his background, his education, and other similar questions, designed to steady him and instill some self-confidence before Webb went into the substance of his trial testimony. At the first break, Fischer told Webb he had to put his hands on his knees to keep them from shaking uncontrollably. Between the easy manner of Webb's approach and the early break in the testimony, Fischer found his footing and testified in the way he was capable of.

The government's case was very long, lasting about 10 weeks. It was a skillfully arranged and implemented prosecution, with Webb interspersing the voluminous bar owner testimony with immunized police officer testimony. Webb did this to avoid the jury getting bored with repetitive bar owner testimony about payments with the more exciting immunized police officer testimony.

The evidence put on by the government in its case in chief was massive, as was the testimony of the bar owners. To gather it, organize it, and present it at trial required enormous mental and physical effort. The trial itself lasted two months. Ask any trial lawyer in America and they will attest to the pressures confronted in such circumstances and the exhaustion that ensues. One defendant pled guilty at the start of the trial while 23 defendants' cases went to the jury, nine of whom testified in their own defense. In effect, there were 23 mini-trials taking place, since each defendant was entitled to separate and distinct consideration as to his guilt or innocence. Webb later recalled that this was probably his most grueling trial experience because of the long days in the courtroom combined with non-stop, late night preparation of the many bar owners who would be called to testify the next day. By the end of the government's case, he was exhausted, but confident his case had gone on well.

As the defense case started, Webb turned his attention to preparing for the likely cross-examination of the lead defendant, Braasch. Webb's early instincts were correct as the police commander decided to testify, giving Webb a chance to cross-examine him. Not unlike Webb's earlier decision to withhold a witness for use in rebuttal for maximum effect in the Gill/Fahey prosecution, the same courtroom instincts were used in the Braasch case. Prior to trial, the government team had gotten ahold of some letters authored by Braasch that revealed a lack of law enforcement and arrests in protected establishments in the 18th District. The government could have introduced those letters in its case in chief as relevant evidence, but Webb and the other prosecutors thought the impact of the letters would be maximized for use in cross-examining Braasch should he choose to testify. If Braasch did not take the stand, the value of the letters could be lost. Reflecting on the decision in the Braasch case, Holderman said, "Dan's always had a sense of what a real person considers persuasive with regard to the facts."

Braasch did testify and he asserted that he was vigilant in ferreting out corruption in his district. In his cross-examination, Webb highlighted for the jury how Braasch's letters graphically showed the 18th District vice squad never made any arrests at the bars participating in the vice club. Any arrests made at those bars were made by the Vice Control Division, a police unit operating out of downtown police headquarters, and not under Braasch's command. Additionally, Webb convincingly argued to the jury that none of the arrests mentioned in those letters were about the big ten bars in Braasch's "big club."

Holderman noted that just before a lunch break, Webb put a stack of arrest reports in front of Braasch and requested that the judge ask the police commander to review the reports during the recess.

"The way [Webb] did that, that heightened the drama and impact of the evidence, and that sunk the case," Holderman said. "Braasch could not recover. He looked guilty from that point forward."

During the trial, there were two major issues. One was the jury's ability to assimilate all the evidence that it would hear and apply it to all of the defendants. With so many defendants, witnesses and charges, Webb knew he needed a way to present his case in a way the jury could understand and remember it. For use in his final argument, Webb prepared a graphic chart in which all of the defendants were compartmentalized as to their roles, their groupings with similarly situated defendants, and the names of witnesses who testified against them. The chart was a visual presentation of the prosecution's case that was easily remembered.

Webb believes "visual aids can make or break a trial." The visual aids don't need to be complicated; they are a simple way to break up the monotony of oral presentation and provide a visual image to help the jury remember what is being said. Webb referred to the chart as his "pyramid" because each level showed the escalation from the street cops up to the sergeant and to Braasch. "I went for three hours in my closing and that pyramid was my rock."

The other concern was whether the jury would believe Braasch's protestations of innocence or whether Webb's cross-examination was effective enough to discredit him. Webb believed, probably correctly, that if they failed to convict

Braasch, the trial would be widely viewed as a significant loss for the government in its efforts to identify and root out corruption. As he described it, "I was on pins and needles while waiting for the verdict."

Of the 23 defendants, 19 were convicted, including Commander Braasch. Webb's cross-examination of Braasch was apparently effective. "He didn't stand up very well," one juror said after the trial of Braasch's testimony on direct and cross-examination.

Nothing described above is meant to suggest that Webb was a one man government band in the investigation and prosecution in the largest single trial in Chicago Federal Court history. As *Chicago Tribune* reporter Robert Davis wrote, "This case rewrote the record book on police corruption in Chicago and outdid the Summerdale scandal of the late 1950s." Two other young prosecutors of exceptional ability, Griffin and Holderman, ably assisted Webb. Countless numbers of FBI special agents and other government lawyers were equally devoted to rooting out Chicago's corruption in its law enforcement ranks.

What cannot be denied, however, is that Webb was at the epicenter of all the necessary investigative efforts to bring about the indictment. In conducting the prosecution, Webb demonstrated his tirelessness and thoroughness in developing relevant evidence in this significant matter after only two years' experience in court. Webb's courtroom presence and conduct matched his elaborate pretrial preparation. By all accounts, his was the commanding presence in a lengthy trial

---

> *I'm this young hillbilly kid from southern Illinois who managed to go to night law school and worm my way into the U.S. Attorney's office," Webb said. "Then, all of sudden, I find myself trying the biggest police corruption case in Chicago's history.*

resulting in the conviction of so many. Even in his modesty, Webb had to acknowledge that the Braasch case put him on the map of successful trial lawyers.

"I'm this young hillbilly kid from southern Illinois who managed to go to night law school and worm my way into the U.S. Attorney's office," Webb said. "Then, all of sudden, I find myself trying the biggest police corruption case in Chicago's history."

A check of records has not revealed any other federal criminal trial where so many defendants have gone to trial at the same time. "To be able to manage a case of that magnitude as a young lawyer out of law school and go through three months of trial against the best defense lawyers in Chicago, and to win the case in a commanding fashion—it was a huge learning experience for me."

Webb not only wanted to be a good lawyer, he knew it was important to be publicly recognized as such. Early in his career, he saw his name in a local newspaper. He was thrilled and said to himself, "Here I am, a guy from a small town in Illinois and my name is in a Chicago paper—that's not bad." The Braasch verdict did more than mention his name in a small paper. The successful outcome was headline material in all of Chicago's major papers, and his picture and those of the other prosecutors were splashed on page one of the *Chicago Tribune*. It was a memorable photo and memorialized a historic legal effort and result. From that day on, Webb had no worries about public mention.

Webb conducting the direct examination of lead drug dealer witness Milton Kelly in the Marquette 10 trial.

United States v. Ambrose, et al.

CHAPTER 5
PROSECUTING THE PROTECTORS

It has been an age-old lament in parts of Chicago that drug users have no difficulty finding drug dealers even as the police are unable to do so. The case that became known as the Marquette 10 supplies at least part of the explanation. It involves the round-the-clock sale of drugs on the west side of Chicago for three years with the aid of a band of Chicago police officers. As a federal judge in Chicago put it, Chicago's finest routinely ignored the many complaints from citizens about the drug dealers flaunting their wares so boldly that the press of customers caused traffic jams.

In early 1979, there was an independent entity in the Chicago Police Department called the Vice Control Division (VCD) that was investigating the Smith-Kelly drug operation, also known as the Avers Avenue group because that was where most of their drug sales occurred. It would later be determined that the Smith-Kelly operation was the largest in Chicago. Captain Jack Hinchy and the VCD brought the case to the U.S. Attorney's office, and Assistant U.S. Attorney James G. Schweitzer led the investigation to build the case, indicting Milton Kelly, Green D. Smith, and 11 other people in the fall of 1979 in a massive illegal drug distribution case.

During the Smith-Kelly trial, one of the witnesses was Kalvin Shannon who had been inside the operation but decided to turn state's evidence and testify against the other dope dealers. Based on his testimony and that of others, the jury convicted the members of the drug operation and they received stiff jail sentences.

While the convictions were important, Shannon's testimony revealed something far more troubling to the prosecutors—there were police officers in the 10th Police District that were taking

> *As the U.S. Attorney in the early 1980s, Webb would have to decide whether to again indict corrupt law enforcement officials. In addition, his office would have to convince a jury to trust convicted drug dealers over police officers.*

payoffs from the drug dealers. That testimony would trigger the investigation of corrupt police officers later dubbed the Marquette 10.

The investigation took time because the potential witnesses were the drug dealers making the payoffs, and prior to their convictions and sentences, they had no incentive to testify against the police officers. The same streets where they sold their drugs were where these police officers patrolled; the success of their drug operation was tied to little or no law enforcement oversight. The U.S. Attorney's office determined that granting immunity to these drug dealers would be the only way to get them to testify. They had already been convicted of drug-related crimes and given long prison sentences. Giving them immunity for their police corruption conduct was a logical step for the U.S. Attorney's office to expose rampant corruption in Chicago's 10th Police District.

What happened next shocked the investigators. One by one, these drug dealers confirmed police corruption in not just the Smith-Kelly operation, but a total of 10 operations within the 10th Police District. While their testimony provided a detailed description of these drug operations and the related police corruption, the investigators recognized the challenge ahead of them. As the U.S. Attorney in the early 1980s, Webb would have to decide whether to again indict corrupt law enforcement officials. In addition, his office would have to convince a jury to trust convicted drug dealers over police officers.

The Marquette 10 case is the story of how some members of the Chicago Police Department not only sold their integrity and violated their oaths to enforce the law but became outlaws themselves. Although it is not necessarily a new story, the size and scope of the illegality made it an important chapter in the annals of law and order in Chicago. Judge John Grady, the experienced judge who presided over the many weeks of trial, confirmed the extraordinary nature of the police officers' unlawful behavior. "These crimes that were committed in this case come about as close to unmitigated evil as anything I have encountered in my lifetime," he said.

As became apparent to federal law enforcement officials, it is difficult for a large, illegal drug enterprise to flourish in the open without official protection. However, investigating and prosecuting police corruption involving drugs was also going to be a significant challenge in large part because of the backgrounds of the witnesses who were making the police payoffs. Who can testify about payoffs to police to buy protection for dealing drugs? Drug dealers, of course. The credibility of these witnesses was a real concern. As one of the defense lawyers later argued to the jury at trial, "This is one of the most unusual prosecutions ever to be brought in this building, and I say that because for the first time you have criminals accusing police. They are criminals, admitted perjurers, people who have no conception of what a sworn oath means."

So it was established from the beginning that the investigation would be as extensive as possible, with as many witnesses developed as could be found. They included Green Smith, Milton Kelly, and C. W. Wilson. Each of the three had been the head of a drug distribution enterprise in Chicago and each had been convicted, along with many of their subordinates, of a variety of serious drug crimes. All three had already been given substantial prison sentences after jury trials.

Upon my induction as a United States District Judge in Chicago on November 24, 1980, I inherited the case of *U.S. v. C. W. Wilson, et al*, which included Wilson and nine of his drug sellers. After a multi-month trial, nine of the 10 defendants were convicted and sentenced. The jury could not agree about the tenth defendant, but he was later convicted after a second trial.

Dan Webb and his assistants knew the names of the major drug dealers and their employees at the outset of the police investigation. Getting them to testify would prove to be another matter. The government was able to amass a substantial number of the witnesses with the selective use of immunity, particularly for the most important witnesses who had previously been convicted.

A 67-count indictment was returned against 10 police officers in November 1981 after an exhaustive investigation. The defendants were accused of accepting $250,000 in cash bribes, guns, narcotics, and other valuables in return for protecting two multi-million-dollar-a-year drug rings operating on the West Side of Chicago. Nine of the defendants were tactical unit investigators and the tenth was assigned to the gang crimes section.

In exchange for money and goods, the defendants were accused of failing to arrest the drug dealers or their employees, warning the drug dealers of impending raids by honest police officers, ignoring many complaints from citizens about drug dealing activities, and beating and threatening to kill a drug dealer who was competing with the protected drug dealers.

U.S. Attorney Webb, at the suggestion of several of his assistants, committed to personally trying the case, along with his exceptionally talented Assistant U.S. Attorney, Jim Schweitzer. Also added to the trial team was a bright young attorney named Michael Siegel. When Webb became U.S. Attorney, he decided that he did not want to be solely a manager. "I thought you could run the office and be a good administrator," he said. "And at the same time, you could still be a leader by showing the office and the community that you could get down in the trenches, try major cases and get your hands dirty. That was important to me."

The trial lasted an exhausting three months and saw close to 100 witnesses testifying on both sides of the case. Webb and his two fellow prosecutors were up against 14 defense lawyers. Webb was known for his comprehensive preparation and it was on full display throughout the case. Schweitzer recalled going into Webb's office at about midnight one evening. Webb was preparing for cross-examination, filling up legal pad after legal pad with questions for the police officers.

"By the time he got up to cross-examine people, he did not even need his notes," Schweitzer said. "He had already gone through the mental gymnastics. Nobody will ever out-prepare Webb."

As an indication of its length and breadth, Judge John Grady afforded each side a total of 14 hours for final arguments. The protocol in U.S. District Court in Chicago is that the government goes first in its final argument followed by the lawyers for each defendant. After all defense counsel have finished, the government gets the last word by virtue of a rebuttal because it has the burden to prove each defendant's guilt beyond a reasonable doubt.

The time given to the government is divided between its opening portion—called summation—and the rebuttal argument. The defense's time is apportioned voluntarily by the defendants and their counsel. While the government summation and all defense counsel's arguments are structured and prepared prior to their delivery in open court, the government's rebuttal must be responsive to the defense arguments. Even though a prosecutor can anticipate some of the arguments defense counsel will make, the prosecutor cannot know the exact arguments that will be made or the emphasis given by each of the defense lawyers.

In the Marquette 10 case, Jim Schweitzer was designated to give the summation for the government. It lasted approximately three hours. Each defense counsel argued for many hours before Webb had a chance to present the government's rebuttal. Even a legal amateur can appreciate the necessity for a trial lawyer to be fully familiar with all the evidence in the case, quick to recall it, and eloquent enough to counter the defense claims with persuasive force.

What follows are portions of Dan Webb's rebuttal argument, showing how difficult it was for him—or any other prosecutor for that matter—to prosecute police officers. The trial drew broad attention and interest. According to Schweitzer, other federal judges in the Dirksen courthouse came to watch Webb deliver his rebuttal.

> *May it please the court, Mrs. Wolfson, and gentlemen of the defense, ladies and gentlemen of the jury.*
>
> *I must tell you that as I have patiently sat in that chair listening to the defense arguments for—if I counted right—about 17 hours, I must tell you that on occasion, because of the emotional, sentimental—on occasion, theatrical—presentations by defense counsel that I was moved by the eloquence of what they were telling us. But then my mind would harken back to the astounding volume of evidence that exists in this case that establishes the wrongdoing of these 10 Chicago police officers. And I would then realize that eloquence and sympathy can never be substituted for evidence in a court of law while we are presenting a case to a jury.*

As the arguments proceeded and I listened to the defense counsel in this case try to explain to you why these defendants should be acquitted by this jury, there was a very simple concept or proposition or saying that we have all heard that kept ringing in my ears, and as the arguments proceeded, it kept getting louder. But it was so simple and so elementary that I thought I ought not to mention it for fear that someone would think I am trying to simplify something when I am really not. But I know that lawyers often make things far more complex than they have to. And so I will tell you what the phrase that kept ringing in my ears was—that two wrongs do not make a right. Those dope peddlers that testified against these police officers are bad, evil people, and they ought to rot in jail. And as long as I am the United States Attorney, I will do everything I can to see that that is what happens to them.

But police officers cannot take the wrongdoing of these people and use it as a barrier or a shield to disguise their own misconduct. These police officers cannot have chosen to participate in graft and corruption with those witnesses and then put up this barrier and say, "innocence, because there are so many wrongdoers that I could never be found or should not be found guilty by a jury of my peers." They cannot do that.

When I became the United States Attorney, to be faced with indicting these 10 men who represent brothers that I have worked with during my entire adult life, I will tell you [that] was the single hardest thing I have ever done as a prosecutor. But I would do it again tomorrow and the next day and the next day because the volume of evidence against these men was so overwhelming. It wasn't even a close call, not even close.

But I learned from these cops that I worked with that there is one thing they don't do—the honest cop, the good cop. He doesn't take that star, that shield, and hide behind it. If he is doing something wrong, he admits it, he stands up, he accepts the conse-

> *I cringed when I heard their lawyers stand up and say to this jury that you must find these defendants not guilty because these 10 men are the only barrier between you and the terrorism on the street. To that, ladies and gentlemen, I say bunk. Poppycock. That simply is not true.*

---

quences of what he has done. As I have sat here and watched this trial proceed, I have watched the artificial light in this courtroom glisten and shimmer off of those badges as they wore them here in this courtroom. And then I cringed when I heard their lawyers stand up and say to this jury that you must find these defendants not guilty because these 10 men are the only barrier between you and the terrorism on the street.

To that, ladies and gentlemen, I say bunk. Poppycock. That simply is not true. These 10 men gave up the right to be our protectors the first day they decided that it was easier to sell their honesty, their integrity, and the stars that they wear here; when they found it was easier to take money from a dope peddler than it was to deal with the narcotics problem.

But ask the honest policeman about the corruption that these 10 men decided to engage in when they sold the thing that they couldn't sell, the oath when they became a policeman. When corruption takes over any police department, any unit inside a police department, it's like a cancer. It starts slowly, but gradually it grows and it grows and the cancer grows and all of a sudden you have a monster, and there is only one thing you can do, and that is cut it out and get it out of the police department. If you don't do that, the devastating destructive force that corruption has inside a major metropolitan police department is probably beyond your comprehension, nor should you ever have to comprehend it.

The reason for it is because of peer pressure. Look at this case. [It started with two policeman becoming dirty], but it grew and grew and grew and all of a sudden in 1978 there's 10 of them.

Do you know what the honest policeman goes through? You remember Lowery's testimony, the defendant Curtis Lowery, about the fight he had or the argument with other officers because they heard he was on the take?

Do you know how hard it is to be a cop out there and work with the scummy dope peddler syndrome and to say to yourself, "I'm not taking a dime from those bums. I'll put them in jail. I'll convict them, or maybe I'll lose but I will not take a dime. I will not buy Mary a new pair of shoes with dope peddler money. I won't become corrupt."

But you know what happens when peer pressure takes over? It's astounding, and there but for the grace of God go a lot of very strong police officers because all of a sudden there's two, there's four, there's six, there's eight policemen on the take, and not only is no one doing anything about it, these men seem to be doing fine.

But that's the evil that has to be dealt with, and that is why police corruption cannot be ignored just because the people who paid them the money have backgrounds that make them such that normally you—or I won't say you—I as a prosecutor would not want to put them on the witness stand.

You are going to hear a lot through my argument. I am so delighted that the defense proceeded in this case with a defense so that you could see [how] some of these police officers tried to defend the conduct that they engaged in on the street. You are going to hear me refer to it frequently.

Henry Jackson was on the stand; while he was testifying, I finally said, "Mr. Jackson, you are an honest cop, aren't you?"

He said, "Yes, I am."

I said, "Mr. Jackson, you are not trying to suggest to this jury that police officers ought to get put into a position where they would know that they could take money as often and as frequently and as much as they wanted from dope peddlers and that they could never be prosecuted for it? Could never be held accountable for their conduct, because the witnesses who would be the witnesses against them were disreputable?"

Do you remember what Mr. Jackson's answer was? He said, "That would be bad."

That is right. That would be bad, and that is why I signed the indictment that brought these 10 policemen here. And that is why you are sitting here as jurors in this case, because that type of attitude that would bestow total and complete immunity on these police officers just because the witnesses that they chose for their criminal partners have backgrounds that are not as good as we would like them to be...if we could never prosecute them—and that is what they are suggesting—then there would be chaos.

There are some very simple facts in life. When police officers do go bad—by the way, the bulk of those 13,000 policemen out there on the street are honest—but when they do, they do not take their payoffs from the local parish priest. I do not end up with witnesses that I can put on the stand who will testify about the corruption that are not involved in criminal activity.

Maybe the best place to start is, what did the defense try to inject into the case and try to bestow upon you to use during your deliberations that they shouldn't have?

These are the 10 cops in the 10th District that we have the evidence on that they're corrupt. There they are. They're sitting there for you to look at.

Just so you understand, once Kalvin Shannon—in December of 1979, in another trial which you've heard about, the Smith-Kelly drug trial—got on the witness stand and blurted out that there were allegedly police payoffs in the 10th District, the whole world knew that we had an investigation, and it hadn't even started.

And, from that day forward, the investigation that ultimately started—and which I'm going to tell you about in a few minutes—from that day forward it would have been impossible to go out and start filming police payoffs.

Dope peddlers and cops transacting their business on the streets, it's impossible to get that kind of evidence. But they tried to tell you that because that evidence doesn't exist, that they ought to be found not guilty. And that's not true.

The two major issues or broad questions that I want to talk about in rebuttal is, number one, did it happen? Now, here's what I mean by "did it happen?" Was there widespread narcotic trafficking in the 10th District that was protected, aided, and assisted in part, at least, by police payoffs? Not necessarily these 10, let's set that aside. But did it happen? I mean, were they drug trafficking out there and were there police officers getting payoffs?

The second broad question, which I'll get to after I finish the first, is, assuming it happened—and you might guess that that is going to be my conclusion ahead of time—but assuming that it happened, did these 10 defendants participate in it [in such a way] that you can find them guilty?

As far as "did it happen?", let's start off and I'm going to take about ten seconds on was there widespread narcotic trafficking? Absolutely.

[There were a] lot of narcotics being sold in the 10th District, but were there police payoffs that aided and assisted?"

Webb reminded the jury of all the testimony and physical evidence of the rampant drug dealing within the 10th Police District. The Smith-Kelly narcotics operation was functioning in the same location 24 hours a day, 365 days a year. Webb would compare their street sales to sales at a vegetable shop and then he shifted his focus to the involvement of the 10 police officers.

How could [the Smith-Kelly operation] even exist if there were not some assistance and help from the police officers that worked right there in the district where it went on?

At least, if you didn't even have a piece of evidence, it's certainly a lot of circumstantial value to [show] that a narcotics operation can operate out there in the streets of Chicago. Lines of cars, lined up; you had to stand in line to buy drugs.

When I first heard about it, I thought it was a joke. But it happened.

Webb used the defense witnesses to make his case. Using the testimony of the other side's witnesses to support your case can be extremely effective and Webb saw an opportunity during rebuttal to do just that.

I'm delighted that the defense decided to proceed by putting some of these witnesses on the stand.

Captain Hinchy, again God bless him, spent his entire life working in narcotics. His entire life, professional life, as a police officer. Heading up what they called the narcotics section of VCD.

They've called him an expert, and I'll say he may be the leading expert in this country on narcotics. And he deserves every bit of that praise.

And it's this expert, Jack Hinchy, do you remember something he said? I thought it was astounding and so important. [He] was talking about a time he remembered when Green Smith, one of these major narcotic operators, had been brought down to 11th and State for some interrogation, as they call it.

And Hinchy turned to Green Smith at some point in time and said, "How much are you paying off the cops to be able to operate out there?"

Jack Hinchy knew. He'd been a cop in the city for 30 years. Jack Hinchy's been in every street in this town. Jack Hinchy knew. He knew the structure of the police department, he knew the 10th

District. Jack Hinchy would have bet his life at that moment that there were police payoffs in the 10th District.

And I'll take that; I'll take Jack Hinchy as a witness any day of the week in this courtroom. Thank you for calling him.

The defense put witnesses on the stand to prove [police payoffs] didn't happen. What they wanted to do was to try to show you that there wasn't any police misconduct out there; and, to do it, they called to the witness stand, I think it was three witnesses from VCD, this group of investigators that operated out of 11th and State.

So, since these people had been out there, the defense thought they might have been able to say they didn't see anything wrong. And since they didn't see anything wrong, maybe you would think nothing happened.

That's a fair attempt on their part.

But why these 10? The defense have told you that it could just as well be another 10. I doubt if that argument made much sense to you, with all due respect to my defense counsel. Think about it. I just want you to think about it for a minute. The defense basically have told you that all of these witnesses, all of them, lied. Now, just think hypothetically: if 50-some witnesses came and lied, what that means is that these people, like a ouija board, sat down and said, "Okay, I am going to pick out some policemen, and I am going to say they are crooked."

Now, think about it for a minute. In the 10th District, there are several hundred policemen just assigned to this tactical unit that

---

> *"There is one thing the defense told you that is true: you do not leave your common sense out here in the courtroom when you go back and deliberate."*

these 10 officers belong to at any given time. There were roughly around 27 to 30 people at any given time on the unit, and there is a turnover. If you take the payoff period from '77 to '80, what have you got, 60 or 70 different guys on and off that tactical unit? Out of 60 or 70 police officers, why is it that these 10 police officers—Frank Derango, Billy Guide, Bob Eatman, Smentek, Haas—why is it that their names keep coming up? Was it just pure coincidence? That, roughly, is one in 10 trillion that 50-some witnesses could sit down, and out of 60 or 70 different bodies, they could just make up the same 10. It is astounding.

[There is] one thing the defense told you that is true: you do not leave your common sense out here in the courtroom when you go back and deliberate. And that argument that was made by some of the defense lawyers in this case is astounding.

The reason I am going to talk about it is that [in] about 90 percent of the defense arguments that you just heard, to the extent that they ever addressed the issues, they talked about the credibility of the witnesses that were called to testify. They basically said they all lied, every one of them lied. That they somehow conspired to lie and they got together and made this whole thing up. They planned it out. That is what they told you. They wanted you to lump together all 55 government witnesses, lump them all together, spell the word, L-I-E, and say they are all bad, get rid of them.

Now, there is a reason why the defense had to do that, because there are so many that they have trouble picking and choosing. If they say that this one told a lie because of this reason, this one told a lie because of this reason—all of it sounds a little stupid. It sounds a little ridiculous. So most of the defense lawyers tried to lump them all together.

Let me talk a little bit about credibility, and maybe some of these things will be helpful to you as you go back and deliberate. First of all, when you consider credibility of the witness, there are some things in the law that the judge will tell you you have a right to consider. One is the demeanor of the witness while he is on the stand. You have an absolute right to consider how he looked, how he testified. Did he give straightforward answers, did he appear to be evasive, did he appear to recall the event?

Then the judge is going to tell you that you can consider something else that probably is very important, and that is motivation. What was the interest or the bias of the witness? Did the witness have some motivation in this trial, not some other trial, but in this trial to lie?

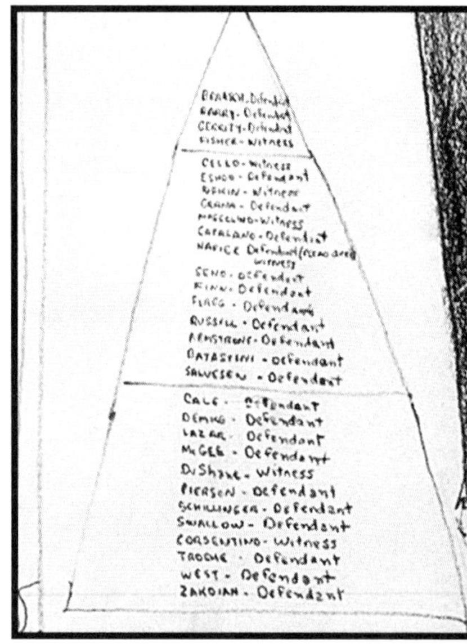

Webb's "pyramid" of witnesses exhibit.

Webb grouped together witnesses with similar motives on a chart to help the jury understand the different types of witnesses and what weight the jury should give to their testimony. Some witnesses had a motive to lie, some had a motive to tell the truth and others were neutral because they didn't have any particular interest one way or another.

The first group of witnesses Webb addressed were the managers of major narcotic operations who are now in a federal penitentiary. Webb reminded the jury that each of these witnesses had been convicted and their common motive was that, in exchange for their truthful testimony in this case, the judge that sentenced them would be informed and may choose to reduce their sentences.

Now, when you think about it for a minute, the defense just jump up and say they all lied because they wanted to get their sentences reduced; but when you think about it logically, just apply some common sense to that. If these people were on trial in this case where your verdict would mean the difference between conviction or acquittal, they clearly would have a motive to lie to you. The only way they are going to get acquitted is to lie.

That is why Milton Kelly told you he lied in his own trial. I am not going to conceal it. He lied because he wanted to snow a jury.

What interest does Kelly [or] Green have in what your verdict is? The answer is none. Their cooperation has nothing to do with your verdict, absolutely nothing. All they had to do is agree to provide the information and come in here and testify. I mean, their cooperation is not hinged upon your verdict, so they do not have any negative motive. They do not have any reason to snow you because they do not have any interest in the outcome of the case.

Let's take it one step further. Just logically apply your common sense. The only benefit they can possibly derive out of even being in this courtroom is that the sentencing judge who sentenced them will say they cooperated, told the truth, trying to amend their past misdeeds. The judge may say that does not reduce their sentence at all, or maybe he says "I am going to reduce it two years." I do not know what that judge is going to do. But what does C. W. [Wilson] know about that? C. W. knows that if, in fact, he were to lie on the witness stand—now, you have got to remember there are a lot of witnesses in this case—if C. W. were going to go on that witness stand and tell a bunch of lies, he knows the likelihood of him getting caught in one of those lies is great. And what is going to happen then? That is hardly going to help C. W. get his sentence reduced, is it?

Next, Webb addressed the 23 government witnesses that were dope dealers at the lower echelon of the organizations. He acknowledged that these witnesses were not sitting in a federal penitentiary and were in their own special category.

Now, what is their motive in testifying here? Well, the defense said they're liars, they're just liars. Well, you have to do more than that. Let's think about it now. I mean, what interest would they have in your verdict in this case?

> *Here's [what] immunity means as far as this case is concerned. The witnesses came in here and they said words, which now we can't use against them. But it doesn't make any difference, because we can indict them and prosecute them tomorrow for drug selling, if they do it.*
>
> *Now, the defense told you that that wouldn't happen. The defense implied to you that somehow, because these witnesses came in here and testified, that somehow they were going to get a license to go out there and sell dope.*
>
> *I just want to remind you, there were no promises to those witnesses. They were on their own. All I did is, I used them as witnesses so you could hear their testimony.*
>
> *If they walked out of this courtroom and sold as much as a dime bag of heroin—jail.*

Webb emphasized his point by recounting what happened to similar cooperating witnesses that were caught selling drugs after testifying and sent to jail—no favors. Webb knew he had to address another credibility issue raised by the defense: that these witnesses were hard core junkies.

> *Out of the entire 50-some witnesses that testified in this courtroom, 50-some witnesses, six of them testified they used heroin within four months of their testimony in this case.*
>
> *I'm not defending them, but to say that you had nothing but wiped-out junkies on the witness stand is a gross misstatement.*
>
> *And, another thing, just so you understand: if there was any medical evidence that people who used heroin are incapable of testifying or recalling events, you can be sure that the defense lawyers in this case would have called witnesses into this courtroom to testify about it. And they didn't.*

Witnesses at trials come to the stand with a variety of traits and loyalties. Many may be the parties to the case themselves, with their motives obvious to all. Their testimony must be viewed in a prism of skepticism because the desire to win is worn on their sleeves. Others may have motives and biases hidden just beneath the surface, to be elicited with careful and sometimes clever questioning. But any trial advocate will tell you that the best types of witnesses to have on your side are those described as "innocent bystanders." These witnesses are not always present at important events, but when they are, their testimony can be pivotal. Of course, it requires good investigative work to find them and concentrated pretrial development to prepare them to testify.

During the government's presentation of evidence, a group of bank employees, mostly tellers, were called to testify. The essence of their testimony was similar. They described the many occasions that defendants came to their bank to exchange cash for cash, an unusual banking transaction. Even more unusual were the small denomination bills—fives, tens, and twenties—the defendants turned in, while asking for fifty and hundred dollar bills in return. The transactions were often in the range of $500 to $1,000.

These tellers came to court without loyalties to either side of the case and did not identify with either side. Their fidelity was to their oaths to tell the truth, rendering their testimony virtually unassailable. They were impervious to any attempts to influence their testimony. Webb leveraged these witnesses to support the testimony of the drug dealers and appeal to the jury's common sense. Are full-time police officers paid at irregular intervals in small denominations? Why would they make regular visits to the bank to exchange cash for cash? Webb would next tie together the tellers' testimony with the evidence of payoffs by drug dealers.

Webb returned to his chart and, pointing to the third group of witnesses—the bank tellers—he explained how this group of neutral witnesses helped corroborate the testimony from the drug dealers.

> *These 23 witnesses on this chart are government witnesses that were not involved in those narcotic operations. Most of these witnesses on this chart are the witnesses that we called to corroborate and to establish to your satisfaction that the witnesses who testified, the dope peddlers, told the truth and that these defendants were guilty beyond a reasonable doubt. These witnesses*

fall into the category of neutral witnesses that had no particular interest or motive, one way or the other.

First of all, in order to win this case, the defense lawyers had to tell you that all of these witnesses also were liars. They had to tell you that, but you know what? They ran into some problems because it wasn't as easy to argue about those witnesses because those are the witnesses [for whom] there is no reason why you should think that they are coming in here and lying to you.

What I'm trying to say as respectfully as I can to the defense lawyers is that in order to get their clients acquitted, when they got into this group of witnesses, they had a real problem. And if they had to go to the length to make it up, they did. The defendants who were incriminated by the exchanging of the bills, whenever they tried to explain that away, they got in trouble.

Now, why would a 10th District police officer be walking into a bank with fives and tens and twenties, often in a crumpled-up condition, and want to exchange, you know, $500 or $800 or $1,000 in his pocket in fives and tens and twenties, and be wanting to convert it to large bills?

Think about it. How many times in your lives, all of you, have you walked into a bank where you had some fives, tens, and twenties, that you built up that you had to go in and cash them in for fifties and hundreds? Now, to the extent that some of you are business people, [one defense lawyer] said that is not uncommon. But when business people walk in with fives, tens,

---

> *"These cops are pulling money out of their pocket and counting it out. These policemen, who get a paycheck every two weeks, have got all this cash. What is the significance of all that cash?"*

and twenties, they have a tally sheet, and they know how much money they have.

These cops are pulling money out of their pocket and counting it out. These policemen, who get a paycheck every two weeks, have got all this cash. What is the significance of all that cash?

The dope peddlers testified in this case that when they paid off these 10 officers that they paid them off in small bills, usually fives, tens, twenties. The reason they paid them off in those small bills is because that is the way they sold the dope. The dope sold for $10 or $15 a bag. So the dope peddlers ended up with all these small bills, and so the dope peddlers gave them to the cops.

Webb explained that the only reason why these police officers were exchanging money was to avoid the possibility of being caught with marked bills from drug transactions. He appealed to the jury's common sense, suggesting that laundering the money through the bank allowed them to trade dirty money for clean.

With the overt acts of money laundering now established, Webb turned the jury's attention to the defendant's acts of omission: arrests.

You have heard a lot about arrests. Throughout the arguments of these defense attorneys, they have talked about how many arrests their clients made. And I think it is important that we actually look at the evidence, not just their statements. I want to look at what the actual evidence is about the arrests that these 10 men say that they did.

The evidence establishes, make no mistake about it, that during the time periods that C. W. and Green Smith and Milton Kelly say that they were making payoffs, not one arrest.

They made some arrests that were illegal in the sense they did not have probable cause, and they probably conducted some searches that did not have what we call probable cause. They are not on trial for that. In fact, they testified that is pretty good police work because that keeps the narcotic peddlers on their toes. Run them in a few times.

Does it strike you as amazing that once they got the cops on the payroll, somehow they were never able to arrest—"they" being the nine 10th District cops—Milton Green or C. W. during the payoff period?

Let me tell you about something else so you can understand what I am talking about. Kelly testified, if you remember, what the deal was for the payoffs. When he put the police officers on the payroll, Kelly knew that the police would have to make some arrests. I mean, they have got to make it look good. If these guys are not banking down any statistics at all, it is going to look awful. So the deal was, in essence, Kelly and Green do not get arrested. You do not hassle them. You can arrest the workers once in a while if you catch them. Just make sure they do not get convicted.

During the entire Avers Avenue operative period, from the fall of '77, late in the year, to August of '79, during that entire two-year period when they were running dope there night and day, none of these nine 10th District cops on trial in this case ever arrested an Avers Avenue drug worker and got a conviction on it. Not one.

Did that deal work out pretty well? They can talk about arrests until they are blue in the face. Kelly got his money's worth, and so did Green Smith. Now, what do they say about that? Well, they say, "You know, you just could not get convictions." That is what they said. Darn it, [defense attorney] Pierce told you, "My guy is not responsible for convictions. He can only make arrests. And the problem is that those dumb courts, the courts throw the case out."

The reason the court threw the case out is because when they made the arrest, they wrote up the case report in such a way that they knew the case would be thrown out the next day. They had total control over it.

To emphasize his point, Webb reminded the jury that other officers in the Vice Control Division, who did not work in the 10th District, were able to convict six workers from the Avers Avenue group. Arrests could be made.

Webb recognized that some defendants may appear to the jury to be more guilty than others. He carefully explained that the jury's job in reviewing the evidence is not to determine who is more guilty.

> *Now, we have talked about motive to fabricate in connection with the government witnesses. Let me just briefly talk about motive to fabricate by the defendants who took the witness stand and testified in this trial.*
>
> *There is no question that of anyone who testified in this entire trial, the witnesses that have the most vital interest in the outcome of this case are the defendants. The strongest motive to fabricate or to lie rests with those defendants.*
>
> *Whether they lied or not is a separate question, but certainly there is no doubt that whether you find them guilty or not guilty is the ultimate issue in the case, and so there is no question that those defendants who did testify clearly have a motive to fabricate. Your responsibility will be to determine whether somebody is in fact guilty.*
>
> *There may be people who are guilty who are more guilty than others, in other words, more culpable, they did more bad things. And that's up to the judge, if he wants to consider that when he imposes the punishment.*
>
> *But you as jurors are not to weigh or grade the degrees of guilt. After you review all the evidence, and you consider nothing but that evidence, if you find a defendant is guilty beyond a reasonable doubt, then you find him so.*

In challenging each defendant's claims, Webb effectively used his witness chart to show how the defenses were often based on scant witness testimony and little or no physical evidence, while the government had produced dozens of witnesses, many of whom were neutral.

One of the defendants was officer Bill Guide. There were 26 government witnesses that testified about Guide exchanging money. With all this evidence against him, Webb noted that Guide's attorney, Jo Ann Wolfson, "knows that if she doesn't explain that to you somehow, you're going to convict Bill Guide. I mean, there are 26 witnesses that incriminate him."

The defense told the jury that Guide's wife, Sally, was the treasurer for a class reunion; they collected some cash in small bills from the participants in the class reunion, and she sometimes would give her husband small bills to exchange for her. Webb recalled testimony from earlier in the trial from Mrs. Guide and used that to discredit her husband's defense as to the source of the exchanged money.

> *Well, on cross-examination I respectfully pointed out to Mrs. Guide that, "Didn't that all take place in 1976 and up to around September of '77?"*
>
> *"Yes, it did."*
>
> *And I said then, "Why is your husband exchanging bills of $500 and $700 up in '78 and '79?"*
>
> *Mrs. Guide said, "I don't know, I don't know why he's doing that."*
>
> *Mrs. Wolfson went to great lengths to try to refute that bank evidence by calling those witnesses. I suppose if she really wanted to refute it and she thought it was untrue, why didn't she call some of those other bank tellers to come in here and say, "[bank teller] Kathy Martinez is a liar, [bank teller] Leonard Dickerson is a liar"?*
>
> *The reason I tell you this, and the reason it's important, is that innocent men do not have to explain their conduct through these type of changing explanations.*

Near the end of his rebuttal arguments, Webb used defendant Joe Pena to illuminate the holes in many of the defense arguments, and closed with a strong example of how the government witnesses can be trusted and the defense's cannot. There were 20 government witnesses against Pena and just him and Raciel Garcia testifying in his defense. Webb also questioned Garcia's testimony by pointing out that during opening statements, Pena's attorney indicated that a witness would testify as to the source of money, but did not identify Garcia.

"We went through this entire trial not knowing who was that witness that was going to explain that $10,000 transaction," Webb said. Webb then recounted the trial testimony to remind the jury who Garcia was. He was deferential in describing him as a "hard-working business man" who owned a pool hall and some apartment buildings. The $10,000 had come from the apartment rents and the pool hall, according to Garcia. Though Webb noted to the jury incredulously, "For some reason it's all in fives, tens, and twenties."

Webb then brought the jury back to the cross-examination of Garcia by AUSA Siegel earlier in the trial. As Webb told the jury, once Siegel began asking Garcia questions, "something just didn't smell right." Webb proceeded to put to rest any doubt about Pena.

> *I think when he came down on Monday morning and he was cross-examined based on full-disclosure of relevant facts that might be helpful to you as jurors in deciding the guilt or innocence of Pena, you got a little different picture of Mr. Garcia.*
>
> *First of all, as far as the $10,000, his testimony that he had accumulated that, if he ever did at all, from rents at a building or profits from a pool hall, that was certainly exploded quickly because we showed him his tax return. In the entire year of '78—in the entire year—he had money to put in his pocket of $6,345 from both those sources.*
>
> *Now, he had five children and a wife to support and apparently a mother. He had bought a $15,000 Lincoln Continental. I am thinking, how can there be, out of that $6,000, how did he get $10,000? How? Couldn't have been.*
>
> *Then we find out that maybe Mr. Garcia had some good reason to be in here helping Mr. Pena. First of all we found out that apparently Mr. Garcia, at least on occasion, engages in criminal activity in the 10th District. So it's nice to have some 10th District police officers as friends, I'm sure, and coming into a courtroom and taking out one of the defendants with a bogus explanation of $10,000 probably doesn't hurt him.*

I wondered why [defense counsel Robert] Bailey didn't tell us about that. I mean, to paint Mr. Garcia as just some citizen off the street who came in here, a businessman, who just happened to have $10,000 that just happened to explain away a very incriminating piece of evidence. And we find all this out, but it doesn't stop there.

Mr. Garcia's criminal activity in the 10th District apparently wasn't limited to gambling. We find out that officer Guide, on trial in this case, and officer DePasquale had arrested Garcia for selling marijuana in front of the pool hall.

So now we have a little different picture. Garcia, we know he didn't have $10,000 from the pool hall and the rents, as he said. He didn't just meet Pena because they were friends; he had been arrested. He himself was convicted of smuggling aliens, and he got arrested by Guide and DePasquale for selling marijuana in the 10th District.

Pena also had to overcome the bank teller witness testimony. Having established these witnesses as being neutral, Webb was able to use sarcasm to make his point that Pena could do nothing other than call the witnesses liars.

"I again most respectfully suggest to you that defendants who are innocent do not have to walk into this courtroom, whether police officers or not, and present a phony defense. In fact, quite frankly, if the man who presents the defense that is phony is a policeman, I think it is a sad day in this courtroom."

Webb concluded by thanking the jury for listening carefully to his rebuttal. In contrast to the defense attorneys asking the jury to "send messages to people," Webb reiterated his trust in the jury to make the right decision.

"I sat through the voir dire examination of you as jurors a couple of weeks ago when there was a question about publicity, and I have never seen a jury that is so dedicated to nothing but reviewing the evidence and reaching whatever verdict you think is proper. And whatever that verdict is, this United States Attorney accepts it. Thank you."

After due deliberations, the jury returned verdicts of guilty as to all 10 defendants.

In reflecting on the trial, Schweitzer noted that during the initial 10 minutes of Webb's rebuttal, he defused hours of the defense argument. "You could just tell that the jury was fixated on everything he said. They understood his 'two wrongs do not make a right' argument."

Vincent J. Connelly was one of the bright young Assistant U.S. Attorneys hired in the later stages of the Bauer and Thompson administrations and was one of many AUSAs in attendance as spectators during the final arguments. Later a partner at Mayer Brown, Connelly reflected on what he witnessed.

> *The defense lawyers varied widely in style and focus but the overriding common theme in their closing arguments was a series of scathing attacks on the federal prosecutors for having "sided" with their witness dope dealers against the defendant Chicago police officers who were portrayed as putting themselves greatly in harm's way to help rid the general population of the disreputable dope dealers.*
>
> *Very quickly, Dan used the device of "the honest police officer" in contrast to the conduct of the ten defendants. By asking the jury to remember "the honest police officer," he had a ready standard to rebut the lengthy defense arguments that the case was a simple choice between siding with their clients or dope dealers and that the U.S. Attorney's Office had chosen to be the ally of dope dealers. "The honest police officer" had an ally in the U.S. Attorney's office and didn't deserve to have his reputation dragged down by the shakedowns of the corrupt defendants.*

Webb noted how closely he had worked with police officers throughout his career. In a few quick strokes, he embraced police officers for their extraordinary work under very trying circumstances. The police officers who were on trial dishonored the great work performed by their lawful colleagues.

By facing and deflating the defense team's strongest emotional arguments in the first few minutes of his rebuttal, Webb had clear sailing to keep the jury focused on the actual evidence for the remainder of his argument.

> *To be loyal to a group you are a part of comes easily. It is a true test of leadership when obedience to a sacred oath supersedes all other considerations. It was personally difficult for the prosecutors because they, too, were members of the law enforcement community.*

There were a number of factors displayed by Webb in his three-plus hour argument to the jury. Some were apparent from the written record, including his thorough knowledge of a massive evidentiary and trial record and the facility of his immediate recall. Another characteristic that comes through is the direct and hard-hitting way he responded to the arguments of the 10 defense lawyers. By taking the defense arguments point by point and often using the defendant's own testimony, Webb was able to provide the jury with the understanding they needed to find the defendants guilty. Webb used simple, everyday examples to effectively counter the defendant's repeated assertions that the government witnesses were liars and were anxious to run into court to testify against police officers.

What the transcript cannot adequately reflect or portray, however, was Webb's energy, appearance, and the sincerity in his delivery. He was passionate in his role, and manifested a genuine belief in the rightness of his position, which allowed the jurors to accept his straightforward arguments and reject those of the defendants.

It took courage to bring this case against police officers who are supposed to be partners of the U.S. Attorney's Office in fighting crime. It would have been acceptable for the U.S. Attorney to direct the prosecution from the comforts of his office. But Webb's decision to personally sit in the first chair emphasized the importance of the case.

To be loyal to a group you are a part of comes easily. It is a true test of leadership when obedience to a sacred oath supersedes all other considerations. It was personally difficult for the prosecutors because they, too, were members of the law enforcement community.

Webb honestly and eloquently described his angst over the decision to prosecute his "brothers" in law enforcement. Those expressions were genuine. The convictions of the Marquette 10 defendants were not occasions to rejoice.

Webb delivering his closing argument in the Operation Greylord trial of Judge John Murphy

United States v. John M. Murphy; United States v Richard F. LeFevour

CHAPTER 6
WHEN JUSTICE WAS BLIND

Upon becoming the top federal prosecutor in Chicago, Webb inherited an investigation into courtroom corruption that could have destroyed his legal career. That investigation, known as Operation Greylord, turned out to be the most significant and successful undercover operation ever conducted. It would be the first time a sitting Illinois judge would be found guilty of judicial corruption. I was privileged to have a front row seat presiding over the first major Greylord trial.

As the investigation was in its infancy, it was assigned to Assistant U.S. Attorney Dan Reidy. Reidy joined the U.S. Attorney's office in 1975, five years after Dan Webb. Reidy quickly rose through the criminal division and was promoted to the Special Prosecutions Unit where he was assigned an unusual case.

The case file consisted largely of notes prepared by FBI special agents and Strike Force lawyers, based on interviews of a criminal defense attorney who practiced regularly in various criminal courtrooms in the Circuit Court of Cook County. The attorney described a number of instances in which criminal cases pending in the Circuit Court were fixed by payments to various court personnel, including allegations involving judges. It was apparent from Reidy's review of the materials that some level of corruption existed—enough to merit fully exploring the evidence. As in any criminal investigation, fundamental questions had to be answered. Who was involved, what were the acts of criminality, how wide did the criminality extend, and how can it be proved? In answering these questions, Reidy would become the architect of the government's approach for the case.

There were two choices open to the prosecutors: search out and identify historical information about crimes already committed and build cases on that basis, or use undercover investigators and personnel with made-up facts and concocted cases to set traps for the corrupt. The choice of approach is often pivotal to the success of a case, and just as the decision in the Braasch case to immunize the collectors allowed the government to build a successful case, this decision in Greylord would prove to be the key to the case.

Reidy, together with U.S. Attorney Thomas P. Sullivan and relevant law enforcement officials in Chicago, debated the pros and cons of the two disparate methods. Developing the case based on historical information involved the least risk. They knew that whatever records existed were not based on fiction; the facts merely had to be discovered along with the testimony of reluctant witnesses with knowledge of the criminal acts. The downside of this approach was that the attendant publicity would hamper efforts to uncover the full scope of the criminality and its participants. Leads would dry up and evidence would disappear.

The other approach had different and more challenging risks. Creating fictional events that used undercover agents and members of the judiciary, while maintaining the utmost secrecy of the law enforcement project, would provide the greatest prospects for identifying the criminals and the scope of criminality. This approach nonetheless posed the greatest risks of failure.

First and foremost it would require that the lawyers involved would file false documents and lie to judges and others to perpetuate the deception. The ethics rules that govern lawyers' conduct prohibit lying to the court, and do not have an exception for law enforcement attorneys lying to judges. The state agencies that regulate lawyers' conduct are separate from the courts, and focus on their behavior rather than the legal rights of the accused. In adopting this approach to the case, there was no guarantee that the issue of ethical misconduct would disappear even if there was no violation of a criminal's rights. Every lawyer participating in the lies to the judges and court personnel would face sanctions, including the risk of losing their law license.

The second risk was the possible failure of the undercover project if criminality was established only for the phony cases and not for the real cases in the system. When assessing the risk, Reidy and his team had to consider the ABSCAM investigation of Congress conducted by the FBI many years before that was highly criticized because the activities that produced the convictions were all made-up and hypothetical.

The third risk was that the undercover operation would be publicly disclosed before it reached a logical conclusion. Any premature publicity would cut short the normal term of the project. Although plans were later made to structure the events and participants in such a way as to limit the fallout from any unwanted disclosure, the risk could not be eliminated.

As Reidy's investigation developed to the decision-making level, U.S. Attorney Sullivan was the man in charge. Sullivan, Reidy and others spent hours upon hours behind closed doors debating about which approach to take and how to go about it. Ultimately, Sullivan agreed with Reidy's recommendation to use an undercover operation. The decision to proceed in this way was an act of courage by Sullivan, Reidy, and all the other government lawyers who would later be involved.

Even with that decision, debate continued as to who should be informed about the operation. Because of the risks to their licenses, they decided to secure the blessing for the undercover operation from ranking officials in the Justice Department in Washington, D.C. and the FBI Director William Webster. After considerable legal research and with guidelines imposed, the plan was given approval by the Justice Department.

Despite the approval, Sullivan, Reidy, and others understood that nobody in the Department of Justice or the FBI could give the participants legal absolution for any of their conduct. Washington's decision to give the go-ahead did, however, afford a level of comfort to the Chicago group. Sullivan predicted that if the undercover operation succeeded, everything would be okay, but if it was a failure, there would be problems for everyone involved.

Whether fateful or merely coincidental, a young Assistant State's Attorney working in the Cook County courts named Terry Hake was developing deep disgust with what he saw taking place in certain courtrooms where he prosecuted. He observed acts he believed to be illegal and that were corrupting the system of criminal justice. In addition to being a person of integrity, Hake was full of idealism. His name and his angst soon came to Reidy's attention.

Reidy set up meetings with Hake to explain the undercover concept and assess Hake as a participant. Reidy explained to him that the Justice Department was committed to seeing the investigation through to whatever end the evidence would reach. Through the meetings, Reidy became convinced Hake would be a valuable part of the operation. While Hake believed Reidy, he had to evaluate the risks involved and contemplate the near certainty that if he participated in this plan, he might never again be able to practice law in the Circuit Court of Cook County. Reidy and his team meanwhile waited anxiously for Hake's decision.

After due consideration of the government's offer to join the effort against corruption, Terry Hake signed on. Hake initially took on the role of a shady Assistant State's Attorney with criminal defense lawyers and others, and soon developed a reputation as a guy on the take. He was enormously successful in that role and gathered considerable evidence against others. As his corrupt reputation grew, he left the State's Attorney's office and became a private criminal defense lawyer believed to be dirty. He bloomed again in this undercover capacity. However, Hake was much more than a successful criminal defense lawyer. Unbeknownst to those he was dealing with, Hake had been secretly sworn in as a Special Agent of the FBI.

In addition to Hake, other FBI agents and lawyers were enlisted in the operation. Hake's success at infiltrating the system in his assumed role inspired sufficient confidence to expand the effort. Aside from the closely controlled FBI undercover agents, a quirk of circumstance added yet another operative to Reidy's growing group of undercover investigators. Because of the backlog in the Cook County courts in processing cases, judges from downstate counties were asked to come up to Chicago for brief periods of time to help. Judge Brocton Lockwood was one such judge. Moved by the corruption he witnessed in traffic court, he independently contacted the FBI. Shortly thereafter, he too was enlisted to act in an undercover capacity and participate in the investigation.

Reidy and Sullivan carefully structured the operation to minimize the risk that it would be publicly disclosed. They decided never to commingle the efforts of Hake, Judge Lockwood, and the other undercover operatives. Each of them and their information would be isolated in its own silo of storage. Each of the operatives would remain ignorant of the efforts of the others. Reidy and Sullivan decided that none of them were to be debriefed in the presence of any other undercover operatives and information provided by one would not be shared among the others.

This informational firewall limited any damage to the investigation in the event of premature discovery. It also provided centralized control of any fallout. Of course, each undercover operative was deeply imbued with the necessity of secrecy in safeguarding their own activity, but Reidy and Sullivan knew there were limits to the covertness.

For example, which outsiders could be told about the operation? Certain officials within the Cook County justice system would have to be told for the plan to succeed. They decided that the presiding Judge of the Circuit Court Criminal Division, Richard Fitzgerald, would be told of the operation. Because of his impeccable reputation for honesty and integrity, he was a perfect choice. Similarly, it was decided that Hake's boss, the Cook County State's Attorney, C. Bernard Carey, had to be told of Hake's undercover role and the nature of his activities.

Richard M. Daley took office as the new State's Attorney of Cook County in January 1981. Nothing in his public life suggested he could not be trusted. And so Daley was told about the undercover operation. Not only was Daley trustworthy in maintaining the secrecy of the operation, he was delighted with it. Daley was morally offended by judicial corruption. Additionally, he was angered that it was his office that was being victimized by having judges rule in favor of criminal defendants whom his office was prosecuting. As Reidy would later say, "Richard M. Daley was one of my heroes; he never violated a confidence."

As the operation progressed, Webb succeeded Sullivan as U.S. Attorney in early 1981. While Sullivan was briefing Webb about pending cases, he made special note of two boxes on the floor in his office. "One of those boxes will destroy your marriage, and one will destroy your career," Webb recalled Sullivan telling him. "That first box over there, that's a secret investigation of John Cardinal Cody for being involved in a fraud scheme...Knowing that your wife is Catholic and your kids are Catholic, that's

---

> *My advice to Webb was win the Greylord cases or we're all going to lose our law licenses.*

not going to do well for you. The second box is a super-secret, undercover project that's going to expose corruption in the Cook County court system, and you'll never practice law again." After that, Webb recalled, Sullivan got up and left.

"The John Cardinal Cody case was a totally no-win situation," Webb said. "If I prosecuted, I'd make a lot of enemies. If I declined, we'd be accused of giving special treatment to the man because he was a cardinal. When he died, the case died too. It made it a lot easier for me, I admit."

Though the Cody case was buried with the cardinal, that other box, Greylord, remained an active operation at the U.S. Attorney's office—even though the stakes were so high for all the lawyers involved. "My advice to [Webb] was win the [Greylord] cases or we're all going to lose our law licenses," recalled Sullivan.

The 1980 election also brought about staffing changes at the U.S. Justice Department in Washington, D.C. Whereas the prior administration ultimately approved of the undercover operation, the new one did not. Members of the new Justice Department came to the conclusion that some of the acts already undertaken in Operation Greylord were neither lawful nor proper. This news created pandemonium among some in the U.S. Attorney's office in Chicago. Would they have to terminate the investigation and thereby reveal its existence? Too much progress in identifying corruption had been made to stop now.

Reidy and the others scheduled a quick trip to Washington and were soon making their case to new and skeptical Justice Department personnel. The legal issues were again debated and analyzed. As the Chicago contingent overcame each of the Justice Department's reservations, they began to breathe easier. The Department finally decided that the scope and methods of the investigation were in fact legal and warranted.

With that hurdle now overcome, the investigation proceeded apace. Hake and the others were making substantial inroads in attempts to follow the trail of money. The operation's secrecy was maintained and additional investigative tools, such as wiretaps, were employed. Recorded conversations are particularly powerful evidence since the person against whom they are used can neither deny the words spoken nor retrieve them. Federal law permits the introduction into evidence at trial any recorded conversations when one party to the conversation consents to the recording.

The undercover practices included phony accident cases, with agents playing the parts of hostile participants as well as the lawyers. As Sullivan noted, "We didn't want to have Terry Hake taking bribes and helping to get people out of real cases and [those people] committing a serious crime."

Helped by the use of wires worn by Hake and others, criminal cases were developed against corrupt lawyers, courtroom personnel, and police officers. As those cases reached the federal indictment stage, these putative defendants often made plea agreements in exchange for their cooperation and testimony against those higher up in the corruption. In some instances, use immunity was bestowed on reluctant witnesses.

At some point, the press got wind of the investigation and the methods being used. There was an immediate hue and cry by the media for confirmation or denial of the investigation, and politicians expressed outrage over the stories, especially those indicating there was wiretapping occurring in the chambers of judges. Critics of the operation demanded that if evidence of criminality existed, indictments should be brought immediately. Even some members of the public said it was time to put up or shut up.

As the U.S. Attorney, Webb was under enormous pressure to respond to the publicity. However, he knew more evidence was needed to render the cases winnable at trial.

Webb was stalwart in his resistance to the outcry for immediate action or explanation of the situation. Even seasoned prosecutors marveled at his resolve in ignoring the calls for action. Webb assured his troops that criminal charges would be filed only when the investigations were developed as far as evidence would permit. While he was an Assistant U.S. Attorney working on Braasch, Gill/Fahey, and other cases, Webb had learned the need for thorough investigation and pretrial preparation, and now as U.S. Attorney he knew the operation's success would depend on the thoroughness of these efforts. He tuned out the media agitation.

Webb withstood the pressure to take action for four months after Greylord's first public disclosure. In the summer of 1983, the first indictments were returned. Two judges, a former judge, two court clerks and a police officer were charged in separate cases. *Chicago Tribune* reporter Maurice Possley, a standout investigative reporter, quoted Webb in announcing the filing of charges: "I believe this will be viewed as one of the most comprehensive, intricate, and difficult undercover projects ever undertaken by a law enforcement agency." The truth of Webb's belief would soon be proved with the help of his investigative team and trial talent.

As the investigation became more involved, additional Assistant United States Attorneys were assigned to work them. Dan Reidy, the principal AUSA who rose to become First Assistant U.S. Attorney, was joined by Scott Lassar, (later to be named United States Attorney), James Schweitzer, Charles Sklarsky, Scott Mendeloff, Candace Fabri, and Sheldon Zenner. Greylord spanned the administrations of four United States Attorneys. In addition to Sullivan and Webb, the others were Anton Valukas and Fred Foreman.

The first Operation Greylord case to go to trial was *United States v. John M. Murphy*. Both the U.S. Attorney's office in Chicago and in the Department of Justice's office in Washington had serious concerns about whether a jury of citizens would convict a sitting state court judge. For that reason, a number of other indictments of judges were held up pending the outcome of the Murphy trial. Webb and officials from the Justice Department, particularly the Deputy Attorney General, had a number of conversations centered on whether other cases could or should be brought if the Murphy case was lost. There was a distinct possibility in Webb's mind that if they could not win the Murphy case, the Greylord investigation would be shut down. Lassar would later say, "It took some courage on [Webb's] part to continue the investigation and the prosecution."

As is tradition in the U.S. Attorney's office, Reidy as the case architect was entitled to be the first chair at the government's table in the first Greylord trial. Selflessly, Reidy declined and instead went to see Webb. Reidy understood the must-win importance of the Murphy case, and though he had demonstrated his own superior courtroom skills, he believed that it was Webb who should personally try the case in order to enhance the likelihood of success. Reidy asked Webb to lead the prosecution team at trial, and Webb agreed.

Webb and his team recognized the importance of the first case. "Judge Murphy was the first judge to go to trial," Webb said. "We all recognized that we were going to sink or swim on that first trial. We wanted to show the men and women who had worked so hard on this case that the U.S. Attorney's office was completely behind the FBI and what everyone had done, and that the U.S. Attorney himself was going to try the case. We also wanted the public to know that the U.S. Attorney was behind the case."

Early on, Webb told Lassar to assign him to whatever part of the case he wanted. "But he was the best trial lawyer in the office as well as being U.S. Attorney," Lassar said, "So, I was very generous in my assignments. I thought if we won that first case, it would tamp down the criticisms of the techniques we used."

Murphy's defense counsel was Matthias A. Lydon, himself a former AUSA in the Chicago office. The assignment of cases in the Northern District of Illinois is random selection, and I was designated to preside over the case. The circumstances of our respective roles were unusual. Webb, Lydon and I were not only former AUSAs who served together for a number of years, we were also good friends. Our families had vacationed together, and the three of us, along with other AUSAs, had gone on weeklong fishing trips to Canada on a number of occasions. Webb and Lydon had practiced law together as partners before the trial and would do so again when Webb returned to private practice. While the bonds of friendship remained and the trial provided a professional reunion of sorts, our respective roles were clearly separate and clearly defined. Webb and Lydon were unmistakable adversaries and I was unmistakably the neutral. None of us had any difficulty in discerning our roles, our different obligations, and to whom and where our loyalties belonged. Members of the press wrote about the relationships, and there was no doubt Judge Murphy was aware of them.

The trial started in late May 1984 and would last for two weeks. In his opening statement to the jury, Webb said,

> *If you would for a moment, go back with me in time to approximately three years ago. The date: July 29th, 1981. On that date, a lawyer in the City of Chicago had a case up in court. His client was a defendant in a criminal case—a felony case. The lawyer went to court on that date, got to the court house; instead of going into a courtroom like this, he went back to the judge's chambers.*
>
> *And at that time he had a secret meeting with the judge. And as the defense lawyer, he told the judge what his case was about;*

he told the judge the result that he wanted; and he got from the judge what he considered to be a commitment to fix the case.

Later that day the case was called. The judge presided. The evidence was heard, and at the end of the evidence the judge immediately ruled in favor of the defense lawyer, in favor of the defendant.

A little later the judge went back into his chambers. The lawyer then went back into the chambers. The two of them had a second meeting, and at that time the lawyer gave the judge $300 to fix that case.

That, ladies and gentlemen, could be considered the essence of this case; the anatomy of a fixed case in court. For, you see, that case was not decided on the merits based on evidence in a court of law as you will ultimately decide this case. As you will find out, what happened in that case was that the case was fixed with a bribe.

[What I told you is] not something out of a fiction book about corruption in the City of Chicago. For you're going to see shortly that those events that I just related to you will be evidence that you will hear during the course of this trial.

For, you see, the judge who presided in that case that I just described to you was the defendant, John Murphy, a Judge of the Circuit Court of Cook County. And the lawyer who fixed the case is a man by the name of Art Cirignani, who will be the government's first witness.

Art Cirignani was not a special agent with the FBI working as an undercover lawyer. The case that he testified he fixed with Judge Murphy was a real one. Cirignani also would testify that he was sometimes assigned under a Chicago Bar Association referral program to help unrepresented defendants in various courts, including Branch 29 of the criminal court where Judge Murphy was assigned.

There were basically two types of courtrooms in Traffic Court. Minor traffic offenses were heard in one set of rooms. These included offenses such as running red lights and speeding violations. The second type of rooms were ones in which

> *The bribes were paid principally by lawyers who would come to be known as "Miracle Workers." These lawyers were regulars in Traffic Court. They would hang around the hallways and other areas waiting to meet clients there. They would take on the cases of the unrepresented defendants and, in many such cases, pay judges and others to achieve favorable rulings.*

more serious offenses were heard, primarily drunk driving or leaving a scene of an accident. When Judge Murphy was in Traffic Court, the Presiding Judge of Traffic Court was Judge Richard LeFevour.

As chief judge, LeFevour supervised about 20 judges in Traffic Court at any given time. It was Judge LeFevour who assigned Judge Murphy to the major courtrooms during his tenure at Traffic Court from 1972 to early 1981.

The evidence at Judge Murphy's trial established that while Judge Murphy presided in one of the major rooms at Traffic Court, he regularly fixed drunk driving and other serious cases in return for bribes paid to himself and at other times paid to Judge Richard LeFevour. The bribes were paid principally by lawyers who would come to be known as "Miracle Workers." These lawyers were regulars in Traffic Court. They would hang around the hallways and other areas waiting to meet clients there. They would take on the cases of the unrepresented defendants and, in many such cases, pay judges and others to achieve favorable rulings.

Prosecutors testified that although they won as many as 90% of their major traffic cases against public defenders, they almost never won a case in which the defendant was represented by one of the Miracle Workers. Occasionally, however, the Miracle Workers would lose for the sake of appearance, to let the judge be viewed as even-handed in his decision making.

The money-making scheme of the Miracle Workers was facilitated by the bail system in Illinois. When a criminal defendant was required to post bail, in most cases they could do so by depositing 10% of the bail in cash. When the defendant was discharged or the case otherwise terminated, the defendant was entitled to a cash bond refund (CBR) of the amount deposited, less a small handling charge. CBRs were routinely assigned by defendants to their lawyers as compensation for legal services. Assignment required the approval of the judge. These defense lawyers, also known as "hustlers," made their money by soliciting the client, receiving an assignment of the CBR and getting the judge's approval.

In describing the scheme to the jury, Webb referred to the participants as the "hustler bribery club." He explained how in exchange for monthly dues of $500, the five lawyers were allowed to solicit clients in the courthouse corridors although hustling violated the lawyers' professional code of ethics as well as the court rules.

When the government rested its case, Judge Murphy exercised his right to present a defense. In addition to some character witnesses, he took the witness stand, firmly denied engaging in the corruption charged and professed his innocence. When Judge Murphy finished testifying on direct examination, Webb got up and began his cross-examination. There was not much time left in the afternoon session before recess, but there was enough left for each man to establish his position. "I made a judgment call," Webb recalled, "that you had to show respect to judges and that I should show respect for Judge Murphy and the office and not be harsh to him." Webb invariably called him "Judge," and did not always press Murphy when his answers were evasive or suggestive of innocence.

The session ended with the cross-examination to continue the following morning. When the trial team came down from court, Reidy spotted Lassar and asked him how it went. Lassar said it went okay, but Webb was not being his usual self on cross, that he was giving Murphy too much latitude in answering his questions and not being forceful enough in confronting him with the hard evidence, particularly the evidence on the wires worn by the undercover agents.

Lassar acknowledged there was nobody like Webb in the courtroom, but the deference that was owed was to Murphy's judicial office and not to him personally. Lassar knew that the evidence presented clearly established Murphy's corruption and that Murphy should be forcefully required to confront that evidence.

Reidy then went into Webb's office to see how he was feeling. For a man who was typically upbeat when on trial, Webb appeared unusually dour. He seemed to recognize he could have done better. "I just felt that it did not click," Webb said. "I didn't think the jurors were paying as much attention as I wanted them to." Reidy then reiterated all of Lassar's comments from moments before and Webb instinctively knew how right they were.

Webb got very little sleep that night. The cross-examination script he had prepared prior to trial had to be scrapped. Webb realized that he had to change his demeanor and attitude, as well as the content of his questions. Rather than being tired by the task, he became reenergized. "I stayed up most of the night redoing the rest of the cross, changing the focus of my questions and making them much more leading and taking a much more aggressive approach," Webb said.

Everything changed the next morning. Webb did not give Murphy the tolerance in answering questions as the day before. He emphasized the tapes and how they showed in Judge Murphy's own words what happened and the strength of the government's case. Webb was able to marry together three key components in his cross: demeanor, attitude, and substance of the questions. For Webb, "A good cross requires you to change the flow of questions to be much more assertive and in the witness' face, as well as being more attuned to making dramatic points and letting the jury know you've made a dramatic point." Webb found his stride and was relentless in bringing it to bear in a cross-examination that lasted a couple of hours.

"He destroyed Murphy," Lassar said. "He went after him and was very effective."

In its rebuttal case, the government responded to Murphy's character evidence with anti-character evidence. Some of the lawyers who were cheated of rightful outcomes in cases they tried by the hustlers at last had a platform to express their view. And express it they did.

One prosecutor testified about a case that was so crass it was almost laughable. Prosecutors who practiced in Traffic Court had a pretty good sense when things were fishy. When they lost cases they knew they should have won based on the evidence, the memory of the loss stuck with them. A prosecutor testified that in one drunken driving case involving a defendant represented by a Miracle Worker, the arresting officer testified that the defendant failed the usual roadside tests of drunkenness and admitted drinking beer before driving. The defendant took the stand and did not deny imbibing. She claimed that the liquor did not affect her ability to drive. Under cross-examination the prosecutor got her to admit that she was feeling the beer. The prosecutor then asked: "And don't you think it is fair to say that you were under the influence of intoxicating liquor?" Her reply was "Yes, I guess that is a fair thing to say."

Judge Murphy threw up his hands and called an immediate recess. Looking at the Miracle Worker, he said: "Counselor, I suggest you talk to your client."

As Murphy left the bench and headed to chambers, the prosecutor heard Murphy yell down the hall, "You won't believe this. The State's Attorney just got the defendant to admit she was drunk." Trial was reconvened shortly thereafter, and the Miracle Worker had to perform a shameless second miracle—have his client commit perjury and recant her testimony. He asked her whether she was drunk; she said no. In closing argument, the prosecutor stressed the defendant's admission. There was no closing argument by the defense. Judge Murphy's ruling: "I still have a reasonable doubt. Not guilty."

In closing arguments, Webb said the prosecution had brought to the light of day the corruption that had long been rumored to exist. "For the first time in the history of this city, something that most of us knew for years existed has been exposed." Webb reminded the jury that Operation Greylord was necessary because lawyers and judges had ignored court corruption for years. He told the jury that Judge Murphy "administered injustice that was governed by corruption. It is time in this city that the judicial corruption you have seen as a jury stop."

The jury of six men and six women convicted Murphy on 24 of the 27 counts in the indictment. The importance of the overwhelming success of the Murphy prosecution cannot be overstated. The first public presentation of evidence gath-

---

> *"The critics of the Greylord investigation were silenced and a sobering reality set in among the citizenry. The public presentation of the evidence and convictions obtained would call for reforms in the system."*

ered over three and a half years established conclusively that public corruption did in fact exist in certain areas of the Circuit Court of Cook County. The evidence also firmly established that the corruption was not limited to isolated instances that involved only one or two participants. There was a structure to the corruption and aspects of it had been institutionalized. The conviction of the first judge brought to trial in Greylord set the stage for the many cases to follow.

"I thought the U.S. Attorney should put himself or herself on the line for something that important and I did," Webb said.

The critics of the Greylord investigation were silenced and a sobering reality set in among the citizenry. The public presentation of the evidence and convictions obtained would call for reforms in the system. The case demonstrated the necessity of these undercover techniques, and the public seemed to come to accept such methods. In Murphy's appeal to the Court of Appeals for the Seventh Circuit, Judge Frank Easterbrook writing for the court said, "The government offered Murphy opportunities to sell the powers of his office and disgrace himself. He accepted with alacrity." The court also noted that "The FBI and prosecutors behaved honorably in establishing and running Operation Greylord. Operation Greylord harmed only the corrupt."

The results in the Murphy case provided an extra level of enthusiasm for the agents and lawyers involved in Greylord. More work remained and Webb and Reidy set the pace. Preparing for the Greylord trials, Webb and Reidy worked 96 days straight, through Mother's Day and the 4th of July. "Webb has endless energy and you can't wear him down," Reidy said. "You don't find Webb exhausted at the end of a trial. You find him renewed and ready to take on the next challenge."

While the Murphy trial took place, investigative work on other judges continued. As was apparent from the evidence presented in the Murphy case, Judge Richard F. LeFevour had some involvement in corrupt matters relevant to the Murphy trial. Because of his supervisory position as Chief of Traffic Court and later as the Chief Judge of the First Municipal District, Judge LeFevour did not have a calendar of cases assigned to him for adjudication or a courtroom to call his own. Because of the differences between his duties and powers and those of Judge Murphy, the contours of Judge LeFevour's corruption differed from Murphy's.

The investigation had to be structured accordingly, since the use of made-up cases with undercover lawyers and agents did not lend themselves to direct consideration by Judge LeFevour. It became apparent through gathered evidence that he was regularly on the receiving end of large amounts of cash. The investigative services of the IRS were enlisted in an effort to track the expenditures made by Judge LeFevour during relevant periods, particularly cash transactions.

A permissible theory of proof in criminal income tax cases is what can be described as the net worth plus expenditures method. Simply stated, when you spend more than you lawfully receive in income and your net worth either increases or stays the same, an inference can be drawn that you had more income than you declared on your income tax return.

The presentation of this type of evidence can both establish criminal tax violations, and be used to suggest a secret and illegal source of income such as bribe payments to a judge. The tax evidence corroborates the bribe evidence, and the two produce a synergistic quality to the entirety of the government's case. Tracking the many cash expenditures by Judge LeFevour and investigating thoroughly his other financial transactions was extremely time consuming.

On November 15, 1984, Judge Richard F. LeFevour was indicted on 59 counts charging violations of the RICO (Racketeer Influenced and Corrupt Organizations) statute, mail fraud, and filing false income tax returns. He was alleged to having engaged in a 14-year career of accepting bribes. Judge LeFevour was the fourth judge to be indicted in Greylord and also the highest ranking. For that reason, the outcome in his trial would leave a significant imprint on Operation Greylord.

As the investigation of LeFevour had evolved through 1984, Dan Webb decided to leave the United States Attorney's position. He believed strongly that a change in the leadership in the office was a healthy policy that should coincide with the presidential elections. During the trial preparation period, however, the DOJ made the unprecedented request for Webb to try the LeFevour case. Although Webb had already accepted a position at Winston & Strawn, he took a leave of absence and accepted the government's invitation to be a special prosecutor.

Reidy and AUSA Candace Fabri would join Webb as the other team members. Reidy's opening statement described Judge LeFevour's years of criminality and of how his illegal acts were determined by the professional position he occupied at any point.

From 1969 to early 1981, Judge LeFevour accepted bribes to dismiss drunk-driving cases. His cousin, James LeFevour, was the principal witness because James was a Chicago policeman assigned to Traffic Court and acted as the judge's bagman. James received cash from crooked lawyers and passed it on to his cousin, keeping a small portion for himself.

Between 1976 and 1982, Judge LeFevour accepted bribes for quashing parking tickets. The period of 1981 to 1983 when LeFevour was presiding Judge of the First Municipal District involved hustling at two of the Branch Courts in his new jurisdiction. The schemes were described in the same way as in Judge Murphy's trial, with $2,000 a month coming to Judge LeFevour and the rest to cousin James.

In addition to these direct items of evidence of corruption, Reidy outlined the results on the meticulous reconstruction of Judge LeFevour's finances. He pointed out that from 1978 to 1983, Judge LeFevour spent $125,000 for which he had "no legitimate source." Reidy told the jury Judge LeFevour rarely saw a week go by without receiving cash bribe payments. The decision to extend the investigation beyond the illegal bribe payments themselves to an exploration of the judge's finances would be a major feature of the trial itself. A final list of all the money spent by LeFevour that was not from a legitimate source was in excess of $143,000, a fact Webb would use to great effect in rebuttal.

In his opening statement on behalf of Judge LeFevour, Patrick Tuite, a highly respected and effective defense attorney with considerable experience, told the jury that the evidence would show that LeFevour had more than $100,000 in personal loans that accounted for the money at issue. Tuite put on witnesses that described LeFevour as a hardworking man who struggled to provide for his family and often had to borrow large sums of money from lawyers, other judges, and friends to make ends meet. Tuite also would use the judge's six sons as witnesses to testify that they had given their parents thousands of dollars in gifts and reimbursements to support the claimed indebtedness of over $100,000.

Webb's rebuttal argument was a direct and hard-hitting response to Tuite's assertions. Webb described the defense's move to put all six sons on the stand as an attempt to get "sympathy like I have never seen in an American courtroom." Webb told the jury, "I have great respect for the love and devotion that a son has for a father. I have less respect for a father who sends his six sons to the stand to do what was really an impossible job in this case."

He went on to remind the jury that "Those six sons were really the only evidence introduced to ... explain away even a small portion of the $143,000. They got on the witness stand, and they wanted to help their father. Who wouldn't? And you can't hold that against them.

"On the other hand, in a court of law, we can't have inaccurate testimony presented to try to defeat a prosecution, and so I'm going to talk about it. But I'm talking about it not in terms that these six sons did anything evil or wrong. I'm talking about it in terms that they had tremendous pressure put on them when they got on that witness stand and, yes, they wanted to help their father, and they knew that explaining away $143,000 was tough."

There were a number of instances during the trial when the testimony of the defendant's sons was challenged. Webb used these challenges to reinforce his argument. Andrew LeFevour was in college and listed as a dependent on Judge LeFevour's tax returns at the time he was supposed to have given his father money.

"Is that the profile of someone who's going to be giving large sums of cash to his father? You know, most of you, or many of you, have raised children or are raising children. When the kids are at home, are they a source of cash? Or is it more likely that because of the love that a parent has for a child that you give them cash?"

Webb continued to call the son's testimony into question.

> *He said, "I made $3,500 caddying, and I kept it in a big piggy bank. And that's where I was going to get all the money whenever I gave my dad all this money."*
>
> *Then he said it wasn't a piggy bank. It was a beer bottle. I don't want to be unfair to him. Maybe he meant it was a bank shaped like a beer bottle, I don't know. All of the money he said he made caddying ... it just was extraordinary. And then to be stuffing it into a beer bottle and then pulling it out to give to his father doesn't make any sense. It just doesn't make any sense.*

> *I don't know if you know how historic this trial is, because what you have seen in this trial, and what was exposed about this Cook County judicial system, is extraordinary.*

> *I went on to point out to him that he went to Ireland when he was 17 years old. No withdrawals from his savings account. Where did you get money to spend in Ireland? To go to Ireland? Piggy bank.*

Next, Webb took aim at Tuite's assertion that the sons provided $30,000 to their father. "I sat down last night, and I went through the testimony. I tried. Where is this $30,000 Mr. Tuite talked about coming from? If Mr. Tuite wanted to put a witness on the witness stand to try to summarize all that testimony into a chart or something, he didn't do any of that. He just pulled it out of the air, and he said, here's $30,000, because he wants you to just generally accept that these kids were a source of huge sums of money." Webb continued, "I went through, for hours, every bit of testimony and every time one of these sons testified about giving money to their father that had any documentation, such as a check, or a withdrawal from a savings account something that you could hold onto, it totaled $11,580."

In concluding his comments to the jury, Webb reminded them, "[Y]ou have sat through a trial; I don't know if you know how historic this trial is, because what you have seen in this trial, and what was exposed about this Cook County judicial system, is extraordinary. And so yes, I was the United States Attorney and I made the decision that judges don't deserve to be corrupt and citizens shouldn't have corrupt judges."

Webb's main concentration in rebuttal was describing the excess expenditures over reported income. He called that evidence "like a rock"—virtually unmovable and unassailable. While witnesses can be challenged as liars for various reasons, Webb emphasized the numbers because numbers don't lie and the defense did nothing to refute them.

As for LeFevour's sons, it would have been unseemly for Webb to attack them directly. Instead, he used examples from their testimony of how, by virtue of their ages, school attendance, and part-time jobs, they could not have been the sources of unreported cash. Webb also appealed to the parents on the jury who know from experience that fathers are the source of cash for kids, not the other way around. The not so subtle argument was that, in addition to being a crook, LeFevour was not such a great dad either, by involving his sons.

When the jury finished its deliberations, Judge LeFevour stood guilty of all 59 counts against him: 53 counts of mail fraud, 5 counts of income tax fraud and 1 count of racketeering. The verdict came after only 4½ hours of deliberation over two days and left attorneys for both sides stunned at how quickly the jury reached a decision. Judge LeFevour was sentenced to 12 years imprisonment. His appeal was unanimously denied by the Seventh Circuit Court of Appeals.

As reported by Maurice Possley in the *Chicago Tribune*, Special U.S. Attorney Webb offered a statement in an impromptu press conference. "In my judgment, this particular conviction of Richard LeFevour is symbolic of being the pinnacle of success of the Greylord undercover project. There's no question in my mind that that project has turned out to be the single most successful undercover operation ever taken. When this trial started eight weeks ago, we told the jury that we believed the evidence against Judge Richard LeFevour was overwhelming. It is now obvious to us that the jury has agreed with that assessment. We are very pleased with the verdict. This is the fastest verdict that I have ever seen at a major case that has lasted this long."

In addition to the verdict of the jury as a whole, a few of the juror's comments buttressed Webb's statement. The jury foreman said, "It really was a difficult case. It took a lot of soul searching." He then added, there was "a lot of overwhelming evidence." As one of the jurors left for home, she said, "There was never any doubt." Another juror was asked whether the decision was difficult to reach. His response: "Look at the time it took us."

As befits the importance of the Greylord investigation, the results achieved, and its lasting effect, the names and duties of the principal prosecutors and law enforcement agents are deserving of mention. As previously described, the investigation began under U.S. Attorney Tom Sullivan, who showed courage in pursuing evidence which had been gathered prior to his taking office. Sullivan put his neck and law license on the line, and demonstrated characteristic skill and foresight in conceiving and implementing the structures to pursue the case.

Assistant U.S. Attorney Dan Reidy inherited the fledgling case from Tom Johnson, an AUSA in the process of transferring to the U.S. Attorney's office in Denver. Reidy would become the chief operating officer of the project whose ultimate size and scope were never imagined. Reidy recruited AUSA Scott Lassar who would not only be assigned certain putative defendants in the development of evidence but would assist in the management of the overall operation. AUSA Charles Sklarsky also was brought aboard to help develop evidence and assist in the management of the operation.

Reidy, Lassar, and Sklarsky were not only among the best and brightest trial lawyers in the office, the problems which regularly arose in this unique and often dangerous undercover operation required the maturity of judgment they were regularly called upon to make.

Reidy later reflected on the importance of the FBI to the operation. "As to FBI agents, there were several of note. First and foremost is Bill Megary. He was the second case agent on the Greylord undercover project. The first was Randall Lamar Jordan, known by his middle name. Lamar did a very good job in helping us in the very early days and is responsible for selecting the name "Greylord," which he picked out of the list of horses racing one day. It sounded appropriate to him given the nature of the project, and did not violate the recently imposed (post-ABSCAM) FBI rule that code names could not suggest what the underlying nature of the project was. Bill Megary transferred into Chicago as Lamar was transferring out. I always had the impression that the FBI put Megary on this matter knowing that it might turn out to be very complex and important and that he was a star."

Reidy later explained that Megary and his team of agents had to create complex scenarios to "fake" a crime on the street in order to generate matters that could lead to paying a corrupt judge to fix the case. The work was sometimes frustrating because of all of the interests which had to be accommodated in every arrest scenario. The fake arrests had to be designed both to allow a judge to rule in favor of the undercover defense lawyer, but not so favorable to the defense that the judge "had to rule in the defense's favor." The latter situation would, of course, damage the strength of the ultimate federal prosecution of the corrupt judge.

A constant concern in all of the concocted scenarios was one of safety to the undercover FBI agents. They had to encounter Chicago police officers as "offenders," and were arrested for drug, gun, theft, and other violations. They had to go to police stations to be booked and questioned and spent hours, or sometimes days, locked up with inmates in custody for actual crimes. Although unnamed, these undercover FBI agents who volunteered for Greylord duty were instrumental to the success of the project.

Operation Greylord resulted in the indictment of 92 people. Of those, 17 were judges, resulting in 15 convictions. Of the others, 48 were lawyers, 10 were deputy sheriffs, eight were policemen, eight were court officials, and one was a state legislator. The FBI hailed Operation Greylord as the most significant and successful undercover operation ever conducted and Webb played a key role in its success. *Chicago Tribune* writers Joseph Tybor and Maurice Possley would later write:

> *When the first round of indictments in the Operation Greylord investigation was announced 3½ years ago, then-U.S. Atty. Dan Webb said that when the investigation was completed it would be viewed "as one of the most comprehensive, intricate, and difficult undercover projects ever undertaken by a law-enforcement agency."*
>
> *The conviction last week of Judge John H. McCollom and testimony during his trial underline the grim truth in Webb's prophecy. There has been no investigation into official corruption on the state or federal level that can match its scope or prosecutorial success.*

"Though we knew the risks of our approach, I did not hesitate for a moment about Operation Greylord," Webb said. "It was an extremely well-operated project. I was proud to be part of it."

Webb in his role as special prosecutor in th
Iran-Contra affair examining Colonel Olive
North as part of the trial of former Nationa
Security Advisor John Poindexter.

United States v. John M. Poindexter

CHAPTER 7
SOME OF THE PRESIDENT'S MEN

On October 5, 1986, a United States cargo plane was shot down over southern Nicaragua. Two of the crewmembers died in the crash but the third, an American named Eugene Hasenfus, parachuted to safety. However, he was captured and led out of the jungle at gunpoint by the Sandinista army, which ruled Nicaragua at the time. Hasenfus's role in a civil war in a Central American country with which the United States had no formal or public involvement triggered an investigation that would ultimately reach the highest levels of our government, cost millions of dollars, and challenge the fundamental structure of our system of government and the loyalties of elected and appointed officials.

Not long after the plane crash, in a country thousands of miles away from Nicaragua and enmeshed in governmental issues of its own, the Lebanese magazine, *Ash-Shiraa*, reported that the United States was engaged in selling arms to Iran for their help in freeing American hostages being held in Lebanon. In response to the magazine story and the avalanche of publicity it inspired, President Ronald Reagan quickly addressed the nation and said, "Those charges are utterly false. The United States has not made concessions to those who hold our people captive in Lebanon. And we will not. The United States has not swapped boatloads or planeloads of American weapons for the return of American hostages. And we will not."

So what was the connection between these two countries, Iran and Nicaragua, located in different parts of the world having little in common with each other? As the evidence unfolded, it was initially established that arms from America would ostensibly be sold to Israel with the understanding that the same or similar arms would then be sold by Israel to Iran. The arms would be priced at a certain level by the United States with the selling price to Iran at a higher figure. As the plan developed, arms were sold directly to Iran from America. Any excess of the sales proceeds over the cost of the arms would then be diverted to Nicaraguan rebels, the Contras, to aid them in their military activities to oust the Sandinistas from power.

The disclosures that followed the news stories brought about the collapse of the clandestine American support for the Contra effort in Nicaragua and the dealings of arms to Iran. Only the later investigation of these two seemingly unrelated events would provide a link between them.

The United States involvement in both prongs of what came to be known as the Iran-Contra affair was problematic for two reasons. First, Reagan was vociferous in his oft-proclaimed position that he would never trade arms for hostages. Second, the Boland Amendment, enacted by Congress and signed by Reagan in 1984, prohibited the United States government or its officials from assisting the Contras in their military or paramilitary activities.

On Nov. 25, 1986, Reagan announced the appointment of former Senator John Tower, joined by former Secretary of State Edmund Muskie and former National Security Adviser Brent Scowcroft, to gather evidence and testimony concerning U.S. involvement in the two incidents. The Tower Commission interviewed 80 witnesses, including Reagan, who answered questions about his own involvement in the matters.

The Tower Commission concluded that the president did not have knowledge of the extent of the programs, especially about the diversion of funds to the Contras. The president was, however, heavily criticized for not properly supervising his subordinates and should have had better control of National Security Council staff.

A Joint House and Senate Congressional Panel was formed to conduct its own investigation of the Iran and Contra activities. The hearings, held from May 5 until August 8, 1987, featured 250 hours of testimony from 32 witnesses. Two of the prominent witnesses from the NSC were Lieutenant Colonel Oliver L. North and Admiral John Poindexter.

The majority report placed ultimate responsibility on the Reagan White House, but suggested a cabal of zealots therein had undermined the powers of

> *As the evidence would later disclose, there was massive destruction and concealment of records as the Iran-Contra project was in its death throes.*

Congress and subverted the Constitution. The minority report signed by eight of the Republicans on the 26-member committee found only errors of judgment, no constitutional crisis, no systematic disrespect for the rule of law, no grand conspiracy, and no administration-wide dishonesty or cover-up.

In late 1986, Judge Lawrence Walsh was appointed as the Independent Counsel and commissioned to lead the Iran-Contra investigation. The Independent Counsel statute was a byproduct of Watergate, where it became apparent that the competing roles of the Attorney General—as a member of the Cabinet and presidential adviser on the one hand and chief law enforcement officer on the other—create an irreconcilable conflict of interest.

Walsh and his legal staff ran into severe investigative difficulties. As the evidence would later disclose, there was massive destruction and concealment of records as the Iran-Contra project was in its death throes.

The destruction of records prior to Judge Walsh's appointment resulted in a loss of information about the executive agencies responsible for regulating clandestine activities, about Congress, and later about the Independent Counsel and his staff. This type of obstructive conduct continued even after the Independent Counsel's investigation got under way.

The second significant impediment to Walsh's investigative efforts concerned the Classified Information Procedures Act, which governs the disclosure of classified information in trials. When it comes to foreign affairs and dealings with foreign officials and agents, a considerable amount of information is rendered classified and unavailable for public disclosure or use of any kind, even in criminal trials brought in the name of the United States. Elaborate procedures must be established to prevent unwarranted access, or if access is permitted, non-approved disclosure of the classified information. It was not an uncommon experience in the North or Poindexter criminal cases for portions of documents otherwise relevant to the issues in the cases to be excised in part, often in critical ways, as to make difficult a complete comprehension of the contents and import of the documents. The use of many other documents at trial was simply precluded.

A third significant obstacle to the development of evidence and its use at trial involved the matter of immunized testimony. As described previously, immunity bestowed upon a witness protects him or her from the use of the immunized testimony, directly or indirectly, in any criminal prosecution. Direct use is easily understood and easily applied; if a witness admits to any act of criminality while testifying under immunity, that testimonial admission cannot be introduced at any criminal trial as evidence of commission of the act. As we shall see, the indirect use of immunized testimony and the full scope of its protection was an evolving concept and its legal meaning would later prove decisive in the outcomes of some cases brought by Judge Walsh.

A serious obstacle to North's prosecution was the immunity granted to him by the congressional committees that investigated the Iran-Contra affair in 1987. North's nationally televised testimony under that grant of use immunity greatly complicated the Independent Counsel's investigation and raised serious questions as to whether North could ever be tried.

Another formidable challenge was whether North would try to "graymail" his prosecution. Graymailing is the practice of discouraging a prosecution from proceeding by contending that a defendant may need to reveal classified or sensitive information as part of a full defense. Such an approach can force the government to choose between dropping the prosecution or allowing the information to be disclosed at a trial.

On March 16, 1988, the grand jury returned a 23-count indictment charging North, Poindexter, retired General Richard Secord, and Iranian businessman Albert Hakim with conspiracy to defraud the government, theft of government property, and wire fraud. North was also charged with obstruction of congressional investigations and false statements to a congressional committee and the attorney general, shredding and altering official documents, acceptance of an illegal gratuity from Secord in the form of a home-security system, conversion of traveler's checks, and tax-fraud conspiracy.

The case was assigned to Judge Gerhard A. Gesell of the U.S. District Court for the District of Columbia. Defense counsel filed over 100 pre-trial motions that, among other things, challenged the validity of the indictment itself. Beyond that, discovery demands required the production of hundreds of thousands of documents to the defendants.

Judge Gesell conducted two days of evidentiary hearings to determine issues related to the immunized testimony. At the conclusion of this Kastigar hearing (the name taken from the case which set forth the requirements involving the scope and use of immunized testimony), Judge Gesell found that there was no improper use made of any immunized testimony.

Each defendant did, however, prevail in his motion for severance of his case from each of the other defendants. The defendants argued that their intention to use the immunized testimony of their co-defendants in their own defense prevented a joint trial. In granting all of the defendants' severance motions, the benefit to the prosecution of charging a broad conspiracy permitting all defendants to be tried together was lost.

The Independent Counsel chose to try North first. A review of the available evidence by Judge Walsh led to the conclusion that North was central to the investigation into the entire Iran-Contra affair. Irrespective of his rank in the formal chain of command and his mid-level position on the NSC staff, it was clear that North had working control of the covert Iran-Contra enterprise. This was true because of, among other reasons, an extraordinary delegation to North by Robert McFarlane and later Poindexter, the heads of the NSC during the relevant period. The force of North's personality was also a factor in his central role.

Judge Walsh's hopes for a shorter investigation were dashed by North's refusal to enter into plea discussions or to cooperate in the investigation. After severance of the defendants and the dismissal of the central conspiracy charges due to classified-information problems, North stood trial on 12 counts. On May 4, 1989, he was found guilty on only three counts: aiding and abetting obstruction of Congress, shredding and altering official documents, and accepting an illegal gratuity from Secord.

Judge Walsh and his staff were quite disappointed with the outcome of the trial. Although the jury returned guilty verdicts on three counts, the nine other not guilty verdicts were for the most serious charges. The Independent Counsel's office spent considerable time and expense developing the case, but the jury's verdict

> *Webb had an unmatched record of success both as a government prosecutor and as a criminal defense lawyer, and was familiar with the pressures of being in the public eye and in a courtroom matched against worthy adversaries. Nothing he had done previously, however, would compare to the intensity and scrutiny of his work on the Poindexter case.*

---

seemed to favor North. These feelings magnified the importance of achieving success in the Poindexter prosecution. Poindexter's station in the chain of command also put pressure on Judge Walsh, as Admiral Poindexter was not only the ranking adviser on national security issues in Reagan's administration, he was also the top official indicted for Iran-Contra activities.

Judge Walsh and his staff scoured the country to find the best lawyer available to head the government prosecution team in the trial of *United States v. John M. Poindexter*. In addition to trial skills, anybody familiar with testimony in congressional hearings under grants of immunity would have been disqualified from consideration for the appointment, as exposure to immunized testimony by a trial team member would constitute an indirect use of the immunized testimony.

The nationwide search resulted in Dan Webb being chosen to be the lead trial lawyer in Poindexter's criminal case. Webb had been engaged in a trial when the highly publicized immunized testimonies of Poindexter and North were given before Congress, therefore the Independent Counsel concluded that he was sufficiently unaware of that testimony.

Webb had an unmatched record of success both as a government prosecutor and as a criminal defense lawyer, and was familiar with the pressures of being in the public eye and in a courtroom matched against worthy adversaries. Nothing he had done previously, however, would compare to the intensity and scrutiny of his work on the Poindexter case. Because of the nature of the case, its high profile in the public arena, and the prospect that a popular ex-president would be called as a witness for the defense, the idea that it would be the legal equivalent of the Super Bowl did not seem far-fetched.

A sporting contest it was not, however, as anyone involved in the criminal justice system would attest. The stakes were high with the reputation and freedom of the defendant pitted against the dignity and respect for the law. The trial itself would test the mettle of all of the participants. The glare of publicity and the keen interest of the nation's citizens would serve to eliminate the faint of heart from any involvement.

Among other things, Webb had to prepare for the possibility of having to cross-examine former President Ronald Reagan. It became clear early on that Poindexter and his able defense team were hoping to present a defense through Reagan's testimony. As a uniquely popular public figure who seemed to grow in respect and appreciation with the passage of time, the prospect of how to approach him as an adversarial witness was not particularly appealing. Adding to the angst was the fact that he was the most direct superior to Poindexter in the chain of command. In any similar command structure, the important actions of an adviser like Poindexter would be within both the knowledge and approval of that sole supervisory official.

Webb thoroughly reviewed the North prosecution, leveraging his enormous experience in trial work, his analytical prowess, and his practical judgment. One of the more obvious things about the trial was its sheer length and the great number of witnesses called by the government to prove the many disparate acts comprising the criminal conspiracy. These witnesses worked under the overall supervision of North; they had been asked to testify against a man they admired and respected. Three of the major prosecution witnesses against North were McFarlane, Hakim, and Secord. Brendan Sullivan, North's counsel, effectively destroyed their value to the prosecution.

The first strategic pre-trial decision Webb made was to call North, an adverse witness, at the beginning of the government's case against Poindexter. In the North case someone had to tell the jury the whole Iran-Contra story. "They used over 30 witnesses to tell the complex tale, including the creation of a private air force, the opening of Swiss bank accounts, the construction of warehouses, the delivery of missiles to Iran, and conversion of funds to the Contras," Webb noted. "I decided to put North on the stand and have him tell the whole Iran-Contra story in a single, unified, non-piecemeal presentation. This would be simpler, more straightforward, and more interesting—and it would take two or three days, rather than two or three weeks."

In some ways, it was similar to Webb's decision in the Braasch case to give immunity to the collectors of extortion payments from the bar owners and force them to testify against all of the others in that conspiracy. Those collectors were the most knowledgeable witnesses available, they were a small number, and they could collectively describe all facets of the conspiracy. Unlike the price paid by the prosecution in the Braasch case—where the immunity bestowed to the collectors came early in the investigation and essentially gave them a pass for their own criminal conduct—North had already gone to trial and been convicted.

The major risk in proceeding first with North and eliminating others was that he would not be a cooperative witness. "There was no way Oliver North would ever testify voluntarily," Webb recalled. "If I wanted to immunize him, fine, said [Brendan] Sullivan, but Oliver North would not speak to me until he took the stand." In addition, his favorable feelings toward Poindexter could outshine the facts of the case. North's motive for refusing to be prepared by Webb was clear: to blow up the prosecution's case.

One of the cardinal rules of trials is that if you have the burden of proof, you should begin your case with an effective witness that you can control; this guarantees that you start on a high note and the jurors will lean in your direction. Calling North first violated this fundamental rule. "I have always believed that trial lawyers need to make critical trial decisions based on a case-specific, risk/reward analysis—and not based on per se safe rules that trial lawyers often rotely follow," Webb said. "I believed the John Poindexter case was going to be very difficult to win, and I was convinced I had to take the major risk of calling North first, and avoid calling all of these other problem witnesses."

Webb developed a different strategy from the original North trial. Poindexter was the person most responsible for directing North in those activities, and North was the most knowledgeable witness about Poindexter's participation in the Iran-Contra affair. Poindexter's defense was going to be that "North did it all and I didn't do anything." Webb decided that "since North would have to admit to much wrongdoing and Poindexter was his boss, I could use the popular view of the boss-worker relationship. The theme I wanted to sell is that the boss is responsible. So my message was this: how could a mere lieutenant colonel—Oliver North—have carried out a complex scheme on two continents without John Poindexter being involved? It was a simple theme: the boss is responsible. John Poindexter was the boss; therefore he was responsible."

Webb had access to and absorbed enormous amounts of prior testimony including that which North gave at his own trial. Although immunized testimony that North and Poindexter gave before congressional committees could not be used by the prosecution as part of its case, if either testified at trial in a manner contrary to the immunized congressional testimony, they could be cross-examined and confronted with the immunized testimony for the jury to assess their believability as a witness. Poindexter and North could also, in theory, be charged with committing perjury because immunity does not protect a witness who lies.

Webb read all of that material himself and used it to prepare cross examination questions designed to induce the same as, or substantially similar to, answers previously given. That was no small task because the material consisted of thousands of pages. "My goal was to craft questions phrased exactly as North's past answers under oath," Webb said. In addition to formulating all of the questions to ask North, Webb organized the cross examination so that North's previous testimony would be immediately available to confront and impeach him when his answers did not square with those given at former trials or hearings. This procedure was the same for all witnesses, but it was crucial for North because there were so many facts and details to be established for the entire Iran-Contra operation to be understood. Any observer of the trial or reviewer of the transcript would have to appreciate another quality of Webb; his sheer tenacity. Webb's questions were meticulous in their detail and logical in their sequence. Webb knew where he was going and how to get there. He anticipated a difficult and formidable opponent in North and that is what he got.

Poindexter had requested that the charges against him be dismissed on the basis that his and his co-defendants' compelled testimony given to the Congressional Select Committees investigating Iran-Contra in July 1987 were under a grant of use immunity.

Judge Harold Greene, to whom the case was transferred, ordered evidentiary hearings to decide the motion. Regarding trial witnesses, Judge Greene took extensive measures to ensure that Poindexter's immunized statements were not used against him. North testified at the pretrial hearing that he was unable to distinguish what he had personally done, observed, or experienced from what he had learned from watching Poindexter's immunized testimony. In effect, North was suggesting that his own knowledge of relevant information came from Poindexter's immunized testimony. As such, North's own putative testimony in the Poindexter case would have been an indirect product of Poindexter's immunized testimony.

Reacting to a claim that Poindexter destroyed a December 1985 Presidential Covert-Action Finding—important evidence in the obstruction of Congress charge—North acknowledged that he had seen Poindexter destroy a piece of paper but insisted that he did not know it was a finding until Poindexter stated that fact in his immunized testimony. Judge Greene did not believe North's testimony and stated that North "appears to have ... embarked upon the calculated course of attempting to assist his former colleague and co-defendant ... by prevaricating on various issues." As to North's testimony about the finding, the judge found it "inherently incredible" that North did not remember "his participation in an event he witnessed firsthand and that was as dramatic, indeed historic, as the tearing up of an extremely rare presidential finding."

After the jurors were selected and sworn in, the lawyers for the prosecution and the defendant made opening statements on March 8, 1990. Long before then, however, Webb had devoted a great deal of time, effort, preparation, and revision of what he would say in his opening statement. All trial lawyers agree that opening statements are important. Where disagreements arise is about the level of their importance. Webb belonged to the school that they were highly important generally, and more so in the Poindexter case because of the number of facts involved, the major participants and the roles they played, and the sheer complexity of the information.

Webb struggled with how to structure his opening statement because of the complexity of the Iran-Contra events. Although he had never before used jury consultants to test an opening statement before trial, he did so for this case. After he delivered his proposed statement to the jury consultants, Webb concluded that the demonstrative exhibits he was using to explain the facts of the case were too

> *If you get the jury leaning in your direction with the opening statement they will often stay on your side throughout the trial.*

---

complicated and he amended his opening statement accordingly. This process took weeks to accomplish, but Webb and the others were eventually satisfied with the level of improvement reached.

Not only is it important what the lawyers say in their openings but how they say it. As it is the jurors' first meaningful exposure to the facts and events outlined to them, it is also their first introduction to the lawyers. Juries make assessments on the lawyers' knowledge of the case, the sincerity of their beliefs in the information they are presenting, and the rightness of the cause they are championing.

While it may not be easy to describe how to give an effective opening, it is important for a lawyer to connect with the jury in a forceful and effective manner. According to Webb, opening statements are underappreciated. "If you get the jury leaning in your direction with the opening statement," he said, "they will often stay on your side throughout the trial."

Dan Webb was 44 years old when the trial began, though his boyish looks belied his courtroom experience and abilities. His job was to convince the jury that an otherwise honorable man, while in the employ of a popular president and while entrusted with some of the weightiest matters given to any government official, subjugated the command of the law to his own view of propriety, and that he did so by lying to and deceiving elected government officials and the public at large.

Richard Beckler, lead counsel for Poindexter, had as his mission in his opening statement to promote the view that a distinguished military officer and honorable public servant, widely viewed and respected, would hardly abandon the character traits of honesty and integrity that marked his service, engage in prohibited conduct, and then lie about it.

At the beginning of his opening statement, Webb outlined the two clandestine operations in Nicaragua and Iran. He then offered to the jury a civics lesson on the branches of our government, especially the rights and responsibilities of the legislative branch "to find out facts that it may need to know about as it makes, or passes, a law." In describing the necessity of all government officials to act with integrity and honesty with each other, irrespective of which branch they were employed in, he stated, "There has to be a free flow of accurate information, sometimes between the different branches of government."

Webb then described the nuts and bolts of his case. "What you're going to hear from the evidence is that certain people who worked in the executive branch of government, in order to conceal and hide and cover up that they, in fact, were carrying on these secret foreign operations—these people lied and made false statements to Congress, concealed and misrepresented facts to Congress, destroyed documents, and obstructed these congressional inquiries." In his detailed opening statement, Webb described the key actors in the case, the offices and functions of government they occupied, and the importance of their work. Of special note were the two key witnesses in the case: former President Reagan and North. Webb established early on that North would be a reluctant witness against his former boss, Poindexter, and that his appearance was being compelled under a grant of immunity.

Webb succinctly addressed the importance of North as a witness. "Oliver North will tell you that he kept John Poindexter advised of everything he was doing for the Contras. You're also going to hear testimony from Oliver North—and I am going to introduce the documents into evidence—that John Poindexter was fully aware that false information was being sent to Congress."

Webb told the jury about the expected trial evidence. "Oliver North will tell you that on August 6, 1986, instructed by Poindexter, he went and appeared before Hamilton's Intelligence Congressional Committee. Oliver North will tell you that at that time he was asked question after question. 'Were you militarily assisting the Contras? Were you engaged in fund-raising activities on behalf of the Contras?' Specific names were used, events, places. North will tell you—and I expect he will tell you as candidly as he can, he's been convicted—he lied, and he lied, and he lied. One false statement after another ... North will tell you, there is no question, every answer he gave was false. And what you are going to hear from the evidence, when Congressman Hamilton comes into this courtroom and testifies, is it worked. It worked like a charm."

As for Poindexter, he received a written memo from an NSC staff member relating all the lies North gave the committee that day. Webb then told the jury,

"Once Admiral Poindexter finds out how successful North was in lying, what does he do? He congratulates North, and he sends him a note saying, 'Well done.'"

Webb explained how Poindexter appeared before the House Intelligence Committee and the Senate Intelligence Committee, where he was asked about the presidential finding signed by Reagan. Webb said that North's testimony would show Poindexter lied in his comments to Congress regarding the finding.

> *Oliver North will tell you [the document] was destroyed and torn up by John Poindexter. It was ripped in two. Oliver North will tell you that he remembers being in Poindexter's office. The signed finding by the President of the United States was locked in a safe. It was brought to the Admiral, and he destroyed it. I don't have the signed finding because it doesn't exist anymore; it was torn up by John Poindexter as part of his involvement in obstructing Congress, lying to Congress, and deceiving Congress about the Iran shipment.*
>
> *In November of 1986, in the middle of all these congressional investigations, Poindexter destroys and deletes all of the stored messages in his computer file that he had sent or received, which include numerous memos involving the Contra affair and the Iran affair. But you are going to hear from the evidence that the FBI discovered, when this investigation got ongoing, there was a backup system. We recovered a lot of those memos.*

Richard Beckler followed Webb's morning presentation in the afternoon session with his own opening statement. He told the jury "[you have] only four things you have to keep looking at throughout this whole case."

His first point was that the Boland restriction didn't apply to the president. Beckler said that "the president himself will tell you that he believed that it did not apply." Because of that, Beckler argued, it made no sense to lie about a statutory prohibition that did not apply to the underlying conduct. While the assertion that the executive branch was exempt from the Boland Amendment was perhaps debatable, the jury may still have had in mind Webb's statement that Poindexter was not charged with violating the Boland Amendment. The crimes he was facing

> *The popularity of the president and the majesty of the office of the presidency had been appropriated for use by the defense.*

---

concerned lying to and obstructing Congress; it was not debatable that lying to Congress was a crime.

Point number two was the caliber of people Poindexter worked with. Beckler said, "I agree with the prosecution, they were some of the highest men in this country, running this country. Admiral Poindexter always followed the orders of President Reagan. Why did he follow those orders? Because President Reagan was his commander in chief." The premise of Beckler's second point was that Poindexter was only following orders, did not engage in acts beyond those which were authorized, and, of the most significance, was fully and truthfully reporting to the president all of the acts he had committed. It was in this way that the popularity of the president and the majesty of the office of the presidency had been appropriated for use by the defense.

Beckler's third point, simply expressed, was "that Admiral Poindexter always believed that every one of his actions were legal, and they were. The prosecution has talked to you about destruction, about lies, about fraudulent, misleading statements. We will disprove every one of those allegations in our evidence. You will find, and keep it in mind, that Admiral Poindexter always told the truth. He never lied to Congress despite what the prosecution says. The evidence will show that he never lied."

Finally, as for the destroyed presidential finding of December 1985, Beckler instead made reference to a finding signed in January 1986 that did not contain the direct arms-for-hostages language that appeared in the 1985 finding. This second finding was coupled to Reagan's expected testimony that the decision to initiate the arms project with Iran was solely the president's, that he was allowed by law to do so, and that Congress need not be informed of the initiative.

True to his promise to the jury and his trial strategy, Webb called North first. As expected, he was a difficult witness who would challenge Webb at every turn. Even the bare transcript reflects the tension between the two men.

At the beginning of his testimony, North acknowledged that he was testifying pursuant to a subpoena and an immunity order. He admitted to refusing to sit down with the government prior to trial to go over his testimony. He stated that he did not know what questions Webb intended to ask, but acknowledged that he had been convicted of certain crimes arising out of the Iran-Contra affair. The crimes included obstruction of Congress and destroying official documents.

A career officer with the United States Marine Corps, Lieutenant Colonel North was detailed in the summer of 1981 to the National Security Council as a staff officer. At some point, North had responsibility for matters pertaining to democracy initiatives in Central America.

Until the passage of the Boland Amendment in October 1984, the CIA had provided supplies and support to the Contras—all appropriated by Congress. A few months before the passage of the Boland Amendment, North was assigned to take on some of the responsibilities in militarily assisting the Contras that had previously been performed by the CIA. It was during this period that the CIA was being phased out and North was being phased in to the Contra activity. North testified that Director William Casey of the CIA told him that he would have to go forward with the effort because the CIA could no longer do it.

North testified that he began to have meetings with Contra leaders even as he was assisting them in the purchase of arms, munitions, equipment, medicine, and uniforms. The Contras were also provided with intelligence information, logistical support, and actual military weapons. North also got in touch with Richard Secord, a retired Air Force Major General and decorated officer from the Vietnam War, who had experience in acquiring military weapons and making airdrops into places like Central America.

When Webb asked North whether Secord set up an operation under North's control that supplied military weapons to the Contras, North answered, "no." It was at this early point that Webb made clear to North that false answers would not be tolerated and that Webb was in possession of transcripts of North's earlier testimony at various proceedings that Webb would use to impeach answers that were inconsistent with that earlier testimony. "What I did with North for the first day or so was, whenever he told me he didn't know or gave me an answer I didn't like, within seconds I could turn to his prior testimony and say 'Didn't you on an earlier occasion testify as follows?' In this way—by smacking him with the transcript—I was mostly able to control the pace and content of the testimony," Webb said. When challenged by his prior testimony, North changed his answer from a "no" to a "yes."

A pattern developed. First, Webb would ask North a question and North's answer would be different than answers previously given under oath. Webb would then give North the prior reference with the different answer; North would then affirm that he so testified previously. Webb would then ask whether his prior answer was truthful. North would affirm that it was. Webb was also helped by the Federal Rules of Evidence in that he could use leading questions with North even though North was a prosecution witness. Normally, a witness called by a party in a case must be examined with non-leading questions, which allows the witness to set forth the details in their response. With witnesses who are adverse or hostile to the party calling them, however, the use of leading questions is permitted and allows the questioning attorney to better control the details of the testimony. The procedure then becomes one of cross-examination in form if not in fact.

In addition to the verbal pattern of the questions, there was also a pattern to Webb's courtroom conduct when he had to refer to North's prior testimony. Webb would turn his back to North, step away from the lectern, walk to a nearby carton and withdraw the relevant reference to challenge his testimony. This process was repeated so often that one can only imagine North's mindset at the moment Webb turned his back to retrieve another document. "My notes were keyed to the transcripts, so every time North strayed, every time I asked a leading question and he disagreed, I'd turn my back; North came to know he was going to get hit with the transcript which contradicted his answer," Webb said. The gesture must have had a certain Pavlovian effect on everybody. In fact, there were times when Webb would turn toward the box and North would simply cave in and give Webb the answer he wanted without the need to use another document.

North's testimony established that he met with Contra leaders to find out what they needed and to pass on their requests to Secord. Companies were set up for various functions, including supplying weapons, establishing warehouses, and providing air drop supplies. The former CIA operation was essentially replicated by North inside the NSC in the White House. Secord hired personnel with prior military experience, purchased weapons from all over the world, and acquired aircraft to fly resupply missions at night. Funds were raised from various sources and bank accounts were set up in Switzerland and elsewhere. North reported to his superiors and kept them advised.

In the summer of 1985, the NSC received two congressional committee inquiries about whether any NSC staff was militarily assisting the Contras or providing fundraising. The letters specifically questioned North's activities in the described topics.

North was assigned to draft a response to the letter from Congressman Hamilton. He testified that he prepared a draft to one of the letters, which was reviewed and substantially revised by Robert McFarlane, who was the National Security Adviser at the time. North described a meeting that was then held between McFarlane and himself in which North said that what McFarlane put in the revised draft was false. North urged McFarlane to request the president to assert executive privilege to the congressional committee inquiries and simply decline to respond. McFarlane rejected North's recommendation and sent the letter with the false information to Congress.

The NSC leadership underwent a change when Poindexter replaced Robert McFarlane in December of 1985, but in other respects everything about Iran-Contra continued as before. The only major change was the diversion of some proceeds from the sale of arms to Iran to the Contra operation. Based on North's testimony, he continued to advise Poindexter about the Contra assistance activities.

In June of 1986, the White House received another congressional inquiry directing the president to provide to the House of Representatives certain information concerning "activities of Lieutenant Colonel Oliver North or any other member of the staff of the National Security Council in support of the Nicaraguan resistance." This was similar to the inquiry Congress made in the summer of 1985. North objected to Poindexter when another staff member was assigned to respond as opposed to himself.

The evidence at trial established that Poindexter signed three letters dated July 21, 1986, referring Congress back to the information that had been given to them in 1985. North testified that the false information given to Congress in 1985 was still false in July of 1986 since the activities in militarily assisting the Contras by North and others was still continuing. North further testified that he had advised Poindexter of the ongoing assistance to the Contras before Poindexter responded to Congress.

North testified that in a memorandum dated only three days after the dates of Poindexter's responsive letters to Congress, North described how large the project had become. North wrote, "The Contra operation has assets of six aircraft, warehouses, supplies, maintenance facilities, ships, boats, leased houses, vehicles, ordnances, munitions, communications equipment, a 6,500 foot runway, and it is valued at over $4.5 million."

North's testimony at the Poindexter trial also established that Poindexter directed North to appear before Congressman Hamilton's committee. In his discussions with Poindexter, North told him that there were some specific things that North would be called upon to reveal and that he could not do so. Poindexter responded, "You can take care of it." When North was asked how he felt about making false statements to Congress, he answered, "Well, I never feel good about making a false statement, and even though it was never perceived to be illegal, it was something that I didn't want to be put in that situation."

At this point, Judge Greene asked a question.

The Court	Did the false statements have to do with your activities on behalf of the Contras?
North	Your Honor, it is hard to say after several years. I hoped when I went down to that meeting in the [situation] room that we would have enough friends of our policy, if you will, members of the committee who were supportive, that they would be able to, I suppose, vector the conversation away from the very sensitive issues, and I left the conversation with the admiral with that hope. I didn't stand up there and walk into the meeting intending to lie. I lied during the meeting.
The Court	What I am trying to find out, Colonel, is your concern about having to make false statements, did they relate to the Contras or India, Pakistan, or whatever?
North	This meeting focused exclusively on the resistance, Your Honor.

For a brief moment, Webb adopted a spectator's status as Judge Greene elicited the testimony from North that he in fact lied to Congressman Hamilton's committee about his involvement in Contra matters. North apparently did not mind sparring with Webb, but chose not to do so with the judge and candidly admitted to his lies.

At another moment during the trial, after a string of obfuscating responses from North, Judge Greene again lashed out. "Why don't you just answer the questions, Colonel North?" he said. "For somebody who quibbles about every little bit that's being asked—whether something happened in July or August—you embroider at other times when it's not necessary. Just answer the question." The cumulative effect of the judge's chastisements certainly neutralized the sympathy of North and the actions he had taken in the eyes of the jury. North painted himself as a patriot and dutiful in his respect for authority and in championing the noble causes of freeing American hostages and displacing an oppressive regime. Yet when Webb asked about the details of his actions, his lies to Congress, and the cover-ups of his actions, he nit-picked in his responses. He was not nearly so forthright and constantly declined to answer as he had under oath on prior occasions. Although called as a witness for the prosecution, he was clearly hostile to the government's position and adversarial to their interests. If so perceived, his helpfulness to Poindexter's position was questionable.

The questioning later turned to the connection between Iran and the Contras.

> *"Why don't you just answer the questions, Colonel North? For somebody who quibbles about every little bit that's being asked whether something happened in July or August, you embroider at other times when it's not necessary. Just answer the question."*

Webb First of all, tell the jury—as far as the Iran project was concerned after it got under way—eventually, was there a linkage or connection between the Iran project and the Contra assistance project?

North Eventually, yes.

Webb Okay. And, essentially, what that linkage was is that eventually some of the funds that were generated from the arms sales to the nation of Iran were in excess of what the United States needed to be paid for the arms, and that created some residual funds that you and this enterprise, you and this organization, were able to use, in part, to assist the Contras. Is that a truthful [and] accurate statement on my part?

North Yes.

The completeness of Webb's question reflected the essence of the Iran connection to what was the Iran-Contra affair. Detailed questioning of North then established the specifics of the Iran initiative, including the nature and timing of arms shipments, the manner in which the shipments were transported, creation of the residual funds, and the secret accounts established for the transfer of funds to the Contras.

North admitted that approximately $16 million in profit was generated by the arms sales, a large amount of which went to militarily assist the Contras. North testified that he had the full permission and authority to transfer the money from Poindexter to the Contras and that these matters were concealed from Congressman Hamilton's committee.

According to North, there were two factors that coalesced to add fuel to the arms-for-hostages agreement. One was Iran's involvement in a bloody war with its neighbor, Iraq. Iran was desperate to get certain types of military equipment to assist them in that war. The United States had stockpiles of missiles and weapons that Iran wanted.

The other relevant factor was the U.S.'s strong relationship with Israel. Government officials learned that Israel, a neighbor of Lebanon, was preparing to make a shipment of over five hundred TOW missiles to Iran. As North testified, he was directed to monitor the shipment of these missiles.

North told Poindexter that the Israelis had arranged to ship 18 Hawk missiles to Iran and planned to move 80 more. Unlike the TOW missiles which were ground-to-ground projectiles and relatively small in size, the ground-to-air Hawk missiles were large and much more difficult to transport.

The Israelis were having great problems in locating a place in a European country where they could change planes and offload the Hawk missiles. North testified that he met with a senior Israeli government official; in phone calls back and forth with McFarlane he was told that the president had authorized American assistance in helping the Israelis get the Hawk missiles to Iran. North's testimony also showed that Poindexter knew of the CIA's direct involvement.

North described a proprietary company, outside the government, that operates as a commercial company and also provides services to the CIA on a contract basis. North got the name of the company from the CIA and gave it to the Israelis and to Secord. As North testified, this was the first time that Secord, who had been involved with the Contras, became involved in the Iran side of the project.

North testified that in November of 1985, after the CIA involvement in the Hawk missile shipment with the use of its proprietary airplane, the CIA wanted compliance with a legal requirement that a presidential finding had to actually be signed by the president, ratifying CIA activities regarding the shipment. North testified that he had a specific discussion with Poindexter about the CIA insistence on a signed presidential finding.

A CIA attorney named Stanley Sporkin—who would later rise to United States District Judge—composed a presidential finding. A draft was sent to North while CIA Director Casey sent the original to John Poindexter with the following message, based on the documentary evidence at trial: "Pursuant to our conversation, this should go to the president for his signature and should not be passed around in any hands below our level."

North testified that in December of 1985, he learned that the president had signed the original finding. According to North, CIA personnel "wanted to be awfully sure that the president actually signed that finding, that [North] checked to make sure it happened, and that he confirmed to them that the president had signed." North also testified that "the original finding was kept in a safe near

Admiral Poindexter's office and that North went to look at the finding to make sure it had been signed by the president."

The 1985 presidential finding was used to justify the Hawk missile shipment in November 1985. The language of the finding said, "As part of these efforts [meaning the Iran initiative], certain foreign materials and munitions may be provided to the government of Iran which is taking steps to facilitate the release of the American hostages."

North testified that he had no involvement in drafting the finding, but because of the damaging language of the 1985 presidential finding, he worked with CIA personnel in drafting language for a new finding to replace the December 1985 document. The president signed a new presidential finding on January 6, 1986, cleansed of its damaging language, which was then replaced by a January 17 document with slightly altered language.

North also testified that he, at Poindexter's direction, participated in preparing a chronology of events about the history of the Iran project. North admitted in his testimony that at some point, the chronology became false. McFarlane inserted a completely fabricated story to cover up U.S. involvement in the Hawk missile shipment. The false chronology of events involving the Iran project was transmitted to Poindexter on November 20, 1986.

Poindexter and Director Casey were scheduled to testify before Congress, prompting a meeting at Poindexter's office attended by high-ranking officials that North admitted was to determine how the story was going to come out.

At this point, Webb directed North's attention to a document about the missile shipment.

Webb	Does that document look familiar to you?
North	Yes.
Webb	That is a one-page description of the United States involvement in this missile shipment that was brought to the meeting by the CIA. Is that correct?
North	I believe that is a CIA document, yes. Just by virtue of the way it is typed.

Webb When the CIA brought that written memorandum to the meeting, you noticed immediately that it falsely described the United States' involvement in the Hawk missile shipment. Is that correct?

North I don't know if I noticed immediately, but it is very clearly false.

Webb then moved to the particularly significant topic of the embarrassing presidential finding signed in late 1985.

Webb Let me move on to a little different topic. We are still in November of 1986, leaving behind your alterations. Let me move on and talk a little bit about what happened to this presidential finding in November of 1986, the one with the embarrassing language in it. Are you with me?

North Yes.

Webb You told us that the original of this document—this one, of course, is not signed, is it, by the president?

North No.

Webb The original of the presidential finding you said had been put in Admiral Poindexter's safe, the one that was signed by the President of the United States?

North As I recall, it was either in his safe or Commander [Paul] Thompson's.

Webb Okay. Now this document, as I understand you told us earlier, when it actually was originally created, it was in November 1985 to justify the Hawk shipment. It was originally created and signed by the president in November or December of 1985?

North Right.

Webb Would you agree that it became even more politically embarrassing by the time we get to [the avalanche of publicity in 1986]?

North	Well, I don't believe I thought of it at the time. As you mentioned it here today, it certainly does.
Webb	Well, this theme that I have been talking to you about, this theme to cover up and hide this finding, did you get the impression that as we proceeded into November further, that the pressure to hide this finding from Congress became greater?
North	Counsel, I don't recall that aspect of it ever being discussed.
Webb	You didn't think there was any problem or any theme at all going on to hide that finding from Congress?
North	No. As I indicated earlier, I all along thought that the whole purpose was to maintain the cover story we had for a year. Protect the lives of the hostages by doing that.
Webb	Even though McFarlane had told you that this finding, we can't use it, rely upon it because it shows arms for hostages. Did that give you a clue there was something going on to cover up this finding? No?
North	I do not recall thinking of that aspect of it.
Webb	Did you testify under oath in your own trial that people up the line from you, including Admiral Poindexter, did not want the finding to be used as a justification for what had happened in 1985 because the finding was itself a political embarrassment because it looked like it was drafted as a straight arms for hostage swap. Did you testify to that?
North	Yes.

Webb was fully prepared and went toe-to-toe with North, according to Howard Pearl, who worked with Webb on the case. "Webb artfully cut him to pieces," he said. "North was never once able to score a point against Webb by having factual knowledge that Webb didn't. I never in my life have seen anyone absorb information as quickly and thoroughly as Webb did."

When North was finished testifying, all of the material operations of Iran-Contra had been put before the jury. He had also testified about the role of the alleged participants, albeit with some reluctance. North was in position to tell the jury all that Poindexter knew, all of the decisions he made, and the falsehoods contained in Poindexter's presentations to members of Congress.

"I got a sense from the jury that I had done what I wanted. I had told the Iran-Contra story. I thought the jury had gotten 'the boss is responsible' theme. After North finished, I walked into the hallway and told Secord, who was ready to go on next, to go home. We cancelled all the background witnesses," Webb said.

Following North, the prosecution was left to present evidence of the crime. Congressman Lee Hamilton and Judge Stanley Sporkin were able to corroborate the key evidence against Poindexter. The electricity in the courtroom created by Webb's examination of North would be absent until later in the trial, when it would reappear with the testimony of President Reagan.

The circumstance of a former president of the United States appearing as a witness for the defense in a criminal trial conducted in the U.S. District Court is unprecedented in American history. That his testimony would be for a high-ranking government official accused of lying to elected members of Congress about matters being "run out of the White House" added to the intrigue. That Reagan would be cross-examined by Webb, a former U.S. Attorney for the Northern District of Illinois once appointed by Reagan to that post added to the uniqueness of the situation.

In early 1990, the period in which the Poindexter trial would be held in Washington, D.C., Reagan was out of office and living in California. This created some logistical problems for Reagan to appear as a witness for the defense. After consideration of the geographic issues, the parties and counsel for both sides decided that Reagan would give a videotaped evidence deposition in the U.S. District Courthouse in Los Angeles, California. This deposition would be in lieu of Reagan's physical presence at the trial in Washington, D.C. and would be shown to the jury and considered in the same way as live testimony would be. This arrangement would therefore require Judge Greene, counsel for the parties and Reagan, and the defendant to travel to California. Webb would describe this compromise as providing the opportunity to preserve Reagan's testimony in a deposition, and he "would not have to go through the embarrassment, hassle, or trauma of being a witness in a criminal case as a live witness." Both sides were happy with the compromise. Reagan's deposition was expected to take one day and would be conducted prior to the start of the trial in Washington, D.C.

The mere presence and support of a popular and much admired former president was a real plus for Poindexter. The pretrial preparation of what questions to ask and how to ask them in cross-examining such a witness was a daunting task. The necessity to review all relevant information was, of course, similar to what had to be done for any witness. Of prime importance would be all of the prior statements Reagan made on related topics in whatever forum they were made, including press conferences.

The more sensitive part of the preparation was how to interact with such a witness. Respect for his office, age, and popularity had to be considered in the formulations of the questions. Webb was not given a chance to meet with Reagan or to find out what he would say. Things would go smoothly if the president answered Webb's questions in ways similar to his prior out-of-court declarations. What was more difficult to contemplate were circumstances in which Reagan's trial testimony would differ from prior statements. It is in these circumstances of unexpected developments that cross-examination can be elevated to an art form.

Although the record doesn't reflect it, the first question to be resolved was the matter of protocol. Normally, when a judge enters the courtroom, the Marshall calls out "Hear ye, hear ye, all rise" and everyone stands. The former president and the presiding judge each represented a different branch of government under our Constitution. So, instead of saying "all rise" the Marshall said, "Everyone remain seated." Webb was surprised, but he recognized that Judge Greene showed great sensitivity in changing the Marshall's call.

As Reagan began to testify, he indicated that he first met Poindexter when he was deputy to National Security Adviser Robert McFarlane. When McFarlane resigned, Poindexter was appointed to succeed him.

The president described the importance of the position. "Well, mainly, each morning we would meet as a part [of] or following the staff meeting, and it would be to apprise me of anything, any international incident that had taken place, or anything that would be of interest or concern to our government. I would get these reports. And then in addition, there would be advice with regard to what actions might be required of us. Admiral Poindexter reported directly to me as President of the United States."

Beckler asked about the president's recollection of the Iran-Contra affair. "It was a covert action that was taken at my behest," Reagan answered.

Beckler then described to Reagan the two sets of actions that the indictment against Poindexter contained, one having to do with letters that Poindexter sent to congressional committees in the summer of 1986 and the other referred to statements that Poindexter made to congressional committees in November of 1986 referring to a shipment of Hawk missiles that took place in November of 1985. Reagan answered, "I only recall learning that there had been at some point a shipment of Hawk missiles by Israel to Iran. And the only concern of ours was that it was customary that we did not or would not replace weapons that were delivered by us to a country if that country then sent them on or sold them to another country. But that is about the extent of my recollection."

The testimony touched on meetings later in 1985 with some of the president's top advisers. Word had gotten back to his advisers "that the Iranians wanted something, some evidence, that would make them confident that they were meeting with people who had access to the top levels of government in our country." Reagan testified that the Iranian representative had suggested a single shipment of TOW anti-tank missiles to be sold to them. He further testified that he sent word to his people that the U.S. had a policy not to do business with a government that supported terrorism.

Reagan then said, "The answer that came back was that these individuals did not support terrorism, and there was some documentation to the effect that they had shown an opposition to terrorism wherever they had an opportunity. In this case, I sent word back, since this shipment of TOW missiles would not have changed the balance in any way in their contest with Iraq, which we behind the scenes had been trying to end that war for a long time. And I made the decision that there was one thing upon which we could base selling them this single order of TOW missiles, and that was that we had some nine hostages being held by the Hezbollah, which had a kind of philosophical relationship with Iran, and that if they would use their efforts to get our hostages freed, yes, we would make this sale."

When Beckler inquired of the president about his recollection in 1986 of being briefed by Poindexter about some Hawk missile spare parts being sent to Iran, he testified that the only thing he was aware of was "learning or hearing that the

Israelis, prior to these other things, had sent some of their Hawk missiles to Iran evidently in that sale. And the thing that makes me remember that is that, apparently, the understanding was that this was going to be in return for some, perhaps, hostages of their own or the people that were held. That if these individuals by the time the plane of delivery had reached a certain point, if these individuals had not been released, the plane would turn and come back without continuing the delivery."

At a later point in his testimony, Reagan was asked about a 1985 Hawk missile shipment and whether he recalled being informed generally about that shipment at that time. He answered, "I actually don't. I don't have any recollection of when I was told about that or who told me."

After establishing the political and social climate in Nicaragua and Central America, Beckler addressed a key question in the trial.

Beckler	In 1985 and 1986, did you know about what Oliver North was doing with regard to helping the situation in Central America vis-à-vis the freedom fighters?
Reagan	Well, you have to have people that can be available to make contact with the leaders of the Contras and so forth, sometimes closer than just writing a letter. And it was my feeling and my understanding—I did not meet individually with him to any extent at all—but it was my understanding because his name would crop up in memos and so forth that that's what he was doing. And I am trying to I think what the other angle ... I know that there was another area too in which he participated. Well, for example, in the meeting with the Iranians, he was involved in that, and I think was actually there in the meetings with them. Whether all of the time or not, I am not familiar.

Notably absent from Reagan's answer was any awareness of North's active involvement in providing an enormous array of military or paramilitary assistance to the Contras, or his preeminent role in getting the Israeli Hawk missile shipment from Israel to Iran.

> *Reagan's testimony that he was in total agreement with Poindexter's response left Webb stunned. 'I thought maybe he made a mistake. I had his interrogatory answers and was trying to bring him back to reality, but he wasn't coming back to reality.'*

As the president's direct examination was nearing its end, Beckler then turned the questioning to the heart of the criminal charges against Poindexter. Beckler showed the president two letters of inquiry, one from Congressman Lee Hamilton, Chairman of the House Permanent Select Committee on Intelligence and one from Congressman Dante Fascell, Chairman of the House Committee on Foreign Affairs. The letters were identical in content and directed the president to respond to the inquiries about Oliver North and the activities he was engaged in. Attached to the letters was a House Resolution of Inquiry that was referenced in the two letters. When Reagan was asked if the letters refreshed his recollection as to the House making inquiry with regard to Oliver North, he said, "It is hard for me to believe that I would not receive letters directed personally to me, and yet I have no memory of these. And if I did finally read them, then I am sure somebody else provided the answer because I wouldn't have known the answer to this."

Reagan was then shown Poindexter's responsive letter.

Beckler Now, Mr. President, this is a letter that I mentioned earlier that is the subject of a couple of different counts in the indictment. And this is a letter that is signed by Admiral Poindexter and sent to Lee Hamilton, and it is dated July 21, 1986. Maybe you could take a minute and just read this letter?

Reagan I am in total agreement. If I had written it myself, I might have used a little profanity.

Beckler Thank you. I have no further questions on the particular letter.

Beckler then established that similar letters were sent to Representatives Fascell and Leslie Aspin. When Beckler asked if the responses of Reagan would be the same as the letter to Congressman Hamilton, he answered, "I'm in complete support of both letters." The direct examination concluded shortly thereafter.

Webb's initial plan for cross-examining Reagan was to be non-agressive, somewhat soft and respectful. However, Reagan's testimony that he was in total agreement with Poindexter's response left him stunned. "I thought maybe he made a mistake. I had his interrogatory answers and was trying to bring him back to reality, but he wasn't coming back to reality," Webb said. Webb's extensive review of the available pretrial materials—including Reagan's written answers under oath to interrogatories—suggested no personal belief in the truth of Poindexter's written response to the congressional inquiries.

"I considered that document to be my strongest piece of evidence—my smoking gun. I thought the letter Poindexter wrote to a congressional committee contained false information. I knew that Reagan, in his interrogatory answers, had said that he had never seen the letter, did not author it, and knew nothing about it. So, I didn't expect anything," Webb said.

The testimony by Reagan that he would have written similar letters to Congress, albeit stronger, was essentially his declaration that Poindexter was not guilty of lying to Congress. The letters Reagan blessed were the anchors of the five criminal charges against Poindexter, and Webb was very concerned that this critical testimony would cause the jury to find Poindexter not guilty. "I was stunned. All of a sudden I realized that the President of the United States had taken away my entire case," Webb said.

If Reagan had testified that he did not know of the material facts of Iran-Contra and did not authorize the acts engaged in by Poindexter, North, and others, Webb could have lived with that. The less the president claimed to know, the less Poindexter could claim he was simply following orders. Webb realized immediately that he had to destroy the credibility of the president or at least the accuracy of some of his answers.

Besides the president's written answers to the interrogatories, there was other information available to Webb that he could use to impeach the president's answer about the Poindexter response letter. The details of the Iran-Contra affair had received extensive public disclosure and commentary in late 1986. Poindexter's resignation had been tendered to the president in the midst of the publicity and the president fired Oliver North at the same time. The Tower Commission, appointed by the president, had conducted public hearings and delivered a 200-page report with its findings to the president. The president's written interrogatory answers were consistent with the Tower Commission's report that concluded the president did not have knowledge of the extent of the Iran-Contra programs.

Additional areas of challenge to the scope of the president's knowledge were criminal cases that preceded his 1990 videotape deposition. Robert McFarlane had pled guilty to withholding information from Congress in his letter sent in mid-1985 in his capacity as National Security Adviser. McFarlane's letter to Congress, although false, was cited approvingly in the Poindexter letter sent to Congress in mid-1986, the letter Reagan said he would have sent. There was a wealth of information available for use by Webb to cross-examine the president but it had to be reviewed, organized, and structured to be used effectively.

Although there was not much time left in the afternoon of Reagan's testimony, Webb had to start his cross-examination right away. Reagan's testimony adopting the Poindexter letter was so unexpected, that Webb began his cross without having the very letter in his possession that Reagan just adopted. Webb was reduced to using the copy of the letter Reagan was still holding.

Webb	Let me start with the last exhibits that Mr. Beckler showed you concerning the letters that John Poindexter sent to Congress on July 21, 1986. Do you still have those in front of you, Mr. President? My question to you is would you have approved the sending of these letters to Congress by John Poindexter if you knew that they adopted false information that had been previously supplied to Congress by Mr. McFarlane?
Reagan	No. But I would have to have it proven to me that they did.
Webb	My question to you is, sir: if you knew that the previous information provided to Congress by Mr. McFarlane was false, would you authorize John Poindexter to reaffirm that false information in these letters?
Reagan	No.

A little later in the questioning, the matter of the diversion of proceeds from Iran arms sales to the Contras was addressed.

Reagan	May I simply point out that I had no knowledge then or now that there had been a diversion, and I never used the term. And all I knew was that there was some money that came from some place in another account, and that the appearance was that it might have been a part of the negotiated sale. And to this day, I don't have any information or knowledge that that wasn't the total amount, or that there was a diversion.
Webb	Let me repeat my question. My question only to you, sir, is: to the extent that there was in fact a diversion of proceeds, did you in any way approve or authorize that while you were President of the United States?
Reagan	For heaven's sake, no. And when I was once asked about that extra money and said if it was an added sum to the purchase price, what would I do, I said I would have given it back.
Webb	So, the answer to my question is that you did not authorize or approve it; is that correct?
Reagan	That's right.
Webb	Thank you.

In an overarching question of whether Reagan authorized or approved the CIA's transfer of responsibilities to the NSC after the passage of the Boland Amendment, Reagan testified that he had "no recollection of that." He also testified to not having any recollection of Poindexter ever requesting permission to do so. Although the cross-examination of Reagan in the short amount of time remaining in the day was helpful to Webb's case, much more work was needed to address his unforeseen testimony.

Regarding the unexpected testimony of Reagan, Webb told Judge Greene, "What just happened here is something I had not expected and I can tell you right now this is going to take some time. We're not going to be done tonight." Judge

> *Webb did not get any sleep that night. The friendly cross-examination questions he had previously prepared had to be abandoned and an entirely new set of hard-hitting questions had to be composed instead.*

Greene ruled that the questioning would continue the next day. Even with more to be done, Webb felt some confidence that Reagan basically took back on cross what he had said on direct examination.

Webb did not get any sleep that night. The friendly cross-examination questions he had previously prepared had to be abandoned and an entirely new set of hard-hitting questions had to be composed instead. For the next day, he had to make extensive use of Reagan's answers to interrogatories. Additionally, his hotel room had to be made secure to allow him to extensively review classified information that he had not planned on using. Webb was a virtual prisoner in his own room with several secret service agents on guard between the two court sessions.

Besides the change in the content of Webb's questions, he needed to adopt a sharper tone in his questioning because many of Reagan's answers were not responsive to Webb's questions. He would show no less respect to the president but less patience would be discernible.

The Saturday session started off, after some pleasantries, with the resumption of discussing North's activities. Webb then pressed Reagan as to what he knew about Contra activities and how he knew it. Webb's questions focused on Reagan's earlier interrogatory answers that established that the former president did not recall details about the Iran-Contra events. Webb did this to suggest to the jury that Reagan didn't know enough about Iran-Contra to accurately testify that Poindexter's congressional letters were truthful.

Reagan testified to being aware of United States officials in contact with American citizens who were offering to help in the Contra effort and advising them how to do so; he denied authorizing any government officials to encourage citizens in such activities. When asked about an American pilot named Gene

Hasenfus being shot down over Nicaragua carrying arms to the Contras, Reagan recalled the incident but could not remember who told him about it.

After reviewing his interrogatory answers, Reagan acknowledged that it was Poindexter who told him about Hasenfus, but he also said Poindexter told him Hasenfus had no connection to the United States government and was not involved in the operation that had been reported in the press. When Webb asked Reagan specifically whether he had since learned Hasenfus was in fact part of North's Project Democracy operation in Nicaragua, he answered, "No."

The cross-examination then referred to McFarlane's 1985 letters to House Committees that had made inquiries about North's activities in support of the Contras. In his testimony, Reagan testified that he did not recall seeing McFarlane's responses when asked, while in his written answers to the grand jury he wrote that he had not authorized or approved McFarlane's letters. Webb then asked the president for his current belief as to the truth or falsity of the statements contained in the McFarlane letters.

Webb	Mr. President, the statement that I just called to your attention—concerning Mr. McFarlane telling Congress on September 12, 1985, when he told Congress that the National Security Council had not been involved in any fundraising activities on behalf of the Contras and had not provided any support directly or indirectly for military or paramilitary activities in Nicaragua—as to those statements, is it your testimony today, as you sit here in this courtroom today, that you believe those to be truthful statements?
Reagan	I have no reason to doubt them except that also I have to say again, I have no recollection of ever seeing this letter before.
Webb	But just so we are clear, I am talking to you today.
Beckler	Objection, your honor. Asked and answered.
Webb	Judge, I think this goes to an issue that the president testified to yesterday about some subsequent letters that Mr. Poindexter sent which he said that he agreed with, and I think I have the right to at least try to show—

The Court	Overruled.
Webb	Mr. President, as far as you sitting here today in this courtroom in this videotape, those statements that North and the NSC did not participate in military and paramilitary assistance to the Contras and raised money, the Tower Commission that you appointed, and you told us yesterday about, advised you as the president that those were not true statements; is that correct?
Reagan	I do not recall that at all.

Reagan was then asked whether the Tower Commission had reported to him that they found evidence that in fact North and the NSC had become heavily involved in rendering assistance to the Contras. Both Beckler and Theodore Olson, the president's counsel, objected to the question on the basis, among others, that it was an improper use of the Tower Commission report.

Webb argued to the judge that he needed the president to clarify his earlier statement that he "agreed with everything said in these letters." Try as he might, Webb never successfully got an answer to his question. When the question was again put to Reagan if he was told by the Tower Commission that North and the NSC were involved in militarily assisting the Contras, the president answered that he did not remember and added, "probably because I was listening for an answer that I never got." Although he conceded that he did not endorse any false statement in the Poindexter letter—a letter that Reagan said he would have written—he never explicitly recanted his answer given on direct.

The cross-examination then addressed the Congressional Resolution passed in the summer of 1986 authorizing the president's inquiry as to whether North or any other NSC staff member was involved in supporting the Nicaraguan resistance. Although agreeing with Webb that he never saw or authorized the letters, Reagan reiterated that he had no quarrel with them. He later added, however, that he would never have authorized or approved any National Security Adviser or other top member of his administration to make false statements to Congress.

The topic of the Hawk missile shipment was then introduced. In addition to Poindexter's letters to Congress, Poindexter's actions regarding this shipment were, at the risk of oversimplification, the frosting on the cake of lies.

Reagan, after being shown a letter from Casey to Poindexter, with an unsigned draft of the presidential finding attached, said, "This initiative, while I do not deny having signed such a finding, I have no current recollection of doing so."

Consistent with much of the rest of his testimony, Reagan also denied any knowledge of excess profits generated from the sale of arms to Iran during the period of the sales. He did testify that Attorney General Ed Meese told him about a diversion of such profits after the events were uncovered.

The end was near.

Webb	Mr. President, I just have a few more questions and then I will be finished. One of the great problems that you were having in November of 1986, as I believe you testified to yesterday, was that you publicly stated time and time again that the Iran initiative was not an arms-for-hostage transaction, but the press and the public simply were not accepting that; is that a fair statement?
Reagan	I think it is a fair statement. I think in this instance, the press was so voluble about all of this that the people took their belief from what they were reading in the press, and I couldn't go to press everyday.
Webb	Did John Poindexter, in November of 1986, ever tell you about the existence of one particular document that on its face clearly established that this in fact was an arms-for-hostage transaction? Did he ever tell you about such a document in November of 1986?
Reagan	I can't recall whether any such thing was told to me.
Webb	Let me try to refresh your memory. Look back at exhibit number 17 that I showed you earlier. Mr. President, the exhibit that I've called your attention back to is this 1985 finding. If you read that finding, do you see where, when the description of what the project is, it states, and I will read it, "as part of these efforts, certain foreign material and munitions may be provided to the government of Iran which is taking steps to

	facilitate the release of the American hostages"? Do you see that there?
Reagan	Yes.
Webb	Okay. My question to you is, Mr. President, at least now as you read that presidential finding, do you now see that at least in that document, whoever drafted the document directly linked the Iranian initiative as arms-for-hostages? Do you at least see that is what it says there?
Reagan	Yes.

Shortly thereafter, Webb's questioning was finished. "Webb had to undermine [Reagan's] testimony," Pearl said. "At the same time, he had to cross-examine him in a way that was respectful of the fact that he's a 79-year-old former president of the United States who was well-liked and twice elected by a wide margin of United States citizens. I've never seen someone balance those two things the way Webb did."

The final arguments in any trial are an opportunity for each side to comment on the evidence, fashion it in a way most conducive to the party represented, and deliver it with a sincerity and belief in the rightness of the cause that is championed. In many ways, it is the best our system of advocacy has to offer. Everyone involved appreciated the severity of the stakes involved in the Poindexter case and the last opportunity to affect the outcome.

Webb follows a routine when preparing closing arguments. The night before, he closes his office door, drafts his remarks, and delivers his closing argument in segments to himself.

> *When I prepare for a closing argument I believe you need to actually prepare the actual script verbatim of what you're going to say—edit it, think about it, and structure your arguments. In this case I had a 50-page document that was everything I was going to say in the exact order I was going to say it and what documents I was going to put up on the screen. I do that meticulously because I believe once you get it in writing you have to think about it. Is that really the way I want to say it?*

Then you have to rehearse it. You can't read from a prepared text, so you have to go through it several times in front of a mirror. By saying it orally you then start to see where you need to make changes to make it smoother. Then I take the 50-75 pages of script and condense it to one piece of paper because I don't want the jury to see me flip a piece of paper. The jury thinks I am talking extemporaneously for hours and all I need to do is walk back to the podium and glance down at my sheet to make sure I'm following the order of my points. That one page is all I have with me at the podium to deliver my closing argument in any case.

Webb's final argument was thorough, direct, hard-hitting and persuasive. Here are portions that capture the flavor of the trial and the momentum produced by the evidence presented.

Cover-up, deception, and concealment. I told you in my opening statement, when we began the trial, that this case would be about a cover-up by high government officials who lied and made false statements to Congress, who misrepresented and concealed facts from Congress, and who destroyed government records.

I told you in my opening statement that I would prove beyond a reasonable doubt that the defendant in this case—John Poindexter—is one of the men, one of the people, who participated in the cover-up, and concealed evidence from Congress, and lied to Congress. And I told you that by establishing that, I would prove to you beyond a reasonable doubt—the legal standard in this case—that in fact the defendant is guilty of the crimes charged in this indictment. I respectfully suggest to you that, as the prosecution in this case, we lived up to that promise that I made to you in our opening statement that we have proven beyond a reasonable doubt that John Poindexter in fact engaged in the five crimes charged in that indictment. In fact, I would suggest to you the evidence is overwhelming.

We put witnesses on the stand who actually had knowledge of the issue. We started with Oliver North. Four days of testimony. Getting Oliver North to testify and reveal to you the information he had was like pulling teeth. He was a reluctant witness. But he also told you exactly what John Poindexter's involvement was in these Iran-Contra events, and most importantly, he told you what John Poindexter's role was in connection with the five crimes that are charged in this indictment.

I listened to Ronald Reagan testify for two days on videotape before you. I listened to Ronald Reagan tell you that he didn't have the slightest clue as to whether John Poindexter did or did not participate in the crimes that are charged in this indictment. Now, Ronald Reagan did tell us a lot of interesting things, but for the life of me, I could not understand what [that] had to do with the issues in this case.

The only way we're ever going to know whether John Poindexter engaged in the crimes charged in this indictment is to put on the witness stand the witnesses the government put on who know what happened.

When the defense went forward with fifteen witnesses, none of whom as far as I can see had any information to give to you, what was the purpose of doing that? After I heard 12 or 13 of those witnesses testify, I could only assume, as a lawyer, a prosecutor in this case, that the only purpose for putting those witnesses on the stand was hopefully to somehow take this scattergun, unfocused, let's throw mud against the wall and see what sticks, and maybe, just maybe, we'll confuse some members of the jury. And then maybe somehow John Poindexter will be found not guilty. I respectfully suggest to you that that type of defense insults your intelligence as jurors in this case.

Anticipating the defense argument, Webb told the jury about those things it would not have to decide. "The fact that maybe it was good or bad to assist the

> *They tried to wrap themselves in the President, I unwrapped them in closing argument.*

Contras in Nicaragua is irrelevant. Whether that was good foreign policy by Reagan and his administration, we can't decide that. Whether or not it was a good idea to sell arms to the terrorist nation of Iran to get hostages released—maybe it was, maybe it was not a good idea. We can't resolve that issue in this courtroom."

Webb then described in detail the components of the two operations, the Contras and Iran, and Poindexter's knowledge and involvement in both. He also described the events in November of 1986 when "people at the National Security Council, including North and Poindexter, went on a document-destruction rampage." Webb explained that the destruction was to cover up the lies told to Congress in 1985 and 1986 in which the activities of Iran-Contra were denied as having existed.

Later, Webb addressed Reagan's testimony:

> *I suppose the star witness that they called is Ronald Reagan. I have to assume that's what Mr. Beckler is going to tell you in his closing argument. I listened for four and a half hours while Mr. Beckler was asking questions on that videotape. I assumed—and you probably assumed—that President Reagan was somehow going to suggest that he authorized John Poindexter to destroy these records, or to lie to Congress, or to do these things he did. Mr. Beckler never asked him those questions.*
>
> *When I got up on cross-examination, I thought you ought to know the answer. I asked him ten questions right in a row. I said, "Mr. President, did you authorize John Poindexter to lie to Congress?" "No." "Did you authorize John Poindexter to destroy documents?" "No." "Did you authorize John Poindexter to obstruct Congress?" "No." I went on and on. President Reagan said he never authorized or instructed Poindexter to do any of those things.*
>
> *How does that testimony help John Poindexter to defend the charges in this indictment? The reason that Ronald Reagan was*

called to the stand was in the hope that if you listened to testimony from a former president and in support of John Poindexter, that instead of looking at the evidence and facts, you'll just assume that because the president testified, you ought to acquit John Poindexter. I again will respectfully suggest that that defense is an insult to your intelligence.

Ronald Reagan didn't seem to remember anything in this courtroom. When Ronald Reagan looked at two of the letters that are in evidence that are false, and he turned on the videotape, and said, "Why, these letters look okay to me except I would have added in some profanity," that was his answer. I got up on cross-examination, and kind of sternly said, "Mr. President, did you know those letters were false?" "No." "Did you know anything about them?" "No." "Did you authorize them?" "No."

He gave that testimony because he hoped it might help John Poindexter when, in fact, he didn't have the foggiest idea that those were false letters that had been sent to obstruct Congress.

At one point during his testimony, Reagan appeared to have winked toward Poindexter. Webb was not averse to pointing this out to the jury. "When people come into court, we expect them to give fair and truthful testimony," he said. "But when a person is so biased that he turns to someone as if to say, 'Did that last answer help you, John?,' I would have expected more from a former president than that."

Upon completion of Webb's argument, Richard Beckler addressed the jury on Poindexter's behalf, and Howard Pearl delivered the rebuttal argument. Judge Greene provided instructions on the law to the jury, and the 12 men and women of the jury received the case for their deliberation.

Unlike the earlier North verdict, the Poindexter jury was unanimous in its findings. Admiral John Poindexter was found guilty on each of the five criminal charges submitted to the jury. Judge Greene sentenced Poindexter to a six-month prison term. "Juror comments suggested the so-called Reagan Strategy backfired," Webb said. "They tried to wrap themselves in the President; I unwrapped them in

> *The trial victory deserved public approval and respect. It would add luster to the lessons taught in every civics class in the country—that no person is above the law—and deflate those cynics who believe the high and the mighty are more equal than others.*

closing argument." The national media quickly recognized Webb's success. "He is about the best prosecutor I've ever laid eyes on," said Nina Totenberg, legal affairs correspondent for National Public Radio. "I call him the killer questioner with the choirboy face."

There were a number of postscripts to the outcome of the Poindexter trial. Perhaps the most immediate was the relief and satisfaction of the Office of Independent Counsel. It was redemption of all of the hard work that went into their efforts as well as a validation of the belief that their mission was a just and important cause. It also removed the yoke of perceived defeat by some citizens and commentators over the North verdict.

For Judge Walsh, it was also a resounding vindication of his choice of Webb as lead prosecutor. Webb performed all of the major trial functions; the result speaks to his ability and performance. According to Webb, "When we talked to the jurors after the trial and conviction, clearly things had gone well for me with cross of President Reagan on the second day."

The trial victory deserved public approval and respect. It would add luster to the lessons taught in every civics class in the country—that no person is above the law—and deflate those cynics who believe the high and the mighty are more equal than others. For Webb, the fact that his resume reflected a long list of major trial successes did not diminish in the slightest his triumph in the biggest case he ever tried. Notwithstanding the feelings of happiness he had, Webb also realized the sadness that would come to a career public servant who served not only the president of the United States but all of the people in the country for all the years of his adult life. There would be no rejoicing over the consequences to Poindexter.

There was a personal postscript to Webb's work as chief prosecutor that had nothing to do with the verdict of the jury. For many years, Webb's parents, who still lived in the small rural community of Bushnell, had observed his career as a trial lawyer in the "big city" with some pride.

They followed the Poindexter trial's progress from their politically conservative area of Illinois. Like Webb, Reagan was born in rural Illinois, and they found the prospect of the former president and their son engaging with each other in the same courtroom quite exciting.

As noted earlier, Reagan's unexpected approval of Poindexter's false written responses to congressional inquiries changed the dynamics of Webb's cross-examination. After the trial was over, the videotape deposition of the two days of testimony was publicly aired.

Immediately after seeing the videotape, Keith Webb called his son. The only words his father said to Webb were, "Did you have to be that hard on the president?" Webb heard a click; the call had ended. His answer died on his tongue.

As Webb pondered his bruised feelings, he realized that his father was being faithful to the principle that a President of the United States was deserving of the utmost respect and deference at all times. Webb, on the other hand, was dedicated to the principle that all witnesses, irrespective of their rank or office, were duty-bound to testify as truthfully and accurately as they were able. Webb was obligated to demand the truth in their recounting of the historical facts as they knew them, and this obligation was inviolate. Webb understood that he and his father had a clash of principles and, when he later explained the reason for his conduct to his father, the love and respect each man had for the other was fully restored.

Jim Thompson recalled that after the deposition, Reagan called him. At the time, Thompson was Winston & Strawn's chairman. Reagan said something to the effect of "Jim, this man of yours, Webb, he's calling me a liar." Thompson replied that could not be true.

Reagan then said that Webb cross-examined him like he did not believe him. "I said, 'Mr. President I'm sure that's not Webb's conclusion. Prosecutors are tough.'"

After hanging up with Reagan, Thompson went to Webb's office and told him he had offended the former president. According to Thompson, Webb responded, "Well, I was just doing my job."

On July 20, 1990, the District of Columbia Court of Appeals announced its decision in Oliver North's appeal of his conviction. North's three convictions were vacated and set aside in an opinion that found that witnesses in his trial might have been impermissibly affected by North's immunized congressional testimony. The opinion in the North case was issued some three months after the jury found Poindexter guilty.

The Court of Appeals held that improper use of immunized testimony includes its use to refresh another witness's recollection or if the immunized testimony in any way "shaped, altered, or affected" another witness's testimony. It held that the standard used by Judge Greene in the Kastigar hearing he held in the Poindexter trial defined "use" too narrowly and failed to make findings consistent with the proper standard of consideration. The opinion emphasized that improper use of immunized testimony was "any" use of that testimony. In fairness to Judge Greene, he did not have the benefit of the Appeals Court decision as to the standard to be employed. The Court of Appeals decision effectively terminated the government's ability to further prosecute Poindexter and North for their Iran-Contra involvement.

Poindexter also appealed his conviction and sentence to the District of Columbia Court of Appeals. In November 1991, Poindexter's convictions were overturned on appeal for reasons similar to the North decision. In December 1992, the United States Supreme Court declined to review the case.

Notwithstanding the Court of Appeals decisions vacating the convictions of North and Poindexter and decreeing the proper legal outcomes in their cases, it was firmly established in the court of public opinion that the Iran-Contra affair was a rogue operation conducted by ranking members of the executive branch of government. The pages of history will record that the operation was concealed from the Congress of the United States, and when some of its members made inquiry as to its existence, they were falsely told there was no such operation.

That deceit would later be exposed by other dedicated men and women outside of government. In the end, respect for the faithful rendition of service to the nation was restored by people whose own sense of honesty and integrity prevailed over the actions of the wayward stewards of government, however well-intentioned they may have been.

Webb, Arnold & Porter's William Baer and General Electric's Jeffrey Kindler, leaders of the elite team against government antitrust claims.

United States v. General Electric Company, et al.

CHAPTER 8
THE PRICE OF DIAMONDS

General Electric is a storied company with a product and service line that covers sectors of industrial and commercial life almost limitless in scope. In 1896, it was one of the original 12 companies listed on the newly formed Dow Jones Average. After 118 years, GE is the only original company remaining on the index.

Though still thought of by some as a maker of light bulbs and refrigerators, it is now a multinational company operating in a range of industry segments, from energy and technology infrastructure to consumer and industrial products. One division of the company is GE Superabrasives, or GES, which holds patents on and is one of the world's leading suppliers of manufactured diamonds. These cubic boron nitride and polycrystalline products are used in a variety of trades such as metalworking, mining, petroleum, and electronics.

By the early 1990s, 80 percent of the industrial diamond market was split between GE and De Beers, the South African diamond conglomerate. It was around this time that these two corporate giants would be accused of an international diamond price-fixing conspiracy befitting a Hollywood blockbuster. The source for this allegation was one man: Edward Russell, a GE executive of 17 years.

Russell joined GE in 1974 and over time had risen to the rank of vice president, corporate officer and head of GES. For Russell, his position meant prestige, money, security, and a company-leased Jaguar. But in November 1991, Russell was dismissed from GE by his boss, Glen Hiner.

Two months later, Russell and his lawyer went to Washington, D.C. and met with two high-ranking members of the United States Justice Department's Antitrust Division. Working from a 40-page document that he had prepared with the assistance of his attorney, the talkative Russell commanded the attention of DOJ officials for several hours.

At this meeting, Russell leveled a number of charges against his former employer, but at the top of his list was a claim that GE had illegally colluded with its main competitor, De Beers, to set prices in the sale of industrial diamonds. This meeting initiated a two-year criminal investigation.

Although grand jury investigations conducted by Justice Department lawyers are required to be secret and field investigations by FBI special agents are not generally publicized, within a couple of months the Justice Department revealed its efforts. Anthony Nanni, the head of the antitrust litigation for the Justice Department, proclaimed in the *Wall Street Journal* that "a very active investigation into allegations of hardcore price-fixing" was underway.

The "very active" investigation part was certainly true. A team of Justice Department lawyers made their way to GE offices in Cincinnati, Columbus, and Worthington, Ohio. Assisted by squads of FBI agents with subpoenas, they confiscated hundreds of thousands of pages of documents and interviewed scores of employees. Whatever lid had once covered the investigation had now been blown off.

Meanwhile, GE suffered an onslaught of civil suits. Russell filed a lawsuit claiming that his termination was unlawful, induced by his whistle-blowing of GE's criminal conduct. Three different shareholder derivative suits alleged that the value of GE stock was adversely affected by illegal acts committed by company employees with the permission of GE executives. It is not uncommon for suits of this type to be filed at the first sign of this kind of alleged activity. Additionally, two customer class action suits were on the horizon, seeking damages from the alleged price-fixing. "That was by far the most nightmarish day of the year for me," said Jeffrey Kindler, GE's in-house counsel, of the simultaneous lawsuits.

No matter what the outcome of the cases would prove to be, the cost to defend them was inestimable and the harm to the company's burnished reputation was excruciating to contemplate. GE was keen not to settle; if they couldn't convince the Justice Department to drop the charges, GE would fight them in court.

Dan Webb was on trial in Arizona at the time in the middle of a cross-examination when his secretary received a call from someone named "Jack Welch" demanding to speak with Webb. She walked over to the courthouse and, Webb recalled, "she said 'Jack Welch wants to talk to you.' I said, 'Who?' She said, 'Jack Welch!' 'Oh, he's from GE! Please tell him I'm on my way back and I'm looking forward to the conversation.'"

GE had already retained the prominent antitrust law firm Arnold & Porter, but Welch, GE's Chairman, wanted another trial lawyer to join the team. He and Webb met in New York in late spring of 1992 and Welch hired him on the spot to become their lead counsel.

The judge in Russell's civil employment case ordered a settlement conference and on February 16, 1994, Webb and the GE team agreed to settle with Russell's lawyers. The terms of the settlement were sealed; however one part that was made public included an affidavit by Russell affirming that he "never had any personal knowledge of any antitrust wrongdoing at GE," a declaration that ran contrary to the heart of the allegations contained in his complaint for wrongful termination.

With the wrongful termination suit resolved, the GE legal team focused on the criminal case. They presented a report to the DOJ outlining the flimsiness of the government's case, with the request that the investigation end. The paper drew on the findings of GE's internal investigation, as well as inconsistencies that came to light during Webb's six-day deposition of Russell during his civil case.

They had identified a number of falsehoods during Russell's testimony; 12 of them, in fact. "We called them the 'dirty dozen,'" said GE general counsel, Benjamin Heineman, Jr. "I never understood how the government could build a case based on the testimony of a known liar."

However, after Russell settled his case with GE, the Justice Department's Antitrust Division head called his lawyer to find out what Russell had agreed to as part of the settlement. Apparently satisfied that Russell was not compromised in any way, GE was indicted with one count of conspiracy to raise prices in violation of Section 1 of the Sherman Act.

The lead government lawyer was Max Gillam, a senior litigation counsel for the Justice Department and a veteran of four antitrust mega trials. Before being retained by the government, he had been a trial lawyer for a major U.S. law firm. Also at the government counsel table were career prosecutors Arnold Celnicker and David Blotner, as well as Joelle Moreno, a Justice Department lawyer trying her first case.

Webb was lead counsel for GE. At counsel table would also be Jeffrey Kindler, a GE Senior Counsel along with William Baer, GE's outside antitrust counsel from Arnold & Porter. Also part of the defense trial team were Winston & Strawn lawyers Lawrence Desideri and Tom Frederick; David Eggert, from Arnold & Porter; and Daniel Costello and James Pohlman, litigation partners from the firm Porter Wright, based in Columbus, Ohio. "That was a very skilled trial team," Webb would later recall. "I had Bill Baer who was one of the best antitrust lawyers in America. I had Jeff Kindler who was extremely smart and later became General Counsel at Pfizer. I also had great young lawyers from Winston and Arnold & Porter, and great local counsel from Columbus, led by Costello."

The defense lawyers' duties were established early on. As chief trial counsel, Webb would handle the opening statement, closing argument, key motions before the judge, and key witnesses. Webb would also handle the cross-examination of Russell. There was excellent cooperation and consultation on the part of defense counsel, with Webb possessing ultimate authority on strategy. Webb prides himself on being a team player even when leading. "I led by doing," he said of his role on the GE case. "I believe if you worked 20 hours a day, other people are going to work 20 hours a day."

As the case was about to begin, Webb was nervous. "When we were going to start this trial in Columbus, Ohio, I felt pressure. I felt I had the entire GE company watching everything I was doing. Not only was GE managing, they had a guy in the courtroom with me trying the case and I felt a lot of pressure."

It was at this point that Webb received an unexpected phone call. "I got a call [on] the morning of my opening statement from Jack Welch and I bet it was only two hours before my statement. He said, 'I just want you to know that I am

---

> *"The government frequently will ask you to substitute guesses and speculation for evidence, and I respectfully ask you not to let that happen."*

so proud of what you've done and how you've worked with this team and what you've done for us. You can win or lose this case.' I thought, Wow! What a smart thing to do because that took the pressure off of me."

Webb understood Welch to be saying that he knew how well Webb and his team had prepared for the trial and that he had the utmost faith in their abilities. Webb knew Welch was a tough guy who strongly believed GE was not guilty of any criminality, but that he had the equanimity to accept the jury's verdict and not blame his lawyers in case of a loss. In addition to the business acumen Welch possessed in abundance, his comment—intending to ease the pressure on his lawyers—showed a deft human touch and sensitivity.

Some of the statements Webb made during his opening would prove prescient.

> *As I listened to Mr. Gillam talk to you for the last three hours, telling you the government's best case against General Electric, there are certain words that started to ring in my ears—guesswork, speculation, conjecture, assumption. There will be—you will see from the evidence—event after event that Mr. Gillam suggested that occurred when, in fact, there will be no evidence that it, in fact, did occur. There will be no document, no witness, no testimony. The government frequently will ask you to substitute guesses and speculation for evidence, and I respectfully ask you not to let that happen.*
>
> *For example, let's take the single critical issue in the case—which Mr. Gillam told you what it was, and I agree—did General Electric and De Beers actually enter into a specific agreement to fix prices? That is the issue in the case. If there was an agreement and the government can prove that beyond a reasonable doubt, General Electric is guilty. And if the government can't prove a specific agreement beyond a reasonable doubt, General Electric should be found not guilty under the law.*
>
> *It doesn't have to be in writing—I agree with Mr. Gillam. They don't have to bring a writing in, but they have to prove to you that an agreement took place. They can't ask you to guess or ask*

you to speculate. For example, if, in fact, there was an agreement between GE and De Beers to fix prices, what are the basics that you, at least, want to know?

One, proof beyond a reasonable doubt as to who was the representative from GE and who was the representative from De Beers that actually authorized or entered into the agreement. That's pretty basic. If you have an agreement, and an agreement is simply an understanding, an agreement between two people to do an illegal act, somebody had to do it.

The second question will be where did the agreement take place? When did it occur? What was said that created the agreement? Those are four very basic issues that you would expect Mr. Gillam to have answered during the past three hours, but let's talk about them for a moment.

Who? Who is the representative of De Beers that entered into this agreement with GE? I listened to Mr. Gillam for three hours, and he never gave you the name of any officer or employee of De Beers that entered into this agreement with GE. I still don't know, as I stand here now, representing a defendant, General Electric, charged with a felony, I don't know to this day who the actual person is from De Beers they contend entered into this agreement. In fact, it is not even clear to me who was the person from General Electric that entered into the agreement.

As Russell outlined the conspiracy to the Justice Department, there were two men central to the plot: Peter Frenz and Philippe Liotier. Frenz was a German citizen who represented GE in Europe as the head of GES sales. Liotier was chief of a Brussels, Belgium company named Diamant Boart Superabrasives, GES's largest European customer. Both had been initially indicted along with GE, but as neither were citizens of or residents in the U.S., they were not amenable to the processes of the American court system and did not voluntarily appear at trial. Webb picked apart the government's opening statement, indicating the dearth of hard facts about who was involved, as well as when and where they allegedly met.

The government says Mr. Frenz was the person over in Europe running around having meetings. But the evidence will be that Mr. Frenz—everyone will agree in this case—he had no authority to set prices. All that authority rested back in Worthington, here in Ohio at corporate headquarters, and the government did not indict any of the corporate big [wigs] back here at Worthington that would have had the authority to enter into a price-fixing agreement.

So, I am not even sure, as I sit or stand here now, who the person from GE is who actually, quote, "entered" into the agreement, and I still don't have any idea who the person is from De Beers after three hours of listening to that statement.

Where did the agreement take place? If I am the prosecution and I am going to contend that I can prove beyond a reasonable doubt that agreement took place, I would at least be able to tell the jury where it took place, and it wouldn't have to be in a room. It could have been on the telephone, in London, in Brussels, in Worthington, somewhere. If they can prove beyond a reasonable doubt that the agreement took place, where did it happen?

When? When did the agreement take place? If the government says to you as jurors, "we will prove to you beyond a reasonable doubt that there is an agreement between GE and De Beers," when did it take place?

Again, when Mr. Gillam was going through that timeline, I thought when he got to November of 1991 that he might say, "and that's where you will find this agreement took place," but he didn't say that. And then I waited until he got to December. He started going through events that occurred in December, and I thought he might say, "Well, on this date, when this occurred" then you as jurors can assume that they will have proven beyond a reasonable doubt that that agreement took place. He didn't say that.

Then, he went to January the next year. Three hours of listening to the government to give you their best case. I don't know, as the lawyer representing General Electric, when they contend that the

> *I start with who, where, when, and what because if, in fact, as the law provides that the government has to prove its case beyond a reasonable doubt and if I were sitting where you are as jurors, I would at least expect that the government in three hours would have answered those four basic questions. And they didn't.*

---

agreement took place. I assume when we get to closing argument or at some point, they will choose to tell us. They haven't yet.

What was said that created the agreement between GE and De Beers? In order for two people to reach an agreement on something, they obviously must communicate some information. They have to say something to each other to show that they are agreeing to do something. The law says that they must have agreed to do an illegal act, which, here, the government is trying to say that GE and De Beers actually agreed to fix prices, to raise prices.

Judge George C. Smith is going to instruct you that this agreement is not something that we can all just say, "well, maybe it just happened," but it must have been proven beyond a reasonable doubt. I start with who, where, when, and what because if, in fact, as the law provides that the government has to prove its case beyond a reasonable doubt and if I were sitting where you are as jurors, I would at least expect that the government in three hours would have answered those four basic questions. And they didn't.

The reason that they didn't is because of guesses, of speculation and conjectures and assumptions—because there are holes that are big. Even though they have no witnesses that will prove an agreement, and they have no documents, somehow GE can be conjectured into a conviction. Respectfully, throughout this trial, I will respectfully ask you not to allow that to happen. The failure to answer those four questions is a major, major gap in their case.

Another consideration in the opening statement is to humanize your client so the jury can relate to them. Even large corporations like GE are made up of hard-working human beings who live normal lives in neighborhoods; no corporation is some inanimate presence undeserving of the same consideration one would give a fellow human being.

As Webb describes the effort, "Jurors want to vote with the little guy in a case. I have to get the jury to think maybe the big guy should win this one. You have to bring to reality that this is a real company with real human beings that put on their socks one at a time, just like you do."

> *Let me tell you something about GE. Mr. Gillam said it was a large company. He is absolutely correct. GE is a big company. It is a parent company, a large company. It is involved in a lot of different types of business operations.*
>
> *When I grew up as a kid, it was like refrigerators. That's what I always thought GE was, but GE today manufactures and sells everything from jet engines to appliances. It is an American corporation headquartered in Fairfield, Connecticut. It is a company that today is involved in a lot of different business activities.*
>
> *It is 100 years old with thousands of employees, and one of the businesses—one of the businesses that General Electric owns—is a business right here in Columbus or Worthington, Ohio called General Electric Superabrasives. You will sometimes hear the lawyers or witnesses call it GES. It is located roughly 10 or 12 miles north of right where we are here, north of the courthouse on Huntley Road in Worthington, Ohio. It's been there for quite some time.*
>
> *Let me show you a photograph. The General Electric Superabrasives business plant and operation is out in Worthington, and that's a picture of it. GES moved to Worthington from Detroit in 1969, and that was a pretty small business at that time. They began production with 20 people, and today the Worthington facility is the international corporate headquarters for this business with approximately 900 employees that work at that facility, and*

they manufacture this product—you have heard about it—called industrial diamonds.

Now, today, the gentleman actually responsible for running that entire business is Mr. Bill Woodburn, and Bill, would you please stand up for a second? Bill is the General Manager today of the superabrasives business here in Ohio. He actually just took this job recently.

Since the trial involved the complex world of the manufacture and sales of industrial diamonds, Webb needed to relate it to the jurors' everyday life. He compared the man-made, synthetic diamonds to those which a juror might "walk into a jewelry store and purchase," which were created naturally from carbon through thousands of years of pressure. He also told the jurors that "your glasses may very well have been polished by industrial diamonds," and that when they went to the dentist, "some of those drills and dental appliances are made by industrial diamonds."

Because the government's theory was that GE and De Beers conspired to fix and raise prices in one particular instance, Webb needed to describe the GES organizational chart and the employees and representatives. The government's theory was that the conduct of Frenz, a GES sales representative, was attributable to GE as a corporation, and that the jury should therefore find GE guilty. Frenz reported to Steve Palovchik, back in Worthington, Ohio. Palovchik reported to Russell as general manager of GES, who in turn reported to Glen Hiner at GE Plastics. Hiner reported up to the parent corporation, GE. Webb described the government's argument and the expected evidence.

The government contends that Mr. Frenz, in running his European sales operation, entered into some kind of agreement with De Beers, whereby a man named Mr. Liotier would be used to, if you will, funnel price information back and forth. That's what the government's theory is. So a fair question you can ask as jurors is, who is Mr. Liotier?

The first question is, does he work for De Beers? The answer will be absolutely not. He's never worked for De Beers; he's never been an officer of De Beers; and I will show you from the evidence, he has never had any, any connection to De Beers.

Here's what the evidence will be. Mr. Liotier spent his career working for [Belgian company] Societe Generale. He never worked for De Beers; he never had any contact with De Beers; and as far as anyone knows, as far as I know, he didn't know anybody at De Beers.

In 1990, Mr. Liotier is transferred from Societe Generale down to this business to become the managing director. Mr. Liotier becomes the person running Diamant Boart. They use our diamonds and they were a big purchaser of our diamonds, our single largest customer in Europe.

Peter Frenz had dealt with that company, dealt with Diamant Boart for over 20 years. Long before Mr. Liotier ever came to work for Diamant Boart, Mr. Frenz would deal with whoever was there. They had a number of managing directors over the years and whoever the managing director was at Diamant Boart, Peter Frenz would deal with because that's who we are selling our diamonds to. It happened to be in mid-1990 that Mr. Liotier came down here to work in Diamant Boart for our customers and he became the number one person at that company. The government is now telling you that because he was meeting with Mr. Liotier, that that somehow is suspicious.

Mr. Frenz never—you will hear his testimony—he never believed or dreamed anybody would contend that Mr. Liotier was somehow actually just De Beers because Liotier had never worked for De Beers, had never had any connection with De Beers, and yet, that's the government's theory, as I understand it. The government's theory in this case is that, although we don't know how it happened because there is no evidence, that Mr. Liotier somehow became De Beers and their theory is whenever Mr. Frenz had a meeting with Liotier, he wasn't really meeting with Diamant Boart, he was meeting with De Beers.

As this case proceeds, we will show you how unfair and ridiculous that allegation is. To say that Peter Frenz could not have meetings with the representative of his single largest customer in Europe is ridiculous.

It is unusual for a lawyer to describe the judge's instructions to the jury in an opening statement. Normally, instructions on the law are given to the jury at the very end of the case, after the evidence is completed and after the judge has conferred with the lawyers as to the appropriate instructions to give based on the evidence presented. However, as long as what the lawyer says is accurate and not objected to, it is permissible to discuss them at other times. Webb decided there was strategic value in reviewing the jury instructions at the outset of the case.

You are going to be instructed by his Honor that in order for you to find GE guilty, you are going to have to find two things. Number one, that the government proves beyond a reasonable doubt that Liotier actually was not from Diamant Boart, but was really from De Beers—which they will have no evidence of—but then you have to prove that Frenz really knew he wasn't from Diamant Boart and that he was from De Beers. That's what the government has to prove beyond a reasonable doubt.

Frenz had been dealing with that company for over 20 years. So when he dealt with Liotier, he thought he was, and believes to this day, he was dealing with Diamant Boart and as far as I can tell from the evidence, he was.

Mr. Gillam told you that the real issue in the case is whether GE made an independent judgment to raise diamond prices or whether it was done collusively as part of an agreement.

Now, Judge Smith will instruct you that the issue in the case is whether there is an agreement to fix prices. It is not a crime for two companies to raise prices. That happens every day of the week. Companies do raise their prices and that's a fact of business.

> *You will be told it is not a crime, for example, for two companies to raise prices in the same amount at the same time. That also happens all the time and it happens particularly in these types of what they call a limited, or concentrated industry.*

There were two pieces of circumstantial, damning evidence against GE. The first was the fact that both GE and De Beers raised their industrial diamond prices to the same level within weeks of each other. Webb tried to blunt that evidence by pointing out that reactions to competitor's market prices are common.

More suspicious were faxes sent by Frenz to his superior, Palovchik, detailing De Beers diamond prices. But as Webb pointed out to the jury, using information such as this to set prices is legal—so long as that information was not obtained from De Beers as part of a price-fixing plan.

> *In a limited market, it's very common that you have what are called parallel price increases. One competitor decides to go up in prices and others follow. That is perfectly legal, perfectly proper and happens every day of the week.*
>
> *The question, though, is whether they actually had some agreement to do that, because that's illegal. You can't sit down and reach an agreement to do that, but if I'm the competitor today, and I see one of my competitors is going up in price and I decide I would also like to go up in price and I do so, that's an independent decision I make and the law is very clear, very, very clear: that's not a crime.*
>
> *So the question is, did GE decide to raise its prices before it ever had any idea what De Beers was doing? Because if the answer to that first question is yes, that should be the end of the case.*
>
> *I will be able to prove to you, through testimony and documents, that by the time you get to the fall of 1991, General Electric had already made an independent decision to raise prices, long before GE received any De Beers price information, any whatsoever.*

Next, Webb described in detail various pieces of evidence the jury would hear that would establish the independence of the decision on the part of GE to raise the prices of industrial diamonds. Webb pointed out the specific evidence indicating GE's purely internal basis for its decision, as well as the government's lacking evidence in support of the criminal charges.

> *The next point I would like to make to show that there was no agreement is the following, it's pretty basic. GE and De Beers never had any discussions with each other regarding industrial diamond prices. Never.*
>
> *You can listen to all the witnesses the government is going to put on the stand, you can look at all the documents, but there will not be one witness that will testify that they ever attended a meeting with De Beers and GE where De Beers and GE discuss prices. Not one witness will say, there will not be one document offered into evidence that will indicate that happened. The fact is, it did not happen. It didn't happen. It's just that simple.*
>
> *The government, after two-and-half years of an investigation, two-and-a-half years, they indicted GE and this sales representative in Europe. The people back in Worthington that were involved in the decision to raise prices were Ed Russell, John Blystone, Steve Palovchik, a man named Peter Foss, a man named Mike Miceli, and a man named Ray Burgess, those and a man named Mr. Dellinger. Those are the six or seven people that, back in Worthington, had the authority to raise prices.*
>
> *They're all going to testify, and they're all going to tell you they had no agreement with De Beers, and the government obviously believes that because they didn't indict them.*
>
> *And, so, the fact that Peter Frenz has no authority to raise prices is clearly an extremely strong factor to indicate that there certainly could not have been [an] agreement to fix prices because he didn't have any authority to do it.*

Most of Webb's opening statement focused on the facts he expected the evidence would show. It was designed to meet the jury's ability to assimilate and understand a lot of unfamiliar information and to apply reason and common sense in its analysis and comprehension. Toward the end of his opening, Webb focused on Russell, the government's star witness.

> *Mr. Russell was the general manager of General Electric Superabrasives back in 1991, and he was separated by—separated or "fired" is a direct term—from General Electric as corporate executive in November of 1991.*
>
> *Shortly thereafter, Mr. Russell made some very, very serious allegations to the Justice Department about Mr. Hiner being involved in fixing prices with De Beers. After a two-year investigation, the Department of Justice did not charge Mr. Hiner in this case. If you look at this indictment, Mr. Hiner's name is not mentioned. He is not named or charged [nor is] anything said about him in this indictment.*
>
> *But, however, as we learned through Mr. Gillam's opening statement here yesterday, Mr. Russell is going to be a witness for the government, and he, apparently, is going to give testimony that makes allegations against Mr. Hiner.*
>
> *I think that you are going to find the testimony that deals with Mr. Russell and Mr. Hiner to be very interesting, and I want to talk about it with you a little bit. Let's talk about who these two people are, and I am going to tell you the Ed Russell story at General Electric.*

Webb told the jury that Russell was a highly paid executive as the general manager of Superabrasives. He had a very generous retirement package, stock options and a good job, but his business unit began to decline between 1990 and 1991. In July 1991, Russell had a business review meeting, attended by Hiner and GE CEO Jack Welch, which ended up being a "disaster."

Webb read a memo from Welch to Hiner, quoting, "Russell has to go. He made a fool of himself. Russell didn't have a handle on the technology issues or know his businesses' numbers." A follow-up meeting in September went even worse. "I don't want to fool with this fellow much longer, but will respect your end-of-the-year time," Webb continued, quoting Welch in the memo. "Bottom line has to be Russell has to go."

> *Jack Welch made that decision as the chairman of this company, based on the fact that he believed that Mr. Russell was not offering the effective leadership to run this business. Mr. Hiner, after receiving that letter from Mr. Welch, did what he was told to do.*
>
> *Mr. Russell and Mr. Hiner had a meeting. Mr. Hiner explained to Mr. Russell that he was being separated from General Electric and he explained why, but he told Ed that—he handed Ed a letter, actually—and told him what the separation would be. Mr. Russell was given an entire year of compensation, so that he had time to find a job, given his whole incentive compensation. I think it actually adds up to $280,000 total between salary and incentive compensation. Guaranteed a stock option, I think it was worth around $300,000. Locked into his retirement, which is well over a million dollars. Gave him all corporate perks. And we'll help you try to find a job, but you can't stay at GE any longer because you're not performing.*
>
> *And this is where the story gets very interesting. In spite of that severance package, which I think Ed would agree was very fair, what happened is that Mr. Russell became very bitter and very, very, very vindictive against Mr. Hiner, particularly. What you're going to find, for example, is that Mr. Russell a few days before he was terminated, he actually got word that he was going to be terminated and sat down and drafted a letter, a memorandum, which you'll see in this case, in which he made up a bunch of lies about a number of people at GE to get even with being terminated.*

Mr. Russell shortly later went to the Department of Justice and told them that Mr. Hiner was involved with price fixing with De Beers. After two years of investigating, the Department of Justice never took any action against Hiner.

But that's not all Mr. Russell did to get back at Mr. Hiner and GE. He filed a federal lawsuit in which he contended that he was not fired for his poor performance, but for being a whistle-blower.

Earlier this year, in February of 1994, as that case was getting ready to go to trial the [civil] matter was resolved. And as part of that resolution, GE refused to resolve that case until Mr. Russell addressed the allegations that he had made because he had to say once and for all were they true or were they not true or else GE was not going to stop and was going to go to trial to prove that nothing happened.

And Mr. Russell did that. Mr. Russell signed an affidavit [on] February, 16, 1994, eight months ago. You'll hear from the evidence that General Electric said, "You must tell us once and for all, are these allegations you're making true?" And Mr. Russell, after consulting with his lawyer, as part of the resolution of the lawsuit in Cincinnati, signed this affidavit.

In this affidavit, Mr. Russell says, "I am now aware that GE removed me based on its view of my performance, and not because I was a whistle-blower." In paragraph two of the affidavit, he says, "During my entire employment at GE I never had any personal knowledge of any antitrust wrongdoing by former GE senior vice president Glen Hiner or anyone else at GE, and I never had any personal knowledge of any other illegal conduct by GE personnel." The third paragraph goes on to say, "In addition, I have no personal knowledge that would indicate that GE personnel have violated antitrust laws or any other laws."

GE relied on those representations and resolved the lawsuit. I have reason to believe the government will put Mr. Russell on the stand shortly. I'd just respectfully ask you to listen to the cross-ex-

amination because Ed Russell's credibility, I respectfully suggest to you, cannot be relied on.

Jim Thompson watched Webb's opening statement in the case. He recognized how Webb humanized GE to the jurors by identifying the company as a local employer and neighbor. "My belief was that the jury started off with an impression of the defendant that they might not have had otherwise," Thompson said. "I thought this was the best introduction of an opening statement and it was classic Webb."

Opening statements in cases are underappreciated, yet critical to winning trials. "I worked very hard on that opening to get the jurors leaning my way and I felt pretty good about it," Webb said. "I watched the jurors in that trial and was pretty convinced they were going to go for GE."

After the opening statement, Desideri told his colleague, Webb, that he thought they would win the case. Webb's reply was, "Let's just get to work. Don't say that."

Frederick, another Winston & Strawn partner on the GE trial team, remarked on Webb's expert preparation, noting his opening statement lasted more than three hours, and "he looked at his notes once."

The transcript sets forth the words spoken and by whom. What is often not captured is the passion displayed, the anger that may be directed at others, the physical appearances and gestures of the participants, and the electricity in the air that often characterizes foes engaged in non-physical combat. A transcript is a cold record and often misses as much as it captures.

There are passages in the transcript of this case, however, that convey much more than the printed words. Many of those passages deal with the examination of Edward Russell, particularly the cross-examination. There can be no doubt that Mr. Russell was the government's star witness. Without him, there would have been no two-year investigation of such great intensity and depth, and no indictment.

The positions of the parties in the wrongful termination suit were clear, straightforward, and incapable of co-existence: either Russell was in fact a whistle-blower and his contentions apparently true, or he was an inept manager who was fired for poor performance. That was the factual polarization. Since the civil case was set for trial around the time GE was indicted, it would have undoubtedly been a significant barometer for the outcome of the criminal case. The settlement removed any such prophecy.

As a consequence of the diametrically opposed factual positions of GE and Russell in the civil case that were also central to the criminal case, it was relevant for the jury to hear evidence about Russell's abilities as the head of GES. Part of the criteria necessary to any assessment of a boss is how well he leads his employees, what they think of him, and his strengths and weaknesses as they perceive them. Also important is how well the unit performs, both in the manufacturing and technical side of the business and in the marketplace.

Shortly before his termination, Hiner conducted a performance review of Russell. Russell testified about this meeting on direct examination by government counsel. Webb turned to the subject on cross.

Webb	Now, Mr. Russell, let me turn to another subject just for a moment. You mentioned in your testimony last week that when you had that operating review meeting with Mr. Hiner on October 23, 1991—are you with me in time?
Russell	Yes, sir.
Webb	After the meeting, you and Mr. Hiner had a private meeting in which you discussed your performance?
Russell	We had a lunch, a quick little lunch that lasted about 15 minutes.

> *"The third area of comments that your coworkers made about you. You see where it says 'his lack of strategic vision'? 'Insecure,' 'wavers on key issues,' 'lacks strategic vision,' 'runs hot and cold on people,' 'not sufficiently trusted,' 'avoided confronting people,' 'held unproductive meetings,' and had 'mixed customer relations,' among other things?"*

Webb	Did you become aware in early 1991 that some members of your staff did not believe you were an effective leader of the business?
Russell	I became aware some members of my staff disagreed with the actions I was taking.

Webb then established that Hiner had recommended to Russell that he use the services of a Dr. Brad Smart, who was billed as a management consultant focusing on team building. Dr. Smart observed Russell and interviewed 13 of his employees, then filed a report to Russell and Hiner.

Webb	Earlier last week when you were testifying before this jury you stated, "Brad Smart never gave any feedback other than positive on the results." Do you recall that testimony?
Russell	That's correct.
Webb	But just so I understand, would it be fair to say that in April, when you sit down with Mr. Smart after he had interviewed those 13 people, he did give you some comments that would have to be viewed as somewhat negative of your performance?
Russell	He gave me both. He gave me positive and negative and then writes me a letter to share with people to show what his overall assessment was.
Webb	Look at the next one, the next page, I think the third area of comments that your coworkers made about you. You see where it says "his lack of strategic vision"? "Insecure," "wavers on key issues," "lacks strategic vision," "runs hot and cold on people," "not sufficiently trusted," "avoided confronting people," "held unproductive meetings," and had "mixed customer relations," among other things?
Russell	Yes.
Webb	And again, did Dr. Smart review some of those comments by your staff with you?
Russell	Yes, sir.

Webb	And, do you agree that it appears that most of those are pretty negative?
Russell	Well, these are the negative ones. I mean, what happens in this process, Mr. Webb, is he sits down, and he goes through, and he gets positive concerns and negative concerns. And he sits down and he, he first goes through these two pages—and I went through this in my deposition—strengths and concerns. And if you read it, I don't know what it is, but the strengths go on for two pages, and then he says, "do you want me to go through the strengths?" I said, "no." He said, "let me go through the concerns."

Webb pointed out a number of other unflattering remarks that Russell's coworkers reported to Smart. "I have never seen anyone at the VP level so insecure. Everybody talks about it," wrote one employee. Other comments went further. "He sneaks around asking people to rat on each other." "Can't look a guy in the eye and tell him he is screwing up." "Does not belong in a VP chair and way down deep realizes it," one employee said, "so, he figures that people conspire against him."

Russell declared these remarks to all be "character assassination," claiming that the document was produced after he was fired in order to smear him. However, Webb was able to get Russell to concede that the remarks were part of the document that Smart had reviewed with him prior to his termination. During this line of questioning, Webb effectively challenged Russell, who became more unhinged, striking out at both Webb and the judge.

Webb	He gave you some fairly negative comments about your decisiveness. Is that fair to say?
Russell	Yes, sir.
Webb	I would just read off a few here.
Russell	Why don't you read them all off?
Webb	You go ahead and read them, if you like.
Russell	No, you read them, Mr. Webb.
Webb	Is there any one that you want read? You are free to do so.

Russell	No. Go ahead, Mr. Webb.
Webb	In fact, does it appear that, at least a number of your coworkers-
Russell	Well, I think what I object to, Mr. Webb-
Webb	Can I just ask the question?
Russell	It was under...Mr. Smart had said-
The Court	Mr. Russell, would you just calm down here and let Mr. Webb-
Russell	I mean, this is-
The Court	Mr. Russell, I know this is unpleasant for you, but-
Russell	It is almost illegal.
The Court	Well-
Russell	Go ahead.
The Court	Please quiet down. And just answer the questions.

In conducting his cross-examination of Russell, Webb had the rare opportunity to have taken Russell's deposition in the civil case for wrongful termination. Webb said he was able to "lock him down on enormous amounts of bias and impeachment that you never get in a criminal case." In addition, Webb recommended settling the civil case once the criminal indictment was released. "We settled that case for a very reasonable amount," Webb said. "But in connection with settling it, I knew that Russell had lied in his deposition. I was not going to settle the case unless Russell basically acknowledged that he did not have any knowledge of criminal wrongdoing by anyone at GE."

Webb then turned his attention to whether Russell's testimony at the criminal trial against GE constituted an about-face from the affidavit he signed as part of the settlement of his civil case in which he admitted that he had no knowledge of antitrust misconduct by GE staff. Webb asked Russell to square that acknowledged claim of ignorance with his testimony for the government in support of its criminal antitrust charges.

Webb	In light of the testimony I heard you give to the jury this morning, isn't it a fact that you are now retracting what you had in the affidavit in paragraph two?

Russell	No, I'm not.
Webb	Didn't you tell the jury this morning that you weren't personally present with Mr. Hiner when you allege that he made some kind of statement to you, which you contend violates antitrust laws?
Russell	Could violate antitrust laws, yes.
Webb	Could violate?
Russell	Yes, but my interpretation of this document, this affidavit, which was carefully worded by the lawyers, was that I had no personal knowledge. I could never attend meetings with De Beers. I can only testify to what Glen Hiner told me, but I had no personal knowledge of the price-fixing allegations, or antitrust, or other activities that took place.

There are a variety of ways to determine a witness's credibility. One is to assess a witness's motive and bias, as was outlined effectively by Webb in his Marquette 10 rebuttal. Another way is to evaluate the witness's consistency. Is what the witness testifies to at trial consistent with his prior statements—statements made before the existence of intervening events and new motivations? Put another way, were the witness's actions and conduct in a non-trial setting the same or similar as what the witness later asserts at trial? Prior inconsistent statements

---

> *"Russell alleged, as fact, that 'Peter Frenz met with Liotier in Brussels for the purpose of fixing prices on industrial diamonds.' On cross-examination, in the criminal case, Russell acknowledged that he was not at the meeting and did not know what had happened."*

and conduct are admissible at trial because their evidentiary or probative value lies in the fact that it differs from trial testimony.

Under the Federal Rules of Evidence, inquiries as to a witness's motive and bias are proper because of their possible bearing on the believability of the witness. It is a common sense rule, as are most of the Federal Rules of Evidence. A witness who harbors a grudge against another or bears intense dislike toward those he is accusing of misconduct leaves open the challenge to his veracity for those very reasons. Similarly, a witness occupying a neutral and objective position in a lawsuit may well be more believable because of the absence of a festering antagonism.

Russell had unkind arrows in his quiver for some of the people he had worked most closely with for years, but it was Hiner he despised the most. The cross-examination also addressed Russell's reaction to his October 23rd meeting with Hiner regarding the inadequacy of his performance.

Webb You were pretty well convinced after this meeting that you would be terminated from General Electric; is that correct?

Russell Absolutely not.

Webb All right. Let me ask you, would it be fair to say, as a result of this meeting that I went through with you, you got very, very upset and angry with Mr. Hiner; is that fair to say?

Russell No, sir.

Webb Let me ask you this. Did you, within a few days after this meeting, did you sit down in your office in Worthington—

Russell Yes, sir.

Webb And prepare a written memorandum?

Russell Yes, sir.

Webb Which contained a personal, scurrilous attack on Mr. Hiner?

Russell It documented what was going on in GE Superabrasives and certainly contained items that were not favorable to Mr. Hiner.

Webb My question is, did you sit down a few days after this meeting and prepare a written memorandum which contained a personal attack on Mr. Hiner? That's my question.

Russell	Included in my comments about him, and some of them were a personal attack, and some of it was activities regarding antitrust.
Webb	For example, did you prepare a memorandum in which you referred to him as "pond scum"?
Russell	Yes, sir.
Webb	Did you refer to other people at GE as "disgusting, a cancer on American industry"?
Russell	Yes, sir.
Webb	Do you consider that a personal attack on somebody?
Russell	You say personal attack—I mean, if you really believe something, and then are you attacking somebody? It can be called a personal attack and it could also be how I felt about him.

On direct examination, Russell testified that he was aware that Frenz had scheduled a meeting with Liotier on October 17, 1991. It had been established that meetings between Frenz and his customers were normal and routine. Russell was neither in attendance nor advised what actually occurred at the meeting. In his own lawsuit for wrongful termination, however, Russell alleged, as fact, that "Peter Frenz met with Liotier in Brussels for the purpose of fixing prices on industrial diamonds." Believing Russell's suspicion was worthy of prosecution, the government signed on to Russell's version of events. On cross-examination, in the criminal case, Russell acknowledged that he was not at the meeting and did not know what had happened.

Beyond the believability issues, the documents told a different story. First, Russell testified that the ultimate authority to set prices for GES products rested with him. That included whether or not to follow any pricing actions by De Beers. The evidence established that with two companies dominating the industrial diamond production market, it was not unusual for one of the two to follow the pricing actions of the other. Another accusation Russell leveled at Hiner in his October 30, 1991, letter was that after Hiner's September 1991 visit with De Beers, Hiner automatically put a pricing increase in the GES budget for 1992. It was Russell's assertion that the price increase was a consequence of Hiner's price-fixing trip to Europe in September 1991. Webb tore into this assertion on cross-examination.

Webb	The allegation you are making there is that Hiner went and had a meeting with De Beers in September, and then you contend he was fixing prices, and he returned and he then made you raise your prices?
Russell	Right.
Webb	And you admitted that you learned that was wrong, isn't it?
Russell	Well, what I said is—that's correct—is automatically entered in my budget in August of '92, but actually it's before he went to the meeting, during the time period where Mr. Hiner and I are having discussion about what he is going to be doing over there.

In further questioning, Russell was asked if in August of 1991 that he specifically instructed his international sales manager, Steve Palovchik, to plan and implement a price increase effective January 1, 1992. Russell conceded that he wrote that instruction to Palovchik. At another point in his testimony, Russell claimed this was merely for his staff to evaluate, although the language used in August 1991 was "plan and implement."

To dispel any notion that the price increase was just a hypothetical test run and offered as a challenge to his staff, Webb presented the irrefutable evidence that a price increase was intended to take place at the direction of Russell.

> “*In his testimony, Russell substituted wrath for reason, conjecture for knowledge, and anger for fairness. The outcome was ordained when he left the witness stand.*”

Webb	My question to you, Mr. Russell, is, did you meet with your boss, Mr. Hiner, on October 23, 1991?
Russell	Yes, I did, sir.
Webb	Thank you. At that time, did you have what is known as an operating review?
Russell	Yes, I did.
Webb	And there had been a document prepared by your business, GES, and that document was called the 1991 Capacity and Operating Review. Is that correct?
Russell	That is correct.
Webb	In this document, your business, General Electric Superabrasives, you set forth on here—I notice the date at the bottom is 10-23-91?
Russell	That is correct, sir.
Webb	You set forth on here the [diamond saw] price increase?
Russell	Yes.
Webb	And you describe in detail what the price changes will be?
Russell	That's correct.
Webb	And you actually set forth when you are going to announce the price increase?
Russell	Right.
Webb	What you said there—it's November 15, 1991?
Russell	Right
Webb	And it is going to be effective January 1, 1992?
Russell	Right.
Webb	Now, that document this jury is now looking at, Mr. Russell, you had reviewed that document before the meeting. Is that correct?
Russell	Yes.
Webb	And you were aware that that document structured into it a price increase?
Russell	Of course; I delivered it.
Webb	You delivered it to Mr. Hiner?

Russell	Yes.
Webb	And you actually supervised your staff in the preparation of this document. Is that correct?
Russell	Correct.
Webb	And you actually reviewed it ahead of time and approved it. Is that correct?
Russell	Correct.
Webb	And you actually spoke in favor of the price increase in this meeting. Is that correct?
Russell	Correct.

Edward Russell was indisputably the government's most important witness. It would be his performance that set the tone for the rest of the trial. Although the material issues in the case transcended his testimony, how he performed left an indelible impression and gave flavor to the government's case. In his testimony, Russell substituted wrath for reason, conjecture for knowledge, and anger for fairness. The outcome was ordained when he left the witness stand.

Baer, another lawyer representing GE in the case, said Webb successfully undermined Russell's credibility during cross-examination. "Dan let Mr. Russell hang himself with his own words," Baer said. "It was a very thoughtful and effective way of letting the witness damage himself."

In the U.S. District Court, a criminal defendant can move, at the close of the government's case, for a judgment of acquittal. It is a request by the defendant to terminate the case immediately in favor of the defendant and eliminate the necessity of the jury's determination of the facts. The standard of review the judge must employ is whether, viewing the evidence in the light most favorable to the prosecution, a jury acting reasonably could find the defendant guilty beyond a reasonable doubt.

Although such motions are rarely granted, it is incumbent on the government to present evidence sufficient to satisfy the standard as to all of the elements of the offense. When making such motions, it is not uncommon for a criminal defendant's lawyer to claim that the requisite amount of proof is lacking as to all of the elements or as to most of them. Experienced and skilled trial lawyers often direct their attack on selected elements of the crime that are the most assailable and concentrate on those rather than a shotgun approach.

It is also unproductive to attack the believability of witnesses in making such a motion, as fertile as such an attack might otherwise be. Credibility of witnesses is generally an appeal to the good sense of juries as opposed to the judge whose constraint on the topic is well established. No matter the failings of Russell as a witness, Webb's appeal to the judge ignored the obvious. Judge Smith afforded each party 30 minutes per side for oral argument on the motion in addition to each party's written submissions.

In his argument, Webb addressed three issues in which the evidence failed to satisfy the government's burden. The first was Webb's claim that the evidence, at best, proved an agreement to exchange price information between GE and De Beers and did not prove a price-fixing agreement. An adjunct of the argument was that the person acting on behalf of GE had to have pricing authority to bind the corporation.

The second issue was the failure of the government to prove that Liotier was acting on behalf of De Beers and entered into a price-fixing conspiracy with GE on their behalf. Additionally, the government had to prove that GE was aware that Liotier was acting on behalf of De Beers.

The third issue was that if Frenz was the alleged conspirator on GE's behalf, then GE was the wrong party to be criminally charged since Frenz worked for GES Europe. There was considerable elaboration of all three issues.

Mr. Gillam argued on behalf of the government. Among other things, Gillam alluded to Liotier's many responsibilities and referred to the relationship among the various corporations involved. In the midst of his explanation, Judge Smith asked a question Webb had posed in his motion. "What evidence—is there any direct evidence or any evidence from which an inference could be made that Mr. Liotier did, in fact, deal with anyone actually at De Beers to get authority to enter into an agreement?"

Gillam responded that he didn't believe De Beers ever authorized Liotier to do so and that "it wasn't the government's position that they authorized Liotier to enter into any kind of agreement." Gillam then proceeded to piece together a variety of events and discussions, all of which constituted circumstantial evidence, to suggest the existence of a criminal conspiracy. None of the evidence alluded to by Gillam addressed the judge's question.

Near the end of Gillam's presentation, the judge again interjected. "Your theory is, or seems to be, that it is Peter Frenz and not anyone else from any of his superiors at GES in Worthington that are involved in this conspiracy. Is that correct?" Gillam's response was, "Yes and no." Gillam then offered up more little pieces of the record—piling up inferences as he went along—in explanation of his ambivalent answer to the direct and straightforward question. At the conclusion of Gillam's argument, Webb had the opportunity to rebut.

> *Let me begin by addressing the issue Mr. Gillam spent the most time addressing, which is the issue about whether or not Liotier had, in fact, been established by sufficient evidence to have been acting as an agent for De Beers. Your Honor, you asked, I guess, a critical question that I would have wanted to ask him, which was did Liotier actually have contact with De Beers and receive authorization to act on their behalf? When you asked him that critical question, if I had taken this down correctly, Mr. Gillam told you something that I am astounded by. His answer was that "it is not the government's theory that De Beers ever authorized Liotier to act on their behalf and enter this agreement."*
>
> *I must tell you as I stand before you, unless I misheard that—I can get the transcript—that I am truly baffled as to what the government's theory of this case is at this point. The government charged, on the face of this indictment, that Liotier acted on behalf of De Beers.*
>
> *Your instructions make it clear that the government must prove that beyond a reasonable doubt. I do not understand, as I stand here now, how the government can possibly survive this case.*
>
> *I would respectfully also suggest to the Court that much of what Mr. Gillam discussed with you had nothing to do with the actual issue, which Your Honor asked, "what is the real evidence*

that De Beers ever authorized Liotier to act on their behalf?" He never answered the question because there is none.

A week later, Judge Smith issued his written decision on GE's motion for a judgment of acquittal. The essence of his decision was that the government failed to show that Liotier acted on De Beers' behalf in pricing matters with GE, that GE knew Liotier was acting on De Beers' behalf in pricing matters with GE, and that documents and communications between GE and Liotier did not show that he acted on De Beers' behalf. Webb said of his approach in the trial, "I milked the devil out of the burden of proof concept. I knew that it was going to be a close case."

With Judge Smith's decision in favor of GE, the criminal case was over. Under the rules, no appeal was possible by the government. What was left for GE, its officers, employees, and lawyers, was a time for quiet celebration. It was GE's view that the case should never have been brought and had no merit whatsoever. Webb believed that Welch's decision to fight the charges, however much they were lacking in merit, took exceptional courage. It was a rare experience for a company not to capitulate to Department of Justice actions and try to resolve these types of charges in the name of expediency. Webb's respect for Welch's decision was profound. Welch's support for the trial team was reciprocated; when the verdict was announced, Welch sent a case of wine and a bouquet of roses to Mrs. Webb as thanks for putting up with her husband's long absences.

"Gillam and Webb would not be a terrible match-up under normal circumstances," wrote William W. Horne in an article for *American Lawyer* magazine. "Both are good with a jury, good with a judge. But Webb had an advantage that became all too clear at trial. Since he had been involved in the case for two years, he knew the whole web of international characters, corporate relationships and allegations like the back of his hand. He could and did use that knowledge—along with his exceptional concentration and earnest manner—to tear down witnesses and build their stories up in a light favorable to GE." It added that, "The government prosecutors were outspent, outnumbered and, in the end, thanks largely to the persuasive talents of Dan Webb, they were outlawyered."

According to the *American Lawyer* article, "When the 12 jurors and two alternates were polled by the judge after the trial ended, 13 indicated they would have acquitted GE if it had been up to them, according to a source who was present at the polling. And two jurors interviewed for this article say, in their opinion, the Justice Department simply failed to make its case."

Baer, who would become the Assistant Attorney General for the U.S. Department of Justice Antitrust Division, described Webb as irreverent and funny and said, "There is a respect he conveys for other people and a certain self-deprecating [style] that makes him very accessible and easy for people to like."

Webb recalled the focus on the successful teamwork by the trial team on the case. "Baer, Kindler, and I were on the cover of the *American Lawyer*. The article focused on our teamwork and that we won the case, which is very rare for criminal antitrust cases. So, when we won and the antitrust division suffered such a huge defeat, it was a big deal. But the thing they emphasized in the article was that we worked together as a team to win the case."

West Division Street in Chicago, the site of the altercation between Richard Vanecko and David Koschman

State of Illinois v. Richard J. Vanecko

CHAPTER 9
ONE PUNCH JUSTICE

Early in the morning of April 25, 2004, on a sidewalk near Division and Dearborn Streets in Chicago, David Koschman hit his head on the pavement when he was knocked to the ground by Richard J. Vanecko. Eleven days later, Koschman died from the resulting injuries. At the time of the incident, Vanecko was 29 years old, 6'3" tall, and weighed 230 lbs. Koschman was 21 years old, 5'5" tall, and weighed 125 lbs.

These stark and straightforward facts would take almost 10 years to be established as true in a court of law. The Chicago police department and the Cook County State's Attorney's office investigated the incident from April 25, 2004 until late May 2004. Early on, it was thought by some that Vanecko, the nephew of then-Chicago Mayor Richard M. Daley, may have received special treatment relating to his role in the confrontation.

The superintendent of the Chicago police department declared in late May 2004 that there was no basis for criminal charges, and the State's Attorney's office agreed. "Based on the witness statements and all the evidence we have, a charge of involuntary manslaughter doesn't fit," the superintendent claimed. "If new evidence came up, we would change. But based on all of the evidence we have now—all the witnesses brought in and lineups conducted—there's no basis for criminal charges."

The superintendent's comments were in response to *Chicago Sun-Times* reporter Fran Spielman's column questioning whether clout played a role in no charges being filed in a fatal fight involving Daley's nephew. In a supplemental Chicago police department report submitted November 10, 2004, it was asserted that David Koschman "was clearly the aggressor as corroborated by all of the witnesses interviewed, in that David Koschman continued to attack the group of people consisting of Bridget McCarthy, Kevin McCarthy, Craig Denham, and Richard Vanecko." From November 2004 until 2011, no investigative activity took place although the case remained open and "in progress" status during that period.

In January 2011, the *Sun-Times* submitted a Freedom of Information Act request for "copies of police reports of the incident of April 25, 2004 at 3:15 a.m. involving David Koschman at 35 W. Division." Around that time, because the original Koschman homicide file was missing and other reports were missing certain information, the police superintendent ordered a re-investigation

On February 28, 2011, the re-investigation concluded. The final police report stated that David Koschman "was clearly the assailant in this incident by breaking away from his group of friends and aggressively going after Vanecko. These aggressive actions caused Vanecko to take action and defend himself. This investigation has shown that Richard Vanecko, alone, punched David Koschman, which caused him to fall backwards and injure his head, which ultimately caused his death."

There were, however, several factors—such as the lack of effort to interview additional witnesses—that called into question the report's reliability. Despite those concerns, a spokesman for the department stated that the 2011 review "revealed that the facts of that investigation remain unchanged since it was initially investigated. The case would be closed shortly."

The same day the final police department report was submitted, *Sun-Times* reporters Tim Novak, Chris Fusco, and Carol Marin authored a front-page article detailing the paper's own findings regarding inconsistencies with the 2004 inves-

---

> *"Reports by two witnesses said that the descriptions of the incident by the Chicago police department and the State's Attorney's office that Koschman was the aggressor in the incident 'is not how it happened.'"*

tigation. Notable in the article were reports by two witnesses that the descriptions of the incident by the Chicago police department and the State's Attorney's office that Koschman was the aggressor in the incident "is not how it happened." In an article published by the *Sun-Times* on March 3, 2011, a bystander to the incident characterized as "a flat-out lie" the claim that all the witnesses involved said that Koschman was the aggressor.

With significant public pressure on the State's Attorney's office, State's Attorney Anita Alvarez considered the need for a new investigation conducted by an outside independent agency. There was concern that the Chicago police department could not fairly investigate the alleged police misconduct aspect of the case. The State's Attorney's office reached out to the Illinois State Police, who declined to become involved, and then to the Cook County Inspector General's office. The Inspector General agreed to partner with the State's Attorney, but it became unnecessary. On December 14, 2011, Nanci Koschman, Susan Pazderski, and Richard Pazderski, David Koschman's mother, aunt, and uncle, respectively, filed a petition for the appointment of a special prosecutor with the Circuit Court of Cook County.

The petitioners were represented by Locke E. Bowman and Alexa VanBrunt of the Roderick MacArthur Justice Center at Northwestern School of Law and G. Flint Taylor of the People's Law Office. Among other things, the petition asserted that State's Attorney Alvarez had a "clear interest in the case based upon her public statements defending the work of the Chicago police department and the Cook County State's Attorney's Felony Review unit, insisting to *Sun-Times* reporters that there was insufficient evidence to charge Vanecko."

Cook County Circuit Judge Michael P. Toomin was designated to hear the petition. Judge Toomin was widely viewed as a judge with integrity, ability, and independence. Such petitions are extremely rare, and rarer still is their success rate. When they are granted, the elected State's Attorney is officially removed from the case and has no official role in the investigation or prosecution of the petition's subject matter. State's Attorney Alvarez opposed the petition, denying that the Koschman investigation was compromised or impeded by any illegal or improper action, and maintained that petitioners had failed to establish any legal or factual basis that warranted her office's disqualification and the appointment of a special prosecutor. Understanding the gravity of the request for the appointment and its consequences, Judge Toomin permitted oral argument in addition to the written submissions of the parties.

After hearing oral arguments, Judge Toomin granted the petition for appointment of a special prosecutor in the matter of the death of David Koschman. Judge Toomin believed the appointment was necessary to maintain the public's confidence in the impartiality and integrity of the criminal justice system.

In reaching his decision, Judge Toomin elaborately described the investigations conducted by the police department as well as various press accounts of its handling of the case. His written opinion and order of appointment noted instances of missing or incomplete police files, press accounts of witnesses at odds with police reports of events, and failure to follow up relevant leads. Judge Toomin's analysis of the law was thorough and amply justified the conclusion he reached.

With the entry of the order granting the petition, the equally important decision of who to appoint as special prosecutor remained. There was no shortage of applicants, but the choice could not just be any able lawyer. Dan Webb was mentioned as the ideal candidate to take the case.

Judge Toomin called Webb and inquired as to his willingness to take the case, even as he harbored doubts of Webb's availability in light of his substantial law practice. To Judge Toomin's surprise, Webb said he would consider the appointment. "I was contacted by two judges I have enormous respect for—Judge Toomin and Judge Paul Biebel—and they asked me to consider serving as special prosecutor and I told my firm that because the allegations were undermining the credibility of law enforcement in Cook County that somebody should stand up and do this," Webb later recalled. "So, I agreed to do it."

Locke Bowman said:

> *We were very gratified when Cook County Circuit Court Judge Michael Toomin ruled that a special prosecutor should be appointed to re-investigate the death of David Koschman and to re-examine police and prosecutors' handling of the original investigation. We knew, though, that the practical significance of Judge Toomin's decision turned on the identity of the person who became special prosecutor. The assignment required someone with considerable*

stature, complete political independence, courage of conviction, and great lawyerly skill. From our standpoint, the list of acceptable candidates was very short.

Dan Webb's name had occurred to me, but I assumed that he wouldn't be willing to do it. For Dan, taking the position involved significant financial sacrifice and a diversion from a national mega-practice. And, of course, this job was utterly thankless. Whatever the result of the special prosecutor's investigation, disappointment and criticism from some quarter was inevitable.

Of course, Judge Toomin did succeed in recruiting Dan. It was only then, when Dan was sworn in, that I felt we'd succeeded in vindicating Nanci Koschman's right to a zealous, fair, and unbiased investigation of the circumstances of her son's death.

On April 23, 2012, Dan Webb was sworn in as special prosecutor in the matter of the death of David Koschman. In doing so, Judge Toomin ordered that Webb investigate two distinct issues related to the Koschman matter. The first issue was "whether criminal charges should be brought against any person in connection with the homicide of David Koschman in the spring of 2004."

The second issue was "whether, from 2004 to the present, employees of the Chicago police department and the Cook County State's Attorney's office acted intentionally to suppress and conceal evidence, furnish false evidence, and generally impede the investigation into Mr. Koschman's death."

Bowman was not alone in his gratification over the choice of Webb. The *Chicago Sun-Times* had been a strong and consistent voice in challenging the quality and depth of the investigation into Koschman's death, the assertion that he was the aggressor, that Vanecko's actions were legally justified as self-defense, and that no criminal charges would be brought against anybody. Following Webb's appointment, the paper editorialized in favor of his selection. By highlighting Webb's involvement in Greylord, Poindexter and other high profile cases, the article set out to allay the fears of those who believed that a special prosecutor wouldn't step on the toes of Chicago's political establishment or would be an outsider, unfamiliar with local politics.

"We fully expect Webb to take the evidence wherever it leads him in the Koschman case, letting the chips fall where they may. And whatever conclusions he ultimately reaches, we expect them to be widely accepted. Webb's credibility precedes him," the article read. "Yes, Webb's first job will be to determine whether criminal charges should be brought against Vanecko. But his more important job will be to restore confidence in the integrity of the city's entire criminal justice system."

In addition to the Webb appointment, Judge Toomin empaneled a special grand jury on June 18, 2012, which would conduct its sessions at Winston & Strawn's offices in downtown Chicago.

In May 2012, the Office of Special Prosecutor engaged as its investigative partner the City of Chicago Inspector General's Office. Joseph Ferguson, the Inspector General, had previously initiated his own investigation into the Koschman matter, and would now cooperate with Webb and his staff. Ferguson, like Webb, was a former prosecutor with the United States Attorney's office for the Northern District of Illinois and was highly regarded by the law enforcement community in Chicago. Webb also engaged the services of a well-known private investigative firm, Kroll Associates, Inc. Kroll's Chicago office was headed by Jeffrey H. Cramer, also a former Assistant U.S. Attorney in Chicago.

During the course of Special Prosecutor Webb's investigation, 146 witnesses provided some type of testimony. A total of 133 witnesses were interviewed, and 24 witnesses personally appeared before the special grand jury. Of those, 10 witnesses would testify only under court-ordered use immunity, relying on the constitutional privilege against self-incrimination.

The special grand jury issued 160 subpoenas for documentary evidence and testimony, and collected more than 22,000 documents totaling over 300,000 pages. Nevertheless, due to the passage of eight years between the date of the incident and the appointment of the special prosecutor, many potentially important records from 2004 proved unavailable. For example, while phone records existed for certain individuals dating back to April 2004, other phone records, such as the personal cell phone records for the lead detective in the 2004 Chicago police department investigation, no longer existed.

Webb's investigation established the following facts. On Saturday, April 24, 2004, David Koschman, then age 21, and three of his friends—Scott Allen, James

Copeland, and David Francis—drove together from their homes in suburban Mount Prospect, Illinois, to Chicago's Humboldt Park neighborhood to visit their friend, Shaun Hageline, at his apartment. Koschman and his friends, who had all gone to high school together, had made plans to go out that night in the city and then attend the Chicago Cubs game the next day. While at Hageline's apartment that evening, the group watched an NBA playoff basketball game, drank beer, and some also smoked marijuana. Later that evening, the Koschman group headed to Division Street, a popular destination on Chicago's near-north side known for its high concentration of bars and clubs. The Koschman group visited several bars in the Division Street area that night, and then around approximately 3:15 a.m. the group left the area and began walking westward down Division Street to make their way back to Hageline's apartment.

That same night, Richard J. Vanecko, Craig Denham, Kevin McCarthy, Bridget McCarthy, and others attended an engagement dinner for Vanecko's cousin, Katherine Daley, at the Adobo Grill in Chicago's Old Town neighborhood. Following dinner, a group of people from the engagement party—including Vanecko, the McCarthys, and Denham—went to a bar in the River North area of Chicago called the Pepper Canister. After a few hours there, the McCarthys, Vanecko, and Denham, planning to go to the bar Butch McGuire's, took a cab to Division Street.

While walking, the Koschman group and the Vanecko group crossed paths on the south sidewalk of Division Street, during which Koschman bumped into Denham. A verbal altercation ensued, and, according to the grand jury testimony of witness James Copeland, Vanecko hit Koschman with "a flush head-on punch that hit Koschman square in the face." Another witness at the scene described that, "[Koschman] came flying back and fell straight back like a dead weight." Koschman's head then struck the pavement. At the time of the incident, Vanecko was six inches taller than and outweighed the younger Koschman.

Immediately after Vanecko hit Koschman, Vanecko and Denham ran from the scene and took a taxi back to the Pepper Canister. Kevin McCarthy was briefly detained by police. When Kevin McCarthy was questioned at the scene, he lied to police, claiming he did not know the identities of the other men who had run (Vanecko and Denham). When released at the scene, Kevin McCarthy and his wife, Bridget McCarthy, entered a taxi on Division Street, conferred with Vanecko by cell phone, and traveled to the Pepper Canister to meet Vanecko and Denham. While the Pepper Canister had been officially closed, someone at the bar allowed the four to enter and meet.

Koschman was taken unconscious by ambulance from Division Street to Northwestern Memorial Hospital. Despite numerous surgeries over the next eleven days, Koschman died on May 6, 2004 from injuries resulting from the fight.

The special grand jury returned an indictment on December 3, 2012, charging Richard J. Vanecko with committing involuntary manslaughter. Shortly after the return of the indictment, Stephen J. Senderowitz, an attorney with Webb, asked for a judge to be appointed from outside of Cook County. "There could be issues raised about impartiality of even the most qualified judge because of the relationships that exist," Senderowitz said.

Judge Toomin agreed and asked Cook County Circuit Court Chief Judge Timothy C. Evans to seek an outside judge. Judge Evans made the request, and Judge Maureen McIntyre, from McHenry County, Illinois, was ultimately designated to preside over the case.

Long before any plea discussions took place between Webb and lawyers on his staff that assisted him, he met with Nanci Koschman and talked with her at some length. "I was very moved by Mrs. Koschman and the suffering she had endured because of the death of her son, and it reinforced my decision to get to the bottom of what happened in my role as special prosecutor," Webb recalled. "As time went on, and particularly at the time of the final plea discussions with Mr. Vanecko's attorneys, I was committed to making sure that Mrs. Koschman could finally put the death of her son to rest. That was a strong contributing factor to my commitment that I would not agree to a plea arrangement that did not include a period of incarceration for Mr. Vanecko. I thought that was the least I could do for this wonderful and endearing mother who had suffered so much for so many years regarding the tragic loss of her son."

A plea agreement was in fact reached between Webb and Vanecko and his lawyers. Webb addressed the judge in recommending acceptance of the plea agreement.

> *I will be brief, your honor. Let me just address briefly the nature of the crime, the nature of Mr. Vanecko's background and also*

what we believe to be the reasonableness of what we're recommending in the way of a proper sentence in this case.

Your Honor, Illinois law requires that someone charged with the crime of involuntary manslaughter be presumed under the law to be entitled to probation as the appropriate punishment unless the nature and circumstances of the offense or the criminal history of the defendant require that imprisonment be imposed.

Now, as far as the nature and circumstances of the offense, I think your Honor is well aware of some of the details of that from the voluminous filings that have been presented to the Court and so I don't think I need to belabor that other than to say in conclusion from our standpoint as special prosecutor we believe the evidence at trial would have established that Mr. Vanecko engaged in reckless and irresponsible conduct that resulted in the death of David Koschman. At the same time, however, the facts are undisputed that Mr. Vanecko's criminal conduct lasted for a few seconds and that when he punched and struck David Koschman and caused him to fall backward and his head hit the pavement and eventually [he] died, that that was an extremely serious course of criminal act, but we also recognize that it lasted for a very brief period of time. The facts are very clear. There was no premeditation, there was no preplanning and it did occur as part of a spontaneous punch in the middle of a heated argument between two groups of people that encountered [one another] in the Rush Street area late at night, and that we have looked into Mr. Vanecko's past and have determined that he does not have any adult criminal history. He has been a productive member of society, so that when we look at the nature of the offense and we look at the background of the defendant, I and my office, as special prosecutor, have determined out of fairness that a presumption of probation cannot be overcome by these facts of the case.

Therefore, we have made a decision to recommend to the Court, and it has been accepted by the Defense, of the maximum amount of probation under the law which will be 30 months' probation. So we are recommending 30 months' probation.

We also would point out to your Honor that Mr. Vanecko is pleading to the entire charge. The felony he is charged with is involuntary manslaughter and he is pleading guilty to that entire charge.

As part of the probation we are recommending to the Court and we believe it's a fair recommendation that some incarceration is required, and we have reached an agreement that total confinement should be four months with two of those months incarcerated in the county jail and two months of the confinement will be under home confinement with electronic monitoring,

As part of this arrangement that we have come to on the agreement, we are recommending full restitution to Mrs. Koschman of all of her out-of-pocket expenses relating to these events. Under Illinois law you can only have restitution for out-of-pocket expenses. The suffering and pain that Mrs. Koschman has been through—no one is suggesting that $20,000 would compensate that and no one is suggesting that—but the law allows us to get full compensation for only out-of-pockets and the defense has agreed to that and so we estimated that at $20,000.

We also, as a condition of probation, have asked for and the defense has agreed that as we go forward here today that Mr. Vanecko will extend an apology to Mrs. Koschman based on the events that occurred here.

As far as whether this is the right or appropriate sentence for Your Honor to impose, we have done a survey of Illinois cases and there are cases similar to this which tend to be called the "one-punch" case where there's an altercation that occurs on a street or in a bar somewhere in which there's a punch thrown and someone gets hurt severely or, in this case, would be killed as a result of that. And based on those cases where there's no premeditation, no preplanning, a very short period of time of the criminal conduct almost all those cases result in straight probation, but because David Koschman obviously died as a result of this horrific series of events that occurred that evening, we believe that probation must include the period of incarceration and confinement that I described to your Honor and that's what we're recommending.

One of the most important things to my office in coming to this recommendation has been Nanci Koschman. She and her lawyers have completely cooperated with the special prosecutor's office over an extended period of time. She is clearly the surviving victim of this set of events that is hard to imagine what she's been through. And she has expressed to me and my office that she has agreed, that she believes this is an appropriate and fair disposition based on the facts and circumstances that have occurred. Therefore, I respectfully suggest or ask your Honor to impose the sentence that we described to your Honor as being a fair and appropriate sentence. And I would respectfully ask if your Honor would hear from Nanci Koschman to be able to address the Court now and to give a statement as the victim of what happened here.

Nanci Koschman was afforded the opportunity to address the Court, and she expressed her anguish and accepted the outcome.

Your Honor, thank you for allowing me to speak on behalf of my son, David. I know most of you never met him, but he was the

---

> *"Today is my first opportunity to see Mr. Vanecko in person. While I know in my heart he did not go out that evening with the intent to hurt my son, it happened. David died 12 days later when life support was turned off."*

light in my eyes, in my heart, and my soul. When his life ended a part of me died, too. I never expected to be here speaking for him. I also never thought his life would have ended so soon.

When he left the house on April 24, 2004 to celebrate with his friends, fate took a terrible turn of events.

Today is my first opportunity to see Mr. Vanecko in person. While I know in my heart he did not go out that evening with the intent to hurt my son, it happened. David died 12 days later when life support was turned off.

I have spent nine and a half years waiting for this day because regardless of whatever my son did that night, he did not deserve to die. I have lived with such guilt and pain because I blamed myself for what happened that night. I just needed to know the truth. I have never been out for revenge. I have just wanted an apology. I needed to hear "I'm sorry." I have said this so many times and now I hope to hear those words. Would it bring back David? Of course not, but I have a little peace of mind knowing I got justice for David. It has always been about David.

I agree with the outcome today. Payback won't change the events of that night, nothing will. I hope Mr. Vanecko can go on with his life and I can continue to face mine without David. I'm glad I fought. I'm very grateful that I had so many wonderful people on my side fighting for me. Thank you for allowing me to speak on David's behalf.

After the passage of almost 10 years and all the immeasurable heartache endured along the way, Nanci Koschman listened to Richard J. Vanecko admit in open court that he caused the death of her son when he forcibly struck David in the face, causing him to fall back and hit his head on the pavement.

Then Venecko was asked if he wanted to speak. "I do your Honor. I have felt terrible about this since the moment I heard that David was injured and when I found out he had passed I was shocked, and I cannot imagine the pain and suffering Mrs. Koschman has gone through and that she has endured since the loss of her son. And I can only say, Mrs. Koschman, that I am sorry. I apologize. If I could undo what was done I would, but I can't and I can just extend my sincerest apology."

Pursuant to the plea agreement between Webb and Vanecko and his lawyers, Judge McIntyre imposed the sentence Webb and his team had recommended. With the sentencing of Richard J. Vanecko, Webb satisfied the first of the two mandates imposed on him.

As for Webb's second mandate in the special prosecutor's appointment order, Webb found that prosecution of any potentially illegal actions by the Chicago police department and the State's Attorney's office in 2004 was barred by the statute of limitations. Although prosecution of any illegal actions taken by those groups in 2011-2012 was not barred by the statute of limitations, Webb found that there was insufficient evidence to prove any criminal intent, and therefore did not seek any additional charges.

In reflecting back on the investigation, Webb noted, "I took the approach that we were going to get to the bottom of what happened. I disagreed with the decision not to indict for the death of David Koschman. I made a different decision. I thoroughly tore apart whether anyone else could be indicted. You can tell from my report that I didn't find evidence that could lead to the indictment of anybody else."

Locke Bowman reflected on the investigation and its results.

> *I have no doubt that the decision to indict Richard Vanecko was right. I also know that what ought to have been a relatively simple and straightforward prosecution was rendered enormously difficult not only because of the intense public scrutiny of the case, but because the original, fraudulent investigation had compromised every single prosecution witness. Thus, the decision to indict was not only right, it was courageous.*
>
> *Any reader of the special prosecutor's report, released following Vanecko's plea, knows that the Webb investigation of the police and prosecutors was systematic, exhaustive, and unstinting. I have enormous respect for the thoroughness and technical compe-*

tence of the investigation and the report. The fact that stones were not left unturned and that the analytics of the report are sound and unbiased is hugely important to public confidence in the justice system.

I will not lie; I hoped there would be criminal charges and I felt that there could have been. But that doesn't diminish one iota my gratitude and respect for Dan's huge public service in this case. He and his team did the work and they did it well. That may sound like a small thing, but actually—it's not. They served justice.

Judge Toomin echoed Bowman's praise. "Dan was the captain of the ship and did a great job. I'm happy with my choice and satisfied with the outcome."

Webb conducting direct examination of Microsoft CEO Bill Gates with government counsel Brendan Sullivan looking on.

United States v. Microsoft Corporation, et al.

CHAPTER 10
COUNSEL FOR THE DEFENSE

As Webb left the United States Attorney's Office in 1985 to enter private practice at the law firm of Winston & Strawn, he could never have imagined what would become the reality of his career. As it turned out, his triumphs as a federal prosecutor were not the capstones of his distinguished career as a trial attorney—they were only the beginning. For the past 30 years in the private sector, Webb has probably had more major jury trials than any other attorney in America. Webb's energy for and commitment to trial work has never waned.

When planning his move into the private sector, he interviewed with several major Chicago-based law firms. He eventually selected Winston & Strawn because it had developed such a strong reputation over the decades as being a true and outstanding "trial firm." Webb was greatly influenced in his decision to join Winston & Strawn because of the presence of two great trial lawyers who were personal friends—Tommy Reynolds, Jr. and Ed Foote. Webb's interviews with them were sometimes held in places trial lawyers have been known to frequent: cocktail lounges and bars. Webb would later note how convincing Reynolds could become after a few drinks.

Webb has frequently commented that joining Winston & Strawn was the best decision he could have made in furthering his career as a trial attorney. As his practice reflects, he often takes on cases that interest him, some of which are controversial. Many of these engagements have involved clients with major problems but who did not have the resources to pay the bills generated by a large law firm. "I am proud of my career as a prosecutor. But I enjoy being a defense lawyer more. It's much more challenging. You have to work harder. It's also more of the highs and lows. I get personally close to my clients in major cases, and many become friends of mine," Webb said.

Winston & Strawn has often looked the other way on fees to allow Webb to take on these cases, and he has been ever grateful. One example of the firm's commitment to its clients is the six-month trial of former Illinois Governor George Ryan. Webb's partners and associates at Winston & Strawn swallowed about $20 million in unpaid legal fees in that case.

In entering the private practice of law, Webb realized that simply defending white collar criminal cases would not be enough to sustain his interests. He thrives on representing American corporations in major commercial litigation that is often more complex and challenging than defending white collar criminal cases. Trials involving the subjects of antitrust law, securities fraud, civil RICO allegations, product liability issues, and intellectual property matters would be a major part of his practice while at Winston & Strawn. Sam Skinner said of Webb, "He wants the challenge of being in the biggest cases with the most challenge and the most interest." Webb's passion to be the best required his entry into the full panoply of the civil litigation marketplace.

During his 30-years and counting at Winston & Strawn, Webb estimates that approximately 75% of his private practice time has been devoted to major commercial litigation and about 25% to white collar crime cases. His corporate clients reflect a veritable who's who in American commerce and industry. Included as clients are such names as Microsoft, Cisco Systems, Philip Morris, General Electric, Verizon, Guggenheim Capital, Alcoa, Abbott Labs, BP Amoco, H. J. Heinz Company, Pfizer, Wyeth/American Home Products, the State of Illinois, Maricopa County, Arizona, the Mormon Church, the Los Angeles Dodgers, the National Football League, American Airlines, the New York Stock Exchange, Ernst and Young, State Farm, Motorola, and a host of other equally recognizable organizations.

Because of his love of the courtroom and his early experiences in criminal cases, Webb also maintains a steady diet of criminal cases. These tend to be tried more quickly than civil cases and, because of the stakes involved, can be more exciting. Webb has been the "go to man" for such high profile criminal defendants as former Illinois Governor George Ryan, former Illinois Congressman Dan Rostenkowski, former Detroit Mayor Kwame Kilpatrick, former United States Congressman Jesse Jackson, Jr., Illinois political powerhouse William Cellini, former Cook County Chief Judge of the Chancery Court David Shields, and many others. Beyond the defense of criminal cases, Webb has attracted famous clients in various civil settings. They include former GE Chairman Jack Welch and the Estate of Washington Redskins owner Jack Kent Cooke.

In the late 20th and early 21st century, business conducted in the industrialized world has become extremely specialized. Webb's clients produce a varied list of products and engage in the rendition of many different services. As specialization in the workplace increases, specialization in the practice of law follows suit. It is quite common for lawyers to list one or two specialties, and the era of generalist lawyers, particularly trial lawyers, is fast disappearing. Dan Webb stands among the few bucking the trend. "Some trial lawyers are terrified of losing and therefore they are not willing to try the hard cases," said Brendan Sullivan. "Dan will try any case when justice and the client require it." Joel Flaum, a Seventh Circuit Court of Appeals Judge, and former Assistant U.S. Attorney who tried a case with Webb said, "Whether the matter is an antitrust case or intellectual property or criminal defense, he simply has the ability to move quickly from one matter to another."

Webb's enormous capacity for work, his willingness to take on any case of interest irrespective of degree of difficulty, subject matter, or commitment of time, and his demonstrated successes at trial are reflected in the rankings he receives by his peers. Webb is consistently listed as a star litigator by a number of publications in the fields of business trial lawyers, antitrust, product liability and mass torts, general commercial litigation, white collar crime, and government investigations. He has also repeatedly received accolades from the leading national and local organizations that review and rate lawyers, including Chambers & Partners, Best Lawyers in America, Super Lawyers, Lawdragon, *Leading Lawyers*, and The Legal 500. These independent organizations have ranked Webb as the No. 1 business litigator in Chicago and Illinois, bet-the-company lawyer of the year, one of the 10 leading trial lawyers in the U.S., and one of the top 25 litigation experts in the world. In naming Webb to its list of the country's top litigators in 2010, the *Business Insider* described him as "One of 11 Trial Lawyers You Definitely Do Not Want to See Across the Aisle."

While the courtroom has been the stage of much of Webb's success, he has had significant achievements outside of it. Webb has been active in the management and governance of Winston & Strawn; for many years he was the chairman of Winston's litigation department, and for the past several years, he's been the Chairman of the firm.

Webb has also been politically active and heavily involved in civic affairs. His mentor and one of his closest friends is former Illinois Governor James Thompson. After Thompson left the governorship, Webb induced him to come to Winston & Strawn, where Thompson would lead as Chairman for many years. Webb then succeeded Thompson as the Chairman when Thompson stepped aside to become Chairman Emeritus. Webb has frequently been seen huddled with Thompson in the Winston offices discussing both legal matters and important local and national political issues.

It is neither possible nor within the province of this book to describe all of the major cases in which Dan Webb has been involved throughout his illustrious career. Interested readers can review a list of his major cases as of this writing in the appendix. I have, however, attempted to give the reader a flavor of the trials which established his credentials and others which contained public dimensions of importance to the nation. What follows are highlights of just a few of the major commercial trials where some of the most successful companies in the world "bet-the-company" on Webb.

PHILIP MORRIS

One corporate survival case occurred when the U.S. Department of Justice brought a multi-billion dollar racketeering suit against the tobacco industry. The DOJ filed the case in September of 1999; U.S. District Judge Gladys Kessler would issue her ruling nearly seven years later, in August of 2006.

As the nation's largest cigarette manufacturer, Philip Morris USA, Inc., was the lead defendant in the case. The DOJ sought the disgorgement of the defendants' alleged ill-gotten gains from 1954 until 2050—along with a host of monitoring measures—from the entire tobacco industry. It is hard to imagine a case with higher stakes.

The government essentially accused the entire industry of fraudulently concealing the dangers of smoking and with violating the RICO Act. Specifically, the DOJ charged that the tobacco companies had engaged in a decades-long conspiracy to, among other things, mislead the public about the risks of smoking and of inhaling secondhand smoke; misrepresent the addictiveness of nicotine while simultaneously manipulating cigarette design to increase nicotine addiction; deceptively market cigarettes characterized as "light" or "low tar," while knowing that those cigarettes were at least as hazardous as full flavored cigarettes; and target youth.

William Ohlemeyer, vice-president and associate general counsel of Altria Group, Inc., the parent company of Philip Morris, named Webb lead trial lawyer for Philip Morris. Webb would defend the tobacco giant in cases brought by attorneys general in a number of states, and he would lead an army of attorneys for the industry in a courtroom clash with the DOJ that he described as "the mother of all trials."

"Dan is a real straight-up guy, that's the reason his name is attached to so many things ... The business people really like him and really respect him," Ohlemeyer said. "He speaks candidly and directly to them. A lot of lawyers don't have the confidence to do that. Dan is the best fit."

The tobacco company lawyers included Kirkland & Ellis partner David Bernick, who was Brown & Williamson Tobacco Corporation's lead trial counsel. He described Webb as "very down-to-earth and easy to get along with. I've never seen him lose his temper or talk down to somebody ... Dan is a guy I genuinely look forward to trying a case with."

It was not only Bernick and the business people who expressed respect for Webb. In an earlier tobacco trial pitting the state of Washington against all of the major U.S. tobacco companies as defendants, in addition to his role as lead counsel for Philip Morris, Webb was also designated as the lead courtroom representative for all of the tobacco company representatives on certain common issues. After 10 weeks of trial before Washington state jurors, the trial ended because of a Master Settlement Agreement between the industry and 46 states, including Washington. Jon Ferguson, deputy attorney general for Washington, led the state's trial team.

Ferguson said, "Webb was highly effective. The jurors really like Webb; he was their favorite." This was praise offered to the chief lawyer for a company that had been described by a leading business journal as one of the most reviled corporations in America.

Aided by a ruling from the District of Columbia Court of Appeals that the racketeering statute allows only forward-looking remedies, disgorgement of gains from past conduct was not available. Instead of a claim of $280 billion (which was itself reduced from a $959 billion demand at the outset of the case), the government revised its demands and sought $130 billion for a national smoking cessation program, billions more for a public education and countermarketing campaign, and the appointment of court monitors to essentially run the defendant companies.

The primary thrust of Webb's argument at trial was one of personal responsibility. "There is absolutely no question that people in the United States have known for over 30 years that smoking can have harmful health effects," he said. "People who smoke absolutely understand the risks they run from the time they begin smoking, and they accept that risk. They have the freedom to make that choice. That is why the tobacco companies win the vast majority of cases that go to trial—jurors understand that people cannot engage in a course of risky conduct for 25 years and then come back and blame the tobacco company for what they did voluntarily."

After a nine-month trial, Judge Kessler issued a final order and a 1,653-page opinion. She found that Philip Morris and the other defendants violated federal

---

> *"In addition to the nine months it took to try the case, it also involved live testimony from 85 witnesses, prior testimony from 162 witnesses, and approximately 14,000 exhibits. By any measure, it was one of the most extensive trials in history and consumed the energies of all of the lawyers involved, as well as Judge Kessler. It was a massive undertaking on all fronts, and Dan Webb was in the middle of all of it."*

racketeering laws and ordered various types of equitable relief. Judge Kessler's ruling included no monetary damages and no court monitors. It did provide for future payment by the defendants into a court fund to be used to improve indexing of information and free public access to tobacco industry document websites. Nevertheless, Webb's advocacy helped the tobacco giant avoid paying billions for smoking cessation programs and an anti-smoking campaign. One leading tobacco industry analyst labeled the result, "a complete and unequivocal win for the U.S. tobacco industry."

Though reviled by some, Webb had praise for Philip Morris. "I have represented Philip Morris for years and I don't know of any other company that has higher integrity and a compliance program that is stronger than Philip Morris."

Whether popular or not, it was an outcome produced by the mandate of the law and in accordance with recognized standards of evidence and procedure. Notwithstanding the judge's ruling, the tobacco companies filed an appeal to the D.C. Circuit Court of Appeals. On May 22, 2009, a three-judge panel of the court issued a unanimous opinion upholding Judge Kessler's judgment and almost all of the remedies she imposed in the case. Both the tobacco companies and the federal government then appealed to the United States Supreme Court, which declined to hear the appeals. In addition to the nine months it took to try the case, it also involved live testimony from 85 witnesses, prior testimony from 162 witnesses, and approximately 14,000 exhibits. By any measure, it was one of the most extensive trials in history and consumed the energies of all of the lawyers involved, as well as Judge Kessler. It was a massive undertaking on all fronts, and Dan Webb was in the middle of all of it.

"Tobacco litigation is an extremely stressful, contentious, and highly visible undertaking," said Charles R. Wall, who was senior vice president and deputy general counsel of Philip Morris. "The challenges are enormous, and can appear to be overwhelming. Yet it is just this type of setting where Dan functions best. He is a trial lawyer with few peers as well as a wise counselor on a wide range of legal issues."

MICROSOFT CORPORATION

It was called the biggest antitrust case since the breakup of Standard Oil a century ago. In 1998, Microsoft was the target of a case by the DOJ and the attorneys general of 20 states. It was only after a U.S. District judge ordered the breakup of Microsoft that Webb was summoned to fight the court's command.

As is well known, Microsoft was the leading developer and maker of computer software programs in the United States. Microsoft was in the forefront of an emerging new technology, and combined with the skill of its product execution, achieved great commercial success in the software market.

The plaintiffs alleged that Microsoft abused monopoly power on Intel-based personal computers in its handling of operating system sales and web browser sales. The central issue in the cases was whether Microsoft was allowed to bundle its flagship Internet Explorer web browser software with its Microsoft Windows operating system. Bundling them together meant that every user of Windows would automatically have Microsoft's Internet Explorer browser. Up until that time there were browser wars for users that pitted Internet Explorer against other dominant browsers, such as Netscape Navigator.

Microsoft asserted that the merging of Microsoft Windows and Internet Explorer was the result of innovation and competition, that the two were now the same product and were inextricably linked together, and that consumers were getting all the benefits of Internet Explorer for free. The plaintiffs argued that the browser was still a distinct and separate product, which did not need to be tied to the operating system since a separate version of Internet Explorer was available for Mac 05. They also asserted that Internet Explorer was not really free because its development and marketing costs may have kept the price of Windows higher than it might otherwise have been.

Attorneys from Sullivan & Cromwell represented Microsoft in the initial May 1998 trial, where U.S. District Court for the District of Columbia Judge Thomas Jackson found that Microsoft's dominance of the personal computer operating systems market constituted a monopoly and that Microsoft had taken actions to crush threats to their dominance.

In April 2000, Judge Jackson issued a ruling stating that Microsoft had committed monopolization, attempted monopolization, and bundled its products in violation of the Sherman Act. His remedy was that Microsoft must be broken into two separate units, one to produce the operating system and one to produce other software applications.

The result of the trial was a deep and complete loss for Microsoft. The company attempted to appeal directly to the U.S. Supreme Court, which declined to hear the appeal and sent the case to the District of Columbia Circuit Court of Appeals. The D.C. Circuit Court of Appeals overturned Judge Jackson's rulings against Microsoft other than his findings of fact. It found that a different remedy should be sought and that Judge Jackson engaged in unethical conduct by giving interviews to the news media while still hearing the case. The case was remanded for consideration of a proper remedy under a more limited scope of liability. Judge Colleen Kollar-Kotelly was designated to hear the case.

Upon remand, Dan Webb was retained by Microsoft to act as co-counsel with Sullivan & Cromwell; his first appearance on the case was at an October 2001 scheduling conference. For Webb, the appeal was the challenge of handling another antitrust case of extreme significance, not only to Microsoft, but one with possible consequence to the applications of new technologies on our horizons. Of historical note was that the Microsoft case was in the same court that decreed the break-up of AT&T and the Baby Bell companies.

Microsoft vice-president and deputy general counsel Thomas Burt said, "Dan is not the silver-tongued orator. I think he comes across to jurors as a highly credible advocate, an everyman sort of person." Burt said that when he hired Webb to join Sullivan & Cromwell on the antitrust team, he "wanted someone who could play well with others. He's not the kind of guy who comes to a meeting or the courtroom with a great deal of ego on his sleeve."

In September 2001, the Justice Department announced that it had reached an agreement to settle the case and would no longer seek to break up Microsoft. Nevertheless, nine of the plaintiff states refused to settle, branding the agreement as merely a slap on the wrist for Microsoft. The non-settling plaintiffs and Microsoft began trial before Judge Kollar-Kotelly in March 2002.

Webb gave the opening statement and closing argument for Microsoft, put CEO Bill Gates on the witness stand, helped to prepare potential witnesses in the case, such as Microsoft president Steve Ballmer, and cross-examined some of the states' witnesses. Brendan Sullivan represented the nine non-settling states and told the judge that tougher remedies than those reached in the Justice Department

> *Webb asked McGready if he had ever compared Microsoft to the Donner Party, a group of 1800s settlers who turned to cannibalism when they were lost in the mountains.*

---

settlement were needed to protect new technologies from a company that left "nothing to chance" in attacking its competitors.

Judge Kollar-Kotelly ordered initial testimony from witnesses to be written and submitted ahead of time. "Being overly theatrical is not called for and not warranted," Webb said of the case. Nevertheless, he—and his opponents at the prosecution table—were annoyed by the requirement. While Webb would be able to use his courtroom skills when cross-examining the other side's witnesses, the written testimony would deprive him of the chance to humanize his own witnesses and help craft their testimony on the stand.

The non-settling states tried to demonstrate to Judge Kollar-Kotelly that Microsoft's anticompetitive behavior demanded stronger remedies and they cited internal memos as evidence Microsoft had continued to thwart its competitors even as it was being found guilty of antitrust violations. They also argued that it was technically feasible for Microsoft to produce a modular version of Windows that could incorporate competitors' features and asked that the software giant reveal the technical plans for its web browser, Internet Explorer.

Sullivan told the court that Microsoft should pay for its anticompetitive actions and asked the judge to give developers complete access to the source code for Internet Explorer. Sullivan said that the browser "is the fruit of Microsoft's statutory violations—it is the fruit, there is no clearer fruit and it should be denied them."

Webb argued that the proposal to create a modular version of Windows that would allow competitors to remove Microsoft features in favor of their own would be impossible to develop. "The only beneficiaries would be Microsoft's competitors," Webb Said. Webb would show that Microsoft competitors Sun Microsystems Inc., AOL Time Warner Inc., and Oracle Corp. were involved in drafting the tougher remedies being requested by the non-settling states.

Among other witnesses, Webb cross-examined three executives who testified on behalf of the states and the District of Colombia in support of stiffer sanctions than those agreed to by the Department of Justice. With each witness, Webb exposed possible biases by showing benefits to the companies they represented from the destruction of Microsoft.

Included among the opposing witnesses was Steve McGeady, an Intel official. Webb's goal on cross was to prove that McGeady had a personal grudge against Microsoft. At one point, Webb asked McGready if he had ever compared Microsoft to the Donner Party, a group of 1800s settlers who turned to cannibalism when they were lost in the mountains. McGeady was forced to admit to the jury that he had. Bruce Braun, Webb's partner and co-counsel on the case, said, "Dan just destroyed the guy's credibility." Webb said at the time, "The non-settling states have completely failed to prove their case."

In November 2002, Judge Kollar-Kotelly ruled in favor of Microsoft and upheld virtually all of its settlement with the DOJ. Microsoft executives considered the final outcome of the district court proceedings a victory. Their feelings were validated when the U.S. Court of Appeals rejected the appeal of the non-settling states and unanimously approved the DOJ settlement in 2004. Industry pundit Robert X. Cringely, who believed that a breakup was no longer possible, commented that, "now the only way Microsoft can die is by suicide."

GOVERNOR GEORGE RYAN

A trip to the courthouse may sometimes appear to be an occupational hazard of being governor of Illinois. Within recent memory, four Illinois governors were indicted on criminal charges after their terms in office ended, and one was criminally charged while in office. One of those five governors was George Ryan, and Dan Webb became his lawyer.

In December 2003, Ryan and Lawrence Warner, a lobbyist and friend of the former governor, were named in a 22-count indictment. The formal charges included racketeering, mail fraud, bribery, extortion, money laundering, and tax fraud.

The gist of the charges was that Ryan steered several state contracts to Warner and other friends, disbursed campaign funds to relatives and to pay personal expenses, and obstructed justice by attempting to end the state investigation of the license-for-bribes scandal which had occurred while he was secretary of state. He was also charged with lying to investigators and accepting cash, gifts, and loans in return for his official actions as governor.

These were serious allegations and the governor was determined to fight them. "There are zero plea discussions going on—none," Webb said at a press conference. "There will not be any plea discussions. Governor Ryan wants to go to trial and be exonerated."

At Webb's request, the trial was delayed until late 2005 so that he could complete the nine-month tobacco industry trial in Washington, D.C. and adequately prepare Governor Ryan's defense. However, at one point U.S. District Judge Rebecca R. Pallmeyer, who would preside over Ryan's case, grew weary of the delays and threatened to begin the trial with or without Webb. The governor personally appealed in federal court for a delay until the tobacco trial was complete. "Dan Webb is irreplaceable," Ryan said. Judge Pallmeyer agreed to wait.

Because of the broad range of charges and the evidence generated by a lengthy investigation, it took approximately four months for the government to present its evidence. The balance of the trial took another two months. The case drew intense media scrutiny because of the participants, the nature of the case, and the dynamics of its presentation.

The lawyers' closing arguments drew standing room only audiences in the courtroom. The quality of lawyering on both sides was outstanding, with Assistant U.S. Attorney Patrick Collins acting as the lead prosecutor. The ebb and flow of the case was often determined by the lawyer at the lectern at any particular time.

Chicago Tribune arts critic Chris Jones wrote of the case as if it were another piece of theater. "[Webb] constantly interrupted himself, starting sentence after sentence after sentence, but failing to finish any of them, seemingly because he was suddenly rhetorically overwhelmed by the gosh-darn unfairness of this prosecution," Jones wrote.

Webb pointed out at trial that the prosecution appeared to be itching to send Ryan to jail. Minor points that shouldn't amount to crimes were brought as charges of lying to federal authorities according to Webb. He recounted during his closing arguments a meeting between the governor and the FBI during which Ryan inaccurately recalled who had recommended Warner to him to serve on the Metropolitan Pier and Exposition Authority board. "This is a good example of how far [prosecutors] try to stretch to nail George Ryan," Webb said.

The governor was also accused of moving the secretary of state police department offices to a building in the western suburbs owned by Warner. "George Ryan would no more know what the value of real estate is in Bellwood than he could walk on the moon," Webb said. He urged the jury to acquit the former governor on all counts, saying, "I've tried to walk through every single event and transaction the government has relied on in this case to show you the government has not met its burden of proof."

Veteran *Chicago Tribune* columnist Eric Zorn said, "Defense attorney Dan Webb was brilliant in closing arguments as he took a verbal wrecking ball to the charges against Ryan in the corruption trial coming to a close this week in the Dirksen U.S. Courthouse."

"Watch this famed lawyer and master at work and it's easy to see why Ryan's defense attorney attracts an SRO crowd of peers, acolytes, and onlookers," wrote Jones in his *Tribune* article. "Like Sophocles' classic tragedy, Antigone, a major trial is a war of competing narratives and warring histories. And Webb's colorful, ebullient storytelling on Ryan's behalf—a studied but seemingly spontaneous blend of folksy explanation and doggedly detailed destruction—was a colossal counter-punch to the government's official version of events."

After five weeks of deliberations—marked by two jurors being excused and replaced by alternates mid-way through the deliberation process—the jury found Ryan and Warner guilty on all counts. The judge later dismissed two of the counts based on insufficient evidence. Webb was convinced that the jury deliberations were faulty because of the dismissal of the two jurors before arriving at a verdict. "We're going to begin working immediately on post-trial motions to try to get this verdict overturned," Webb said. An appeal by the defendants was denied on August 21, 2007, by a three-member panel of the Seventh Circuit Court of Appeals, with one dissent. The convictions were, accordingly, affirmed.

Every trial lawyer will lose cases and Webb has lost some, but he is quick to note "you can't accept defeat. No matter what happens, you never get used to it. As a trial lawyer you must soldier on. You never stop jumping through hoops. There's no such thing as resting on your laurels or reputation; you must be a winner or people will not hire you. Of course, you can lose a case now and then—everybody does—but the fact is you're only as good as your last case. If you ever believe otherwise, you're in deep trouble as a trial lawyer."

***

In reminiscing recently over a career in the law that continues to flourish, Webb said that he has had a great trial practice. "Whether in criminal, civil, or administrative law cases, I have always liked the variety and challenges of trying many different types of cases in many different forums. It keeps me from getting bored. I have always believed that one of the major goals of practicing law is to avoid boredom. I am happiest and most content when I am actually in the courtroom on trial."

As for the sheer amount of time spent in a courtroom, Brendan Sullivan wrote, "I doubt one could find another trial lawyer who has spent more hours in a courtroom. He lives there." As Webb has said, "I have some frequent flier miles in the courtroom." Indeed, Webb's resume includes at least 10 cases in his career that have lasted three months or more. Any trial lawyer in the country can tell you the physical and mental toll long trials exact from its participants, particularly those sitting in the first chair at counsel table when the stakes are high, the glare of publicity bright, and the outcomes nowhere near certain.

In his public service career, Webb was involved with a number of landmark cases including Operation Greylord, Iran-Contra, and others. In his decades of private practice, Webb has maintained this high profile, having represented major defendants in lengthy trials with crucial verdicts. These include his representation of General Electric, Microsoft, and Philip Morris. Webb's legal opposition in each of the cases was of the highest caliber and each trial was vigorously contested.

Almost any lawyer would treasure the opportunity to be involved with just one of those watershed cases. But to have had a leading role in all of them might have been beyond anyone's imagination—maybe even Dan Webb's. Then again, perhaps not.

CHAPTER 11
CLOSING ARGUMENT

The particular trials discussed in this book represent only a small number of the criminal and civil cases Dan Webb has been involved in as chief trial counsel in a career which continues unabated to this day. In addition to the trials described in the preceding chapters, a number of others of importance to the public and to the parties appear in the appendix.

Webb's representation of private companies and individuals has necessitated court appearances in many states and in other countries around the world. As a plaintiff's lawyer, Webb has secured millions of dollars' worth of verdicts for his clients in different lawsuits. As a trial lawyer representing corporate defendants in civil litigation, he has staved off claims against his clients for billions of dollars.

Like many other successful people, Webb can point to one person and one event which changed his life and put him on the path of his life's work. Webb says he became a trial lawyer because of Josephine Johnson, the high school guidance counselor who gifted him the legal biographies of Darrow and Rogers after witnessing his performance in debate class. Loyal to her influence, Webb kept in touch with Ms. Johnson through the years; when she passed away, he delivered the eulogy at her funeral. Her long ago gift to him remains one of his favorite memories.

Throughout his career, Webb has adopted Johnson's lessons of helping others and offering guidance. He has worked with young lawyers for over 25 years at Winston & Strawn in passing on hard-won lessons learned and methods developed in trying cases. Webb also took his experience in the courtroom and brought it to the classroom. He has taught law at his alma mater, Loyola University

Chicago School of Law, as well as at Northwestern University College of Law, DePaul University School of Law and The John Marshall Law School.

This passion for the law comes from Webb's personal sense of justice. He believes that "being a lawyer is such a great profession because you are a part of that group of people who have been entrusted with going into a courtroom and dealing with whether the laws have been transgressed or complied with. You are part of the resolution process, which is the natural outcome of having laws."

As for his success in the courtroom, that is underpinned by his deep love of the adversary system. Much of life involves a search for truth, and America's adversarial system of dispute resolution is, arguably, as good as any human system can be. Several elements are necessary to attain the truth in court: the best possible lawyers for all of the parties, a judge of the greatest skill and integrity, and a jury of common citizens sworn to fairness and objectivity.

Webb is blessed with the ability to adapt quickly to unforeseen circumstances when they develop at trial. One example was the cross-examination of former President Ronald Reagan. Torn between appropriate respect for the witness and his former office and the necessity to establish the facts as they truly existed, Dan's performance reached the heights of great theater and drama. It would take an exhaustive search to find a greater real life performance in a courtroom than that put on between these two mighty adversaries, a former popular President of the United States and a young, able, and relentless cross-examiner devoted to the rule of law above all else.

Another example was the cross-examination of Edward Russell in the criminal case against General Electric. Webb's cross produced one of the rare events of real life trials—a meltdown of the government's star witness. What may be standard fare in trials depicted in movies is not normally the stuff of reality. Webb used the critical, unflattering comments by Russell's subordinates to deftly bait Russell into destroying his own credibility. Webb's cross-examination left the jury questioning Russell's testimony, and rendered the prosecution's case devoid of substance in the process.

Following his success with Greylord and upon leaving the U.S. Attorney's office, there was speculation that Webb would vie for public office. The *Chicago Tribune* even ran an editorial urging him to run for mayor of Chicago. "I thought about it—I like the action of politics—but ultimately I didn't want to do it," Webb said. "I wasn't afraid of losing; fear and losing has never played a significant role in my life. I just truly loved being in the courtroom. If I followed a career in politics, I'd be pulled away from the law and probably never get back to it again."

The lives of gifted people are invariably accompanied by devotion to their profession or discipline. Webb's devotion to the law is complete. Notwithstanding the untold hours he has spent preparing for and trying cases, he has managed to maintain a balance in his life. He and his wife, Laura, have raised five adopted children. Webb has been a strong force in their lives, and he delights in them. He also has many good friends and rejoices in their friendships. One of his strongest qualities is his value of loyalty. His good friends will attest to how he regularly practices it.

Dan Webb and I were fortunate to be members of a United States Attorney's office which represented the people of the Northern District of Illinois as ably and successfully as any in its history. Research will disclose the names of cases of great importance to the citizens of the community. As evidence of their stellar contributions, many of those lawyers had noted careers once they left the office.

James R. Thompson would be elected Governor of the State of Illinois a record four times. William J. Bauer would become a United States District Judge and, thereafter, a judge of the United States Court of Appeals for the Seventh Circuit. Joel Flaum, Ilana Rovner, and Ann Williams would follow Judge Bauer's path as judges on the District Court followed by service on the Court of Appeals.

Sam Skinner became United States Secretary of Transportation and then Chief of Staff to President George H. W. Bush. Tyrone Fahner would become Illinois Attorney General. Skinner, Valukas and Lassar were appointed United States Attorneys. United States District judgeships awaited James Holderman and me. Jeff Cole would become a United States Magistrate Judge. Webb, Valukas, Fahner, and Reidy all became managing partners at large and respected law firms. James Montana would become general counsel to Illinois Governor Jim Edgar.

In addition to those named, there were many other lawyers and staff who contributed their outstanding talents to the success of the United States Attorney's office during the Bauer and Thompson administrations. Their hard work and trial skills were the driving forces behind that illustrious period and it was in the courtrooms where their individual reputations were made. Not to be overlooked were the talents of all the investigative agents vital to the results in all the trials.

The best expression of the times came from Judge Ilana Rovner. "I remember one day when we were all having our picture taken and I thought to myself, 'We're the most fortunate group of people who has ever lived. We have the opportunity to do public service and at the same time work with each other.' I remember my heart just sort of swelling."

Rovner went on to praise Webb's work in front of jurors. "I don't think anyone held a candle to him," she said. "You immediately felt that the jurors trusted him. Watching him was like watching a maestro. He was always prepared, always at the top of his game."

Webb himself concedes to a personal preference for working before a jury. "Jury trials are much more rewarding than bench trials," he said. "I am constantly amazed at how jurors can cut through irrelevant material, how they can get to the nub of a case." The use of ordinary citizens from all walks of life, strangers to the facts, is both a unique and unequalled method of decision making and has served our nation well.

By whatever measure there is, Dan Webb is not only an extraordinary lawyer, he is also an extraordinary person. I have been blessed with his friendship for almost fifty years and realize my good fortune in sharing it. This book is my way of saying thank you.

"May it please the Court" is the traditional salutation to the judge that lawyers use when beginning their opening statements or closing arguments at trial. It should neither be lightly given nor lightly received. For a lawyer, trying cases is a special calling. In our country, trials are the supreme exercise in the sometimes elusive search for truth—a worthy pursuit.

Webb stands alone among trial lawyers in America. He has tried scores of cases before judges and juries, both criminal and civil. Many of the cases were the most significant of the times, and the hours he has spent in the courtroom are incalculable. The stakes in his cases have always been high and the pressures they produced were not easy to bear. The successes he has enjoyed and the outcomes achieved were matchless. His devotion to his clients is complete, whether popular or not, and every engagement he has been given saw him invest the fullness of his pretrial work ethic and courtroom artistry.

There is no scientific way to measure greatness, although the virtues described above supply reasonable criteria. Perhaps the greatness of trial lawyers is like the beauty life offers, appreciated only in the eye of the beholder.

Whatever the case, I have had the benefit of having been a trial lawyer and of seeing the work of hundreds of trial lawyers in my thirty-four years as a judge on the bench. Even though it would have taken more than one volume to present all of the available evidence to support the firm opinion I hold about Dan Webb, I submit that what has been described in this book is sufficient to support my conclusion. I offer it to the reader. Dan K. Webb has been the greatest trial lawyer in America these past forty years.

I rest my case.

Annual fishing outings were a long-held tradition for Webb and his friends from his early years in the U.S. Attorney's office in Chicago. Pictured on a trip in the early 1970s to Lake Nueltin in Canada's Northwest Territories are from left, the author Charles P. Kocoras; Winston & Strawn partner Matt Lydon; Mayer Brown partner and former chairman Tyrone Fahner, Jenner & Block chairman Anton Valukas; Webb; and the late Howard M. Hoffmann of Duane Morris.

APPENDIX:
SIGNIFICANT TRIALS OF DAN K. WEBB

Case: *United States v. Edward J. Barrett*
Date: February 1973–March 1973
Type: Criminal jury trial
Jurisdiction: United States District Court, Northern District of Illinois
Representing: Government

See Chapter 3: **The True Cost of Free Elections**

Edward J. Barrett, former Clerk of Cook County and Treasurer of the State of Illinois, was indicted on various counts of bribery and mail fraud in connection with the purchase of voting machines while he was the elected Clerk of Cook County. The trial lasted several weeks and involved serious charges of political corruption by a prominent public office holder. Barrett was convicted by the jury, which hopefully had a deterrent impact on other elected officials who might consider accepting bribes in the performance of their duties. Barrett was sentenced to jail by Judge Richard Austin. Webb prepared this case for trial which consisted of preparing approximately 10 witnesses to testify and the organization of voluminous documents and exhibits. During the trial, Webb conducted direct examination of the major government witnesses who testified concerning the bribery scheme. Webb prepared and gave the closing argument for the government, which lasted approximately one hour and which led to a successful conclusion when the jury found the defendant guilty on all counts.

Case: *United States v. Clarence E. Braasch, et al.*
Date: August 1973–October 1973
Type: Criminal jury trial
Jurisdiction: United States District Court, Northern District of Illinois
Representing: Government

See Chapter 4: **Taking Down the Big Club**

Clarence E. Braasch, the fourth highest ranking police officer in the City of Chicago, and 23 other policemen, were indicted for conspiracy, extortion, and perjury in connection with an extensive tavern/police pay-off scheme. Webb conducted an exhaustive 12-month grand jury investigation that led to the return of this indictment. All defendants were tried in the same case, and the trial lasted approximately three months, involving the testimony of over 100 witnesses. From the standpoint of the number of defendants, it may have been the biggest trial ever held in a United States District Court. All but three of the policemen were convicted by the jury and sentenced to various jail terms by Judge William J. Bauer. The lead defendant, Clarence E. Braasch, was sentenced to six years' incarceration for his role in the conspiracy. Many observers believe this case led to several significant reforms within the Chicago Police Department which have played a substantial role in reducing police corruption since the date of the convictions. Webb prepared and conducted direct examination of approximately 60 witnesses who testified on behalf of the government. In addition, Webb conducted direct examination of five Chicago police officers who were granted immunity to testify about their knowledge of police corruption and extensively cross-examined approximately 10 defendants who denied their involvement in the extortion conspiracy. Webb gave the opening statement and the closing argument for the government.

Case: *United States v. Irwin Weiner, et al.*
Date: February 1975–April 1975
Type: Criminal jury trial
Jurisdiction: United States District Court, Northern District of Illinois
Representing: Government

Several representatives of the Central and Southwest Areas Teamsters Pension Fund, including Alan Dorfman, and several alleged organized crime figures, including mafia leaders Tony Spilotro and Ronald De Angeles, were indicted for conspiracy and mail fraud in connection with fraudulent loans made by the pension fund. The trial lasted three months and involved a complex financial fraud scheme that required testimony from over 70 witnesses and the introduction into evidence of thousands of documents. Unfortunately, all defendants were acquitted, probably because of the exceptionally complex nature of the evidence. However, because of the abuses exposed during the trial, substantial reforms in the management of this pension fund occurred, including the complete removal of the Board of Trustees that administered the fund. Webb conducted direct examination of approximately 40 witnesses during the course of this fraud trial. Because of the complex nature of the evidence and the large number of documentary exhibits that had to be introduced, the direct examination of these witnesses was difficult and lengthy. During the defense case, Webb cross-examined numerous defense witnesses. Webb gave the closing argument for the government which lasted several hours and was quite challenging because it required him to simplify for the jury complicated financial transactions that were part of the fraud scheme.

Case: *United States v. Robert Craig, et al.*
Date: April 1976–June 1976
Type: Criminal jury trial
Jurisdiction: United States District Court, Northern District of Illinois
Representing: Government

Six elected legislators of the Illinois General Assembly along with several executives of major ready-mix construction firms were indicted for bribery in connection with a pay-off scheme to secure passage of legislation. The trial lasted approximately 10 weeks and involved over 70 witnesses and hundreds of documents. Five of the legislators were convicted and sentenced to jail terms. This trial exposed rampant corruption in the Illinois Legislature and has hopefully had a deterrent impact on legislators selling their votes to pass bills. Webb conducted direct examination of approximately 35 government witnesses, including several elected legislators, who testified about the bribery scheme. The direct examination of some of these witnesses was complicated by a serious evidentiary problem arising from the speech and debate clause of the Federal and Illinois Constitutions. Several of the defendant legislators took the witness stand in the defense case, and Webb was responsible for their cross-examination. This required him to master and cross-examine the legislators about intricate and confusing legislative procedure rules and regulations that were related to the contentions of the defense to the bribery charges. Webb gave the closing argument for the government summarizing the evidence against the eight defendants on trial.

Case: *United States v. Commonwealth Edison, et al.*
Date: 1980 (summer)
Type: Criminal jury trial
Jurisdiction: United States District Court, Southern District of Illinois
Representing: Nicholas Kalivianakis

Webb's client, Nicholas Kalivianakis, was the Chief Executive Officer and responsible for the operation of Commonwealth Edison's nuclear power station in the Quad Cities in west central Illinois. Mr. Kalivianakis and Commonwealth Edison Company were indicted for allegedly filing false statements with the United States Nuclear Regulatory Commission relating to security violations at the nuclear station. The trial involved complex federal nuclear security regulations, and the proof consisted of approximately 40 witnesses and several hundred exhibits. At trial, Webb established that the Nuclear Regulatory Commission had engaged in confusing and ill-conceived enforcement efforts, and that Webb's client, far more than the Nuclear Regulatory Commission, had insured that this nuclear plant was the safest in the nation. This, combined with Webb's contention that the case had resulted from an overreaction to the Three Mile Island nuclear incident by the Justice Department, resulted in Mr. Kalivianakis being acquitted of all charges by the jury. This was the first and to date the only case in which a nuclear power station and its officers have been indicted. Webb began the trial by giving an opening statement, and then conducted the cross-examination of approximately 30 government witnesses, including several expert witnesses from the Nuclear Regulatory Commission. Webb prepared and conducted the direct examination of his client, who testified on his own behalf in order to establish his innocence. Webb gave the closing argument, which was quite lengthy and required a detailed discussion and analysis of complex Nuclear Regulatory Commission regulations that were being relied upon by the government. This closing argument was a major factor in convincing the jury to find Webb's client not guilty of all charges.

Case:	*Rice Foundation, et al. v. Northwestern University, et al.*
Date:	1980 (winter)
Type:	Civil bench trial
Jurisdiction:	Circuit Court of Cook County, Illinois, Chancery Division
Representing:	Illinois Attorney General

Webb was retained by the Attorney General of Illinois to act as chief trial counsel in protecting the assets of a charitable foundation in a trial involving excessive legal fees being charged to the foundation by the Chicago law firm of Reuben and Proctor. The trial lasted several weeks and involved complicated proof relating to extensive litigation that has resulted from the probate of a $70 million DuPage County estate. Judge Harold Siegan awarded the law firm a judgment of $1.6 million in legal fees based on a contingent fee theory. Webb was retained by the Attorney General of Illinois to conduct the trial of this case at the last moment just before the trial began. This required him to study and evaluate several related cases that were pending in other federal and state courts. Because there had been several years of litigation that had preceded Webb's involvement in the case, Webb was required to evaluate and master a great deal of materials in a short period of time in order to try this case. Webb conducted direct and cross-examination of numerous witnesses, including several attorneys who testified during this trial. Several of the witnesses were trustees of a charitable foundation, and their examination was difficult and complex. Webb gave the closing argument for Webb's client, which required a detailed analysis of voluminous documents that had been received into evidence.

Case:	*United States v. Ambrose, et al.*
Date:	February 1982–April 1982
Type:	Criminal jury trial
Jurisdiction:	United States District Court, Northern District of Illinois
Representing:	Government

See Chapter 5: **Prosecuting the Protectors**

Ten Chicago police officers were charged with various counts of bribery and narcotic violations in connection with a pervasive scheme of pay-offs to the ten defendants from a substantial number of heroin dealers. The trial lasted three months, and was quite controversial because the government's main witnesses were convicted heroin dealers testifying against Chicago police officers. All ten police officers were convicted and sentenced to various periods of time of incarceration up to 25 years. Webb prepared this case for trial which consisted of preparing approximately 50 witnesses to testify and the organization of thousands of exhibits. During the trial, Webb conducted the direct examination of approximately 50 witnesses, and the cross-examination of approximately 15 witnesses. Webb prepared and delivered the rebuttal argument for the government, which lasted approximately seven hours.

Case:	*United States v. James Lewis*
Date:	1983 (summer)
Type:	Criminal jury trial
Jurisdiction:	United States District Court, Northern District of Illinois
Representing:	Government

James Lewis is the only person charged with a crime as a result of the Tylenol murders in the City of Chicago. After eight people died from ingesting cyanide-laced Tylenol capsules, James Lewis was accused of sending an extortion letter to the manufacturer of Tylenol, Johnson & Johnson, demanding $1 million in order to stop the murders. While Lewis was suspected by various law enforcement agencies of being the Tylenol murderer, the only charge currently brought against him was this extortion case. The trial lasted two weeks, and resulted in the conviction of the defendant. Chief Judge McGarr imposed the maximum sentence of ten years' incarceration. Webb conducted the investigation, the subsequent preparation for trial, the direct and cross-examination of numerous witnesses, and delivered a two-hour rebuttal argument.

Case: *United States v. John M. Murphy*
Date: 1984 (spring)
Type: Criminal jury trial
Jurisdiction: United States District Court, Northern District of Illinois
Representing: Government

See Chapter 6: **When Justice Was Blind**

John M. Murphy was a judge of the Circuit Court of Cook County charged with various acts of judicial corruption. This case was quite significant because it was the first judge to go to trial in connection with the Government's 4½-year undercover judicial corruption investigation, commonly known as Operation Greylord. The trial lasted several weeks, and resulted in the conviction of the defendant on all charges. Judge Charles Kocoras imposed a 10-year jail sentence. Webb supervised this sensitive undercover investigation, and prepared this case for trial. Webb conducted the direct examination of numerous witnesses, including several corrupt attorneys and court personnel who revealed extensive corruption within the Circuit Court of Cook County. Webb also cross-examined numerous witnesses, including an extensive two day cross-examination of Judge Murphy. Webb also prepared and delivered the rebuttal argument for the government, which lasted several hours.

Case: *United States v. Richard F. LeFevour*
Date: June 1985
Type: Criminal jury trial
Jurisdiction: United States District Court, Northern District of Illinois
Representing: Government

See Chapter 6: **When Justice Was Blind**

Richard F. LeFevour held various high-ranking positions within the Circuit Court of Cook County, including Chief of Traffic Court and Chief Judge of the First Municipal District. He was generally viewed as the second highest ranking judge within the Circuit Court of Cook County. The case was considered the pinnacle of a 4½-year judicial corruption undercover project conducted by the United States Attorney's office during the time that Webb served as United States Attorney. This case went to trial after Webb resigned as United States Attorney and returned to private practice, however, at the request of the Justice Department, Webb returned to be chief trial counsel because of his prior knowledge concerning the case. The trial lasted approximately three months, and was a very difficult case to try before a jury because of the complexities of the documentary evidence introduced by the government to establish a net worth tax case against the defendant. After extensive deliberations, the jury convicted Judge LeFevour of all 70 counts of the indictment, including charges of racketeering, bribery, mail fraud, and tax fraud. Judge Charles Norgle imposed a 12-year jail sentence. Webb supervised the investigation that led to the return of this indictment and was chief counsel in the preparation and trial of the matter. Webb conducted the direct examination of approximately 35 witnesses, including the main trial witness, Judge James LeFevour, who was on the witness stand for approximately seven days. Webb also cross-examined numerous witnesses called by the defense, and delivered a four-hour rebuttal argument.

Case: *Automated Transit Systems Group v. MATRA, S.A., and the City of Chicago*
Date: October 1985
Type: Civil bench trial
Jurisdiction: Circuit Court of Cook County, Illinois, Chancery Division
Representing: MATRA, S.A.

This case involved a $150 million contract to design and build an automated transit system at O'Hare International Airport. This was the largest contract ever entered into by the City of Chicago, and the City originally awarded the contract to the Automated Transit Systems Group which was a competitor of Webb's client, MATRA. Webb filed a lawsuit to block the awarding of the contract to the ATS Group, and was eventually successful in convincing the city that MATRA was the lowest responsible bidder. After the city reversed positions and awarded the contract to MATRA, the ATS Group filed a lawsuit to obtain a preliminary injunction against the City of Chicago and MATRA. Because of the significance and urgency of this matter to the City of Chicago, Judge David Shields set aside approximately two to three days each week, and the case took approximately 11 weeks to try on this schedule. At the conclusion of the trial, Judge Shields denied the request for a preliminary injunction, and MATRA was awarded this contract by the City of Chicago. This was a very difficult trial because of the complexities of both factual and legal issues. Hundreds of documents were admitted into evidence, and numerous experts were called by the ATS Group to establish its case. Webb prepared the case and was chief counsel at trial. Webb conducted the cross-examination of approximately 10 witnesses called by the plaintiff, and delivered both the opening statement and the closing argument to the court. The cross-examinations of the expert witnesses called by the plaintiff were particularly difficult cross-examinations because of the complexities of their testimony as transportation experts.

Case: *Ohio-Sealy Mattress Manufacturing Company, et al., and Sealy Mattress Company of Michigan, Inc. v. Sealy, Inc. and Morris A. Kaplan, et al.*
Date: June 1986
Type: Civil jury trial
Jurisdiction: United States District Court, Northern District of Illinois
Representing: Sealy Mattress Company of Michigan, Inc.

This case was a major antitrust jury trial involving an alleged illegal market distribution system by Sealy, Inc. This was an extremely complex trial involving thousands of documents and presenting complex factual and legal issues. Webb prepared the case for trial and was chief trial counsel. After a three-month jury trial, Webb obtained a $45 million verdict against the defendant. Webb subsequently settled the judgment for $37 million.

Case: *United States v. Lisa Hall Huckaby*
Date: October 1986
Type: Criminal jury trial
Jurisdiction: United States District Court, Central District of Illinois
Representing: Lisa Hall Huckaby

Huckaby was a public official with the State of Illinois who was charged with receiving bribe payments to influence official acts. The trial lasted three weeks, and Webb was successful in preventing her conviction. The jury ended up deadlocked eight to four in the defendant's favor. Subsequently, Webb was able to negotiate a plea agreement regarding a much lesser charge. Webb prepared the case for trial and delivered the opening statement, closing argument, and examined and cross-examined approximately 35 witnesses.

Case: *MidAmerica Commodity Exchange v. First Commodity Corp. of Boston*
Date: February 1987
Type: Administrative trial
Jurisdiction: MidAmerica Commodity Exchange
Representing: MidAmerica Commodity Exchange

This was the largest and most comprehensive administrative/disciplinary proceeding ever undertaken by the MidAmerica Commodity Exchange. The defendant was charged with defrauding hundreds of customers in connection with commodities trading. The trial lasted approximately eight weeks and resulted in the defendant being found guilty of all charges. Ultimately, the defendant was fined $3 million, the largest fine ever imposed by a commodity exchange in the United States. The case was eventually affirmed by the Commodity Futures Trading Commission. Webb prepared the case for trial and delivered the opening statement, closing argument, and examined and cross-examined approximately 50 witnesses.

Case: *Farmland Industries, Inc. v. Frazier-Parrott Commodities, Inc., et al.*
Date: October 1987
Type: Civil jury trial
Jurisdiction: United States District Court, Western District of Missouri
Representing: Horace Seixas and John Dunn

Webb's clients were charged with serious acts of fraud in connection with trading large quantities of crude oil in the futures market on the New York Mercantile Exchange. This was a very complicated case involving an alleged $50 million fraud scheme. Webb successfully defended his clients, and the jury returned a verdict of not guilty on all counts for each. Webb prepared the case for trial, delivered the opening statement, closing argument and examined and cross-examined approximately 20 witnesses. It was a very complex trial, lasting approximately six weeks.

Case: *Commonwealth Edison Company Proposed General Increase in Electric Rates*
Date: November 1987–February 1988
Type: Administrative proceeding
Jurisdiction: Illinois Commerce Commission
Representing: Commonwealth Edison Company

This case involved a several hundred million dollar rate increase request by Commonwealth Edison resulting from the addition of three nuclear units to Commonwealth Edison's rate base. It was an extremely complex and vigorously contested administrative proceeding with significant consequences to the financial structure of Commonwealth Edison. Webb worked with another law firm in preparing this case for trial. Webb was assigned certain specialized witnesses, primarily utility economists, to examine and cross-examine. The case was extremely complex, involving a 20-year history of nuclear expansion with this utility.

Case:	*United States v. Thompson B. Sanders*
Date:	September 1988
Type:	Criminal jury trial
Jurisdiction:	United States District Court, Northern District of Illinois
Representing:	Thompson B. Sanders

This was a criminal commodity fraud jury trial, which involved the expert testimony of a number of commodity trading experts. Webb examined and cross-examined numerous witnesses during the course of the trial. The jury found Webb's client guilty and he was sentenced to jail.

Case:	*Anthony R. Gold, PC Brand, Inc., et al. v. Ziff Communications Company, d/b/a Ziff-Davis Publishing Company*
Date:	November 1988
Type:	Civil bench trial
Jurisdiction:	Circuit Court of Cook County
Representing:	PC Brand, Inc.

This was a complex contract dispute between an advertiser and a large publishing company involving the leading computer magazine in the United States. Webb's client prevailed at trial, and the matter has now been affirmed on appeal.

Case: *United States v. Angelo Commito*
Date: January 1989
Type: Criminal jury trial
Jurisdiction: United States District Court, Northern District of Illinois
Representing: Angelo Commito

Webb's client was charged with fraud in connection with his operation of a large health care business that did substantial work for many of the larger labor unions in the United States. Webb examined and cross-examined many witnesses during the course of this trial. At the conclusion of the trial, Webb's client was found not guilty of all charges.

Case: *United States of America v. Norby Walters and Lloyd Bloom*
Date: March 1989–April 1989
Type: Criminal jury trial
Jurisdiction: United States District Court, Northern District of Illinois
Representing: Lloyd Bloom

Based on a novel prosecution theory, Webb's client, a sports agent, was prosecuted for defrauding various universities as a result of the manner in which he signed college football players to representation agreements before their college eligibility expired. This was a very difficult trial, and Webb examined and cross-examined numerous witnesses. After a six-week jury trial, Webb's client was found guilty of some charges and not guilty of other charges. On appeal, the conviction was completely reversed in favor of Webb's client.

Case: *United States of America v. John Poindexter*
Date: February 1990–March 1990
Type: Criminal jury trial
Jurisdiction: United States District Court, District of Columbia
Representing: Government

See Chapter 7: **Some of the President's Men**

Webb represented the government in the prosecution of John Poindexter, the National Security Advisor during the presidency of Ronald Reagan. Poindexter was charged with obstructing Congress in connection with the Iran-Contra Affair. During the course of this trial, Webb cross-examined Oliver North and former President Ronald Reagan. The jury ruled in favor of the government and Poindexter was convicted of all five felony charges. The conviction was reversed on appeal.

Case: *United States v. Chan Wing Yeung, et al.*
Date: March 1991–July 1991
Type: Criminal jury trial
Jurisdiction: United States District Court, Northern District of Illinois
Representing: Chan Wing Yeung

Webb represented Chan Wing Yeung in the prosecution of him and 17 other individuals who were charged with participating in an alleged large-scale Chinese gambling operation. After a four-month trial, the jury was split 10 to two for acquittal, and the case ended in a hung jury.

Case: *United States v. David Shields*
Date: August 1991–September 1991
Type: Criminal jury trial
Jurisdiction: United States District Court, Northern District of Illinois
Representing: David Shields

The defendant was a judge of the Circuit Court of Cook County who was alleged to have taken a bribe in connection with the performance of his judicial duties. After a three week trial, the jury found the defendant guilty of all charges.

Case: *People of the State of Illinois, ex rel., Roland Burris, Illinois Attorney General v. George H. Ryan, et al.*
Date: January 1992
Type: Civil and administrative trial
Jurisdiction: The Illinois Legislative Redistricting Commission; The Illinois Supreme Court
Representing: George H. Ryan, Secretary of State and other related parties

In 1991 the Illinois Legislative Redistricting Commission, carrying out its constitutional authority, remapped the political subdivisions of the State of Illinois. Webb represented various parties whose interests were aligned with the Illinois Republican Party in defending this new political map against various legal challenges. Webb acted as chief trial counsel in a trial before the Illinois Legislative Redistricting Commission in which he examined and cross-examined numerous election and redistricting experts. The Commission ruled in favor of Webb's clients. The matter went by direct appeal to the Illinois Supreme Court and Webb was successful in winning the case on appeal.

Case: *The Illinois Legislative Redistricting Commission, et al. v. Gary Lapille, et al.*
Date: February 1992
Type: Federal political redistricting case
Jurisdiction: United States District Court, Northern District of Illinois
Representing: The Illinois Legislative Redistricting Commission and related parties

This was a federal political redistricting trial that resulted from the redistricting process that had occurred in 1991 in the State of Illinois. Webb was defending the redistricting map approved by the Illinois Legislative Redistricting Commission against several legal challenges. During the course of the trial, Webb examined and cross-examined several election and redistricting experts. Webb was successful in obtaining a judgment in favor of his clients and the new political map was put into effect by the State of Illinois for the 1992 elections.

Case: *Shields, et al. v. Keating, Jr., et al.*
Date: March 1992–July 1992
Type: Civil jury trial
Jurisdiction: United States District Court, District of Arizona
Representing: Lexecon, Inc.

This was a class action civil jury trial that resulted from the failure of Lincoln Savings, the S & L institution owned and operated by Charles Keating, Jr. The class action plaintiffs sued numerous professional firms, including accounting firms, law firms and economic consulting firms. Lexecon is an economic consulting firm headquartered in Chicago. This was a very complex civil jury trial involving outstanding attorneys from across the country. At the end of all the evidence, Webb was successful in obtaining a judgment of dismissal against Lexecon.

Case: *Burroughs Wellcome Co. v. Barr Laboratories, Inc.*
Date: June 1993–July 1993
Type: Civil jury trial
Jurisdiction: United States District Court, Eastern District of North Carolina
Representing: Barr Laboratories, Inc.

This was a major patent jury trial involving the patent ownership of AZT, the drug of choice to treat AIDS patients. Webb represented Barr Laboratories, Inc. who was challenging the AZT patent rights of Burroughs Wellcome. This case involved very complex patent legal issues, and after several weeks of trial, Judge Howard dismissed the jury without a verdict. Several legal issues were appealed to the Federal Circuit Court of Appeals.

Case: *Shields v. The First National Bank of Chicago*
Date: March 1994
Type: Civil jury trial
Jurisdiction: United States District Court, Northern District of Illinois
Representing: The First National Bank of Chicago

This was a major civil RICO case, with the plaintiff requesting approximately $300 million in damages. The evidence involved a complex business transaction related to the financing of a cellular telephone business, and had numerous complex legal and evidentiary issues that needed to be addressed. After three weeks of trial, the case settled favorably for the defense.

Case: *United States v. General Electric Company, et al.*
Date: October 1994–December 1994
Type: Criminal jury trial
Jurisdiction: United States District Court, Southern District of Ohio
Representing: General Electric Company

See Chapter 8: **The Price of Diamonds**

This was a major antitrust criminal case in which the Department of Justice alleged that General Electric and DeBeers had conspired to fix the worldwide prices for industrial diamonds. The Department of Justice contended that GE and DeBeers had used a common customer in Europe as a conduit to fix prices. Webb led the trial team, which consisted of trial lawyers from three law firms, and included one GE in-house litigation attorney. The trial team aggressively challenged the government's evidence at every turn and were successful in severely damaging the government's case, which was heavily dependent on circumstantial evidence. After seven weeks of trial, the judge granted GE's motion for a Rule 29 Judgment of acquittal and discharged the jury.

Case: *Bell Atlantic Corporation & DSC Communications Corporation v. AT&T Corporation & Lucent Technologies, Inc.*
Date: April 1997
Type: Civil jury trial
Jurisdiction: United States District Court, Eastern District of Texas
Representing: Bell Atlantic

This was a major civil antitrust case in which Bell Atlantic sued AT&T and Lucent for alleged antitrust violations regarding the defendants' manufacturing and sale of telephone network equipment. Webb supervised a substantial discovery plan that was efficiently executed, and the case was prepared to go to trial within one year of the filing of the lawsuit–a speed almost unheard of in major commercial antitrust litigation. During the opening statement and jury selection process, the case settled on terms that were quite satisfactory to Bell Atlantic as the plaintiff that filed the lawsuit.

Case: *State of Texas v. American Tobacco Co., et al.*
Date: January 1998
Type: Civil jury trial
Jurisdiction: United States District Court, Eastern District of Texas
Representing: Philip Morris Companies Inc.

This was a massive civil liability case brought by the State of Texas in which all of the major U.S. tobacco companies were defendants. Webb was chief trial counsel for Philip Morris, and was also designated as the lead courtroom representative for all the tobacco company defendants on certain common issues. This case involved an overwhelming pretrial discovery schedule that included hundreds of witnesses and tens of thousands of documents. Webb supervised and participated in substantial trial preparation activities that involved setting up a trial site in Texarkana, Texas that housed approximately 75 lawyers representing the tobacco company defendants. Just prior to jury selection, the case settled for $15 billion–which for years was the largest settlement of a civil case in U.S. history.

Case: *State of Washington v. American Tobacco Co., et al.*
Date: November 1998
Type: Civil jury trial
Jurisdiction: Superior Court of Washington, King County
Representing: Philip Morris Companies Inc.

This was a complex civil liability case brought by the State of Washington in which all of the major U.S. tobacco companies were defendants. Webb was chief trial counsel for Philip Morris, and was also designated as the lead courtroom representative for all the tobacco company defendants on certain common issues. This case involved an overwhelming pretrial discovery schedule that included hundreds of witnesses and tens of thousands of documents. Webb supervised and participated in substantial trial preparation activities that involved setting up a trial site in Seattle, Washington, that housed approximately 60 lawyers representing the tobacco company defendants. After two months of trial the case settled for approximately $4.5 billion.

Case: *CTC Communications Corp. v. Bell Atlantic Corporation*
Date: February 1999
Type: Civil jury trial
Jurisdiction: United States District Court, District of Maine
Representing: Bell Atlantic

The two parties in this lawsuit were both large telecommunications companies serving customers in the Northeast region of the United States. CTC sought to recover commissions earned from Bell Atlantic, for whom it acted as a sales agent. The case settled with CTC receiving cash and other considerations.

Case: *Bell Atlantic Corporation, Cellco Partnership and GTE Corporation v. AirTouch Communications, Inc. and WMC Partners, L.P.*
Date: August 1999
Type: Civil jury trial
Jurisdiction: United States District Court, Northern District of California
Representing: Bell Atlantic

Bell Atlantic sued the defendants in federal court in California to void non-compete clauses in two agreements. AirTouch filed counterclaims, including allegations that Bell Atlantic engaged in unlawful, unfair, or fraudulent business practices violating state law. Application for preliminary injunction was denied. The case settled and did not go to final verdict.

Case: *Howard A. Engle, M.D., et. al., v. R.J. Reynolds Tobacco Company, et. al.*
Date: September 1999–January 2001
Type: Civil jury trial
Jurisdiction: Circuit Court of the 11th Judicial District in and for Dade County, Florida
Representing: Philip Morris Companies, Inc.

Webb represented Philip Morris as lead counsel in the first class action brought by cigarette smokers for punitive damages to be tried to a verdict. The case involved a certified state-wide class of cigarette smokers who claimed to have suffered illnesses and diseases as a result of their addiction to cigarette smoking. Webb assumed the role of primary trial counsel for the punitive damages phase of the case. Webb cross-examined many of the plaintiffs' witnesses and acted as lead lawyer for the industry in the numerous court hearings throughout the trial. The trial lasted ten months, and the large punitive damage verdict was completely reversed on appeal with no remand.

Case: *McCook Metals L.L.C. v. Alcoa, Inc.*
Date: June 2001
Case: Civil bench trial
Jurisdiction: United States District Court, Northern District of Illinois
Representing: Alcoa, Inc.

McCook Metals L.L.C. sued Alcoa, Inc. after Alcoa refused to renew a license that allowed McCook to manufacture an aluminum alloy used in the construction of airplane wings. Alcoa had two patents that protected a high strength aluminum alloy it developed that was resistant to exfoliation, a form of corrosion unique to aluminum. McCook alleged various antitrust violations premised on an allegation that the two patents were invalid for a variety of reasons and could not be lawfully enforced. Webb represented Alcoa as chief trial counsel during a four-week bench trial in June 2001. Before the Court rendered its decision, McCook filed for bankruptcy and the bankruptcy trustee dismissed the case.

Case: *United States of America v. Microsoft Corporation*
Date: March 2002
Type: Civil bench trial
Jurisdiction: United States District Court, District of Columbia
Representing: Microsoft Corporation

See Chapter 10: **Counsel for the Defense**

Webb was retained by Microsoft Corporation as co-lead counsel in connection with a series of highly publicized antitrust claims brought by various federal and state government entities. Webb defended the company in connection with the remedies being pursued by the nine non-settling states. Webb gave the opening statement and closing argument for Microsoft, put CEO Bill Gates on the witness stand, and cross-examined some of the states' witnesses before Judge Colleen Kollar-Kotelly. In November 2002, Judge Kollar-Kotelly ruled in Microsoft's favor, upholding the settlement reached by Microsoft and the U.S. Department of Justice.

Case: *Westside Cingular, Inc. d/b/a Cellnet of Ohio v. New Par, et al.*
Date: March 2003
Type: Civil jury trial
Jurisdiction: Court of Common Pleas Cuyahoga County, Ohio
Representing: Cingular Wireless

Webb was retained by Cingular Wireless in connection with a unique trial that resulted from a regulatory proceeding that created significant potential liability for Cingular. Webb was hired shortly before the trial was scheduled to commence and quickly prepared for trial. During jury selection, the case settled on terms very satisfactory for Cingular.

Case: *Debra Wolinsky v. Wyeth*
Date: July 2003
Type: Civil jury trial
Jurisdiction: Circuit Court of Cook County, Chicago, Illinois
Representing: Wyeth

Webb represented Wyeth in connection with a substantial number of product liability cases resulting from the manufacture and sale of the diet drug, Fen-Phen. After extensive trial preparation, right before opening statements were to commence, the case settled.

Case: *WorldCom, Inc. et al.*
Date: September 2003
Type: Bankruptcy court bench trial
Jurisdiction: Southern District of New York
Representing: A large group of MCI Debenture Holders

Webb was retained to represent a large group of MCI Debenture Holders to challenge the bankruptcy plan of confirmation for WorldCom, Inc. The case was prepared for trial in record time, and involved very complicated factual and legal issues related to the WorldCom bankruptcy. After presentation of written opening statements, the case settled on terms very satisfactory for Webb's clients.

Case: *Vickie Carol Campbell Reese, et al. (Nusted) v. Wyeth*
Date: May 2004–June 2004
Type: Civil jury trial
Jurisdiction: District Court of Upshur County, Texas
Representing: Wyeth

Webb represented Wyeth in this Fen Phen product liability jury trial. Webb gave the opening statement and cross-examined several of the plaintiffs' expert witnesses. After three weeks of trial, the case settled.

Case: *Verizon Directories v. Yellow Book USA, Inc.*
Date: July 2004–August 2004
Type: Civil bench trial
Jurisdiction: Eastern District of New York
Representing: Verizon Directories Corp.

Verizon filed suit requesting an injunction prohibiting Yellow Book from continuing a nationwide advertising campaign that Verizon alleged was false and misleading. This was a three week bench trial before Federal District Court Judge Jack Weinstein. Webb was chief trial counsel for Verizon and gave the opening statement and conducted examinations of the major fact and expert witnesses. At the conclusion of the trial, Judge Weinstein ruled in favor of Verizon and the advertising campaign was terminated.

Case: *United States v. Philip Morris USA, Inc., et al.*
Date: September 2004–June 2005
Type: Civil bench trial
Jurisdiction: U.S. District Court for the District of Columbia
Representing: Philip Morris USA and Altria Group

See Chapter 10: Counsel for the Defense

On August 17, 2006, D.C. federal district judge Gladys Kessler issued her ruling in United States v. Philip Morris USA in which Webb represented Philip Morris USA and its parent company, Altria Group, since its filing by the Justice Department in September 1999, including during a nine-month bench trial that lasted from September 2004 to June 2005. At the outset of trial, the government sought $280 billion in disgorgement (reduced from its $959 billion demand at the outset of the case). When the D.C. Circuit dismissed that claim on interlocutory appeal during trial, the government revised its demands to seek $130 billion for a national smoking cessation program, billions more for a public education and countermarketing campaign, and the appointment of court monitors essentially to run the defendant companies. In her 1,653-page opinion, Judge Kessler found the defendants liable for violations of federal racketeering laws and ordered various types of equitable relief. Judge Kessler's ruling included no monetary damages and no court monitors. The trial itself was one of the most extensive in history, involving live testimony from 85 witnesses, prior testimony from 162 witnesses, and approximately 14,000 exhibits.

Case: *United States v. Lawrence E. Warner and George H. Ryan, Sr.*
Date: September 2005–April 2006
Type: Criminal jury trial
Jurisdiction: Northern District of Illinois
Representing: George H. Ryan, Sr.

See Chapter 10: Counsel for the Defense

Webb represented former Governor of Illinois George H. Ryan in his six-month jury trial on public corruption charges, including racketeering, mail fraud, and income tax fraud. The charges relate to actions he took while serving as Illinois Secretary of State and later as Governor. In April 2006, Ryan was found guilty by a jury after five weeks of deliberations that saw two jurors excused and replaced by alternate jurors mid-way through the deliberation process. On May 27, 2008, the Supreme Court of the United States denied a request to review the conviction, despite a call for such a review based on allegations of jury misconduct and the government's novel use of the mail fraud statute.

Case: *Verizon Communications v. Vonage Holdings Corp.*
Date: February 2007–March 2007
Type: Civil jury trial
Jurisdiction: Eastern District of Virginia
Representing: Verizon Communications, Inc.

Webb obtained a $58 million verdict for Verizon Communications in this complicated case against Vonage Holdings Corp. and Vonage America, Inc. for infringement of five Verizon patents related to sending telephone calls over the Internet. A Virginia federal court jury of four men and four women found that Vonage infringed three of the five Verizon patents asserted. The jury also found all five of Verizon's patents valid and determined that if Vonage was not enjoined from continuing to infringe Verizon's patents, it would have to pay a royalty of 5.5 percent on all of its future sales. Immediately after the verdict was read and the jury was excused, Webb moved the Court for a permanent injunction seeking to prevent any further infringement by Vonage of Verizon's patents. The court granted the request, but issued a partial stay allowing Vonage to continue servicing its customers. The Federal Circuit later issued a full stay of the permanent injunction pending an appeal.

Case: *Rowatt, Forrester and Scofield v. Wyeth*
Date: September 2007–October 2007
Type: Civil jury trial
Jurisdiction: 2nd Judicial District Court of Nevada, Washoe County
Representing: Wyeth

This was a six-week product liability jury trial in Reno, Nevada. Webb was co-chief trial counsel and participated in both the opening statement and the closing arguments. Webb conducted direct and cross examinations of a number of witnesses. The verdict was in favor of the plaintiffs and a bid for appeal was denied.

Case: *Woods and Woodhouse v. Wyeth*
Date: July 2008
Type: Civil jury trial
Jurisdiction: 8th Judicial District Court of Nevada, Clark County
Representing: Wyeth

This was a major product liability jury trial in Las Vegas, Nevada. After two weeks of jury selection, the case settled.

Case: *Altria Group Inc. v. United States*
Date: June 2009–July 2009
Type: Civil jury trial
Jurisdiction: Southern District of New York
Representing: Altria Group Inc.

Altria and the IRS had a major dispute about a number of tax deductions taken by Altria regarding a large number of leveraged lease transactions. There were several hundred million dollars in tax liability at issue. For certain tax years, Altria paid the claimed past-due taxes and filed a complaint in Federal District Court in the Southern District of New York for a refund. The jury trial lasted approximately three weeks. It was a very complex case and Webb did the direct exam and cross exam of most of the major experts. The jury returned a verdict in favor of the government.

Case: *United States vs. William Cellini*
Date: October 2011
Type: Federal criminal jury trial
Jurisdiction: United States District Court for the Northern District of Illinois
Representing: William Cellini

The government alleged that the defendant was an Illinois insider political powerhouse who had engaged in a conspiracy to defraud the Illinois Teachers Retirement Fund (TRS) by agreeing to use his influence and relationship with Illinois public officials to cause TRS to make investments with firms selected by Mr. Cellini and other co-conspirators. Mr. Cellini's co-conspirators were alleged to have used their influence with Illinois Governor Rod Blagojevich to defeat certain proposals that would have affected the business activities of TRS. Webb gave the opening statement and closing argument, and cross-examined the major government witnesses. The jury deliberated for four days and reached a split verdict. The jury acquitted Mr. Cellini on the more serious charges, and convicted him on two lesser charges. The district court judge imposed a sentence well under the guideline range and Mr. Cellini chose not to pursue an appeal.

Case: *HealthSouth vs. Ernst & Young*
Date: July 2010–December 2012
Type: Arbitration Trial
Jurisdiction: AAA Arbitration Trial
Representing: Ernst & Young

Ernst & Young was HealthSouth's independent auditor. HealthSouth filed an arbitration complaint in which it alleged that Ernst & Young was negligent and committed fraud in its role as outside auditor in failing to detect and stop a major fraud scheme committed by HealthSouth's senior management, officers, and directors. HealthSouth and its senior management had inflated the company's reported earnings by several billion dollars and it was one of the most brazen fraud schemes in United States corporate history. The arbitration trial involved the testimony of 76 witnesses (15 live witnesses; 61 witnesses by video designation), with thousands of exhibits. This was the largest auditor malpractice case to go to trial and judgment, with HealthSouth seeking damages in excess of $2.5 billion. In December 2012, the three judge arbitration panel unanimously rejected HealthSouth's attempt to hold Ernst & Young responsible for the consequences of its own misconduct. The panel entered judgment on all claims for Ernst & Young with no damages awarded. On appeal, the Supreme Court of Alabama unanimously affirmed the decision of the arbitration panel. Webb delivered the opening statement for Ernst & Young, and did the direct examinations and cross-examinations of several major witnesses.

Case: *in the Matter of the Death of David Koschman*
Date: April 2012–Januart 2014
Type: Special Prosecution (Criminal)
Jurisdiction: Circuit Court of Cook County
Representing: Government

See Chapter 9: **One Punch Justice**

David Koschman died after a single punch from Richard J. Vanecko on April 25, 2004. No charges were brought against Vanecko by the Chicago Police Department or the Cook County State's Attorney. In April of 2012, the Circuit Court of Cook County appointed Webb as a Special Prosecutor charged with conducting an independent investigation into the death of David Koschman and the investigation by the Chicago Police Department. Webb's report led to Vanecko pleading guilty to a single charge of involuntary manslaughter. The Webb report also identified failings of the police and prosecutors, but did not bring any new indictments.

INDEX